CRITICAL
INSIGHTS
Jane Eyre

CRITICAL
INSIGHTS
Jane Eyre

Editor
Katie R. Peel
University of North Carolina Wilmington

SALEM PRESS
A Division of EBSCO Information Services, Inc.
Ipswich, Massachusetts

GREY HOUSE PUBLISHING

Library of Congress Cataloging-in-Publication Data

Jane Eyre / editor, Katie R. Peel. -- [1st ed.].
    p. : ill. ; cm. -- (Critical insights)
Includes bibliographical references and index.
ISBN: 978-1-61925-218-9
1. Brontë, Charlotte, 1816-1855. Jane Eyre. 2. Classism in literature. 3. Feminism in literature. I. Peel, Katie R. II. Series: Critical insights.

PR4167.J33 J26 2013
823/.8

Contents _____

About This Volume, Katie Peel   ix

The Book and Author _____
(Still) On *Jane Eyre*, Katie Peel   3
Biography of Charlotte Brontë, Joanne Cordón   14

Critical Contexts _____
HISTORICAL BACKGROUND
Souvenirs of Sadism: Mahogany Furniture, Deforestation,
     and Slavery in *Jane Eyre*, Elaine Freedgood (Reprint)   23

CRITICAL RECEPTION
From Myth to Materiality: Critical Reception of Charlotte
     Brontë's *Jane Eyre* from the 1840s to the 2010s, John O'Hara   50

CRITICAL LENS
Shameful Signification: Narrative and Feeling
     in *Jane Eyre*, Ashly Bennett (Reprint)   64

COMPARATIVE ANALYSIS
Passion and Economics in *Jane Eyre* and *North and South*, Thomas Recchio   99

Critical Readings _____
Women's Place: Home, Sanctuary, and the Big House
     in *Jane Eyre*, Katherine Montwieler   113
'Sins of the Mother: Adèle's Genetic and National Burden
     in *Jane Eyre*, Mara Reisman   128
'That Better Part Which Cannot Be Taken From You': Varieties
     of Christian Experience in *Jane Eyre*, Jennie-Rebecca Falcetta   145
Right Obedience and Milton's Abdiel in *Jane Eyre*, Jonathan Kotchian 161
Abrupt, Absurd, Unconventional: Jane and Rochester
     Against the Victorian Conversational Landscape, Cala Zubair   176
Jane Laughs Last: Developing Feminist Humor in
     Charlotte Brontë's *Jane Eyre*, Amanda T. Smith   192

Playing with Dramatic Adaptations: Charades as an Approach to
    John Brougham's 1849 Adaptation of *Jane Eyre*, Mary Isbell   210
'A Solemn and Strange and Perilous Thing': Rereading a
    Reading of *Jane Eyre*, Meghan Sweeney   227
Re-reading Jane Eyre: Not a Romantic Marriage Plot but a
    Tale of Evolving Feminist Consciousness, Barbara Waxman   243

Resources _____

Chronology of Charlotte Brontë's Life   263
Works by Charlotte Brontë   265
Bibliography   266

About the Editor   269
Contributors   270
Index   273

Dedication

For Amy

To my mom, Sharon, who introduced me to *Jane Eyre*, and
to my mentors, Margaret Sönser Breen and
Katherine Montwieler, thank you.
In memory of Karen L. Cajka
and Angela M. Bellardini.

About This Volume

Katie R. Peel

As I invited scholars to contribute to this volume, despite the deterrent of a quick turnaround time that conflicted with the academic calendar ("against my better judgment," and "although it conflicts with my sense of sanity and self-preservation," wrote contributors who shall remain nameless here), the most common response was "but it's *Jane Eyre*!" There is something about this novel, even if it is merely nostalgia-inspiring, that makes the offer to participate in a project like this too tempting to turn down. We find ourselves unable to resist returning to *Jane Eyre*.

I am thrilled to present the contributions to this volume. All but two essays consist of new scholarship, and the two reprints are among the strongest recent essays on *Jane Eyre*. The pieces here provide multiple approaches, including—and this is a novelty for a collection of literary scholarship – a linguistic analysis of the conversation between Jane Eyre and Rochester. The essays here also represent various stages of relationships with *Jane Eyre*. Some authors have been reading and working with *Jane Eyre* across decades, and some come from scholarship in other fields to work with the novel for the first time. In some cases, the authors are using the same passages to argue very different points. The fact that we are still producing new scholarship about *Jane Eyre* indicates how compelling, complex, and perhaps unsettling the novel is. To continue this conversation is to find new ways to think about the novel, make new connections, and come to new understandings.

Critical Insights: Jane Eyre is divided into four sections: an introductory section, a "Critical Contexts" section, a "Critical Readings" section, and a "Resources" section. The introduction considers why we still turn to *Jane Eyre*. It takes a New Historical approach that connects a passage in the novel to an image that would be familiar to its contemporary readers. Joanne Cordón's biography of Charlotte Brontë traces both her life and literary experiences, offering some personal context for the work that we are familiar with. The "Resources" section at the end offers a basic chronology of Brontë's life, as well as a list of her major works. It also includes a bibliography of secondary sources for further reading and research about *Jane Eyre*.

The "Critical Contexts" section takes four distinct approaches to the novel. "Souvenirs of Sadism: Mahogany Furniture, Deforestation, and Slavery in *Jane Eyre*" comes from Elaine Freedgood's *The Ideas in Things: Fugitive Meaning in the Victorian Novel*. Freedgood connects objects in the home with the industry of empire and its violent history. She reads the objects as well as the act of decorating in ways that intersect with feminist, postcolonial, psychoanalytical, and ecocritical readings of *Jane Eyre*.

In his essay on the critical reception of *Jane Eyre*, John O'Hara traces the reception of the novel from its early reviews to present-day scholarship, across time and schools of thought.

In "Passion and Economics in *Jane Eyre* and *North and South*," Thomas Recchio uses Lucasta Miller's comparison of the passive Ruth (from Elizabeth Gaskell's *Ruth*) with passionate Lucy Snowe (from Brontë's *Villette*) as the premise for his comparison of *North and South*'s Margaret Hale with Jane Eyre. His exploration of the intersections of passion and economic inequalities demonstrates interesting overlaps in the works of these two friends, with narrative results that are significantly different.

The "Critical Contexts" section ends with "Shameful Signification: Narrative and Feeling in Jane Eyre," in which Ashly Bennett examines the narrative function of shame as a mediator between anger and sympathy, and "an alternative for shaping individuated, intimate social relations."

The "Critical Readings" section consists of nine new essays that take a range of approaches to various topics in *Jane Eyre*. Katherine Montwieler takes a psychoanalytic approach in reading the inherited traumas of the house in her essay "Women's Place: Home, Sanctuary, and the Big House in *Jane Eyre*." She reads houses as ambivalent, looking at how they are both sites of containment and sanctuary, maintaining the scars of trauma, but also consoling the women within. We move from the sins of the patriarchy to the perceived sins of the mother in Mara Reisman's "Sins of the Mother: Adèle's Genetic and National Burden in *Jane Eyre*." Reisman shifts the postcolonial critical gaze from Bertha to Adèle, and reads the young girl as a site of national anxieties. Like Jane, Adèle is a liminal figure, but unlike Jane, she remains outside of the domestic space at the end of the narrative. Reisman accounts for this with Adèle's French mother, whose legacy ultimately keeps Adèle from being fully anglicized.

The project of anglicization is represented in the mission of St. John Rivers, a character whom many critics have struggled to read. In "'That Better Part Which Cannot Be Taken From You': Varieties of Christian Experience in *Jane Eyre*," Jennie-Rebecca Falcetta reads *Jane Eyre* as offering multiple kinds of Christianities. She also provides a reconsideration of St. John Rivers, recovering him from reductive readings that discuss him as merely Rochester's romantic rival. Jonathan Kotchian also examines St. John's role in his "Right Obedience and Milton's Abdiel in Jane Eyre." Kotchian, a scholar of Renaissance literature, applies Abdiel, a character in Milton's *Paradise Lost*, ("the only angel in Satan's rank to reject sin and remain faithful to God") as a model to use in reading both the tension between Jane's obedience and her resistance, and St. John's narrative function.

This conflict between obedience and resistance, submission and dominance, surfaces in conversation in *Jane Eyre*, and Cala Zubair examines the verbal sparring between Jane and Rochester. In "Abrupt, Absurd, Unconventional: Jane and Rochester Against the Victorian Conversational Landscape," Zubair takes a linguist's approach to the conversation between Jane and Rochester and argues that Jane achieves equality via her conversational prowess and maneuverings, acts that have implications for both gender and socioeconomic class.

Amanda T. Smith also looks at Jane's conversation and responses to situations in her own development of humor as a coping mechanism. In "Jane Laughs Last: Developing Feminist Humor in Charlotte Brontë's *Jane Eyre*", Smith argues that *Jane Eyre* is, indeed, a book of humor. She traces the development of

Jane's own sense of humor as a survival skill, one that connects her to the laughing Bertha and is ultimately an indicator of her triumph.

Mary Isbell looks at John Brougham's 1849 stage adaptation of *Jane Eyre* and compares audience response to such adaptations with spectator involvement in the game of charades. She uses Brontë's own model, the charades passage in *Jane Eyre*, to consider the role of viewer interpretation in the performance and reception of an adaptation. To do so offers a window into contemporary commentary (in this case, commentary having to do with socioeconomic class), indicating the potential richness to be found in such adaptations.

While all of these essays result from multiple readings, the final two are explicitly about rereading the novel across time and experience. The last two pieces offer examples of reader-response criticism, as two contributors consider rereadings of *Jane Eyre*. Meghan Sweeney considers not only a rereading of the novel, but also a rereading of her own undergraduate paper on *Jane Eyre*. Sweeney, whose work currently examines issues of marriage and weddings in narratives for young readers, considers her position today, both as a scholar and teacher of undergraduate students, as well as a former undergraduate student tasked with writing about *Jane Eyre*. This conversation with her undergraduate work can be useful in terms of considering revision as we revisit both a primary text and our own responses to it.

Barbara Waxman's essay charts her own reading of *Jane Eyre* across the years, from her first encounter with it as a young girl in 1960s New York, to a recent reading of it as a full professor in North Carolina. Waxman positions Jane as a model for the developing reader, and demonstrates the ways in which our own relationships with a narrative can change and, ultimately, become enhanced. Both essays convey the pleasures of returning to a work and the potentials for one's own experiences with the novel.

One might think that all has been said with respect to *Jane Eyre*, but these essays indicate that the conversation continues in important ways. We hope that this collection of essays not only provides useful resources, but also inspires your own engagement with the novel.

THE BOOK
AND
AUTHOR

(Still) on *Jane Eyre*

Katie R. Peel

Charlotte Brontë's *Jane Eyre* has been a contentious novel since its publication in 1847. While today's book covers and film trailers tout it as one of the greatest love stories of all time, twenty-first century readers and viewers often forget—or were never aware of— the novel's initial controversies. Early reviews of *Jane Eyre* were generally positive, nearly all remarking specifically on the "power" and "passion" of the novel, while inspiring speculation as to the true identity of "Currer Bell," the author listed. (Charlotte Brontë did not claim the authorship of *Jane Eyre* publicly until her 19 September 1850 preface to an edition of Emily Brontë's *Wuthering Heights*.) Many of the book's aspects that otherwise would have gone unremarked upon became "coarse" once readers suspected that a woman had written it. The *Christian Remembrancer* review notes that in *Jane Eyre* "there is an intimate acquaintance with the worst parts of human nature [. . .] startling of one in the softer sex" (89). In her now infamous review, Elizabeth Rigby, Lady Eastlake, writes that the novel is anti-Christian, in that it challenges the hierarchies established by God (109), and that "we have no remembrance of another combining such genuine power with such horrid taste" (106). This, however, did little to curb the novel's appeal. Brontë's challenges to institutional hierarchies, the ways she articulates spirituality and female desire, her madwoman character, the threat of bigamy, and nighttime arson all made *Jane Eyre* incredibly popular in the mid- and late-nineteenth century. According to her diaries, Queen Victoria read the novel at least twice, the first time staying up late at night to read it with Albert and the second time noting that she found "[t]he description of the mysterious maniac's nightly appearances awfully thrilling" (390).

Today, over one hundred fifty years later, *Jane Eyre* remains a cultural touchstone. Several film adaptations exist, including the most recent—a 2011 production—starring Mia Wasikowska in the title role. Scholarship addresses the book's global readership in countries including China, Japan, Argentina, Portugal, and Germany. The novel has even merited mention on television's *Law and Order*, a true indication of Pop Culture achievement. *Jane Eyre* even surfaces on bookshelves in the forms of graphic novels and board books. As demonstrated by the frequency with which these board books (notably light on plot and bearing no mention of Bertha) appear at English faculty baby showers, these are intended more to evoke the adult reader's nostalgia than to edify the baby or illuminate the narrative itself.

Jane Eyre has a near cult-like following, particularly amongst female readers who have identified with the character Jane and her sense of being wronged. I still have my "Illustrated Junior Library" edition, given to me by my mother, who, while tucking me in one night, told me the story of Jane and Rochester. I distinctly remember her telling me, in a hushed voice, about Bertha and the arson, and I also distinctly recall my own sense of horror. Although I have not yet forgiven her for the spoilers, it was clear to me even then how invested she was in the story of the fierce, young girl who ultimately marries well.

The scholarship of *Jane Eyre* has also proven canonical, and, like the novel's enduring presence in popular culture, is an indicator of its readership's restlessness. Sandra M. Gilbert and Susan Gubar's landmark *The Madwoman in the Attic: The Woman Writer and the Nineteenth-Century Literary Imagination* pioneered the feminist approach to *Jane Eyre* and several other nineteenth-century narratives. For generations of scholars, Gilbert and Gubar's work not only forged a place for second-wave feminism in the academy, but also serves as a model. In the words of a contributor to this collection, Katherine Montwieler, for so many of us, "it is why we have jobs." Many of us are indebted to not only Charlotte Brontë and *Jane Eyre*, but also to the scholarship inaugurated by Gilbert and Gubar. To tackle this scholarship, then, is a delicate task; we appreciate the work of those who came before us, while at the same time applying a critical lens, as evident in Annette R. Federico's collection *Gilbert and Gubar's* The Madwoman in the Attic *After Thirty Years*. There is a lot at stake in literary, cultural, and scholarly senses, and yet we find ourselves unable to resist returning to *Jane Eyre*.

What keeps us coming back? *Jane Eyre* is a novel whose richness continues to invite new readings and innovative theoretical approaches. Most recently, *The Madwoman and Blindman:* Jane Eyre, *Discourse, Disability*, edited by David Bolt, Julia Miele Rodas, and Elizabeth J. Donaldson, uses developments in disability studies to reconsider the novel, and *A Breath of Fresh Eyre: Intertextual and Intermedial Reworkings of* Jane Eyre (edited by Margarete Rubik and Elke Mettinger-Schartmann) looks at various adaptations and iterations of *Jane Eyre*. Some of the most interesting readings of *Jane Eyre* draw on multiple approaches, and these remind us of the complexity of the narrative. Remembering and valuing *Jane Eyre* primarily as a romance, which is often the angle popular culture references take, itself should not be dismissed. In *Reading the Romance: Women, Patriarchy, and Popular Literature*, a study of female readers and romance novels, Janice Radway demonstrates that the allure of the romantic plot has to do not only with readers' desire for escape, but specifically with their own lack of fulfillment by the patriarchal institutions and structures that the novels seem to celebrate. We read romances in light of our own experiences, and Radway finds that the popularity of such narratives is quite telling in terms of our own dissatisfactions.

Considering *Jane Eyre* solely as a romance, however, does not always allow appreciation of Brontë's savvy narrative. For example, while many readers remember "Reader, I married him" as the narrative closure, fewer recall that the novel actually ends with St. John Rivers. This brings me to frustrations with *Jane Eyre*. While *The Madwoman in the Attic* offers a new way to understand nineteenth-century female literary experience, other developments in theory, notably postcolonial and queer theories, have further complicated our readings of *Jane Eyre*. For example, how do we understand Jane, particularly her marriage and status at the end of the novel, with respect to Bertha and to Rochester's sins of Empire? How do we reconcile these frustrations with our own nostalgia for and appreciation of the fierce, young, female protagonist, who is both wronged and resilient? What appeals to so many readers about Jane's voice and struggles for agency from childhood through adulthood? This question of the novel's appeal is one reason why her articulation, "Reader, I married him," is so significant: Jane is the subject, and Rochester the object. Can readers celebrate this, even if they do not appreciate Rochester as the object of her action and affection? While today we might read the marriage plot as narrative capitulation, in 1847, the plight of the white, working woman would have been more culturally salient, and thus Brontë's narrative closure could have been read more immediately as a narrative coup for working women characters. What we can celebrate, then, is what Jane's statement to the reader means on a very practical level to a working Victorian woman.

Today, in terms of narrative, Jane's marriage to the fallen patriarch appears to be not just compensation for the various wrongs in the book. In fact, it is tempting to read *Villette* (1853) in some ways as a re-visioning (à la Adrienne Rich) of *Jane Eyre*'s narrative closure. Charlotte Brontë allows Lucy Snowe the ending that we might want for Jane Eyre: independence, success, and appreciation (love, even!) without having to be completely inscribed within patriarchal systems, the most notable of which is marriage.

While Jane's integration into patriarchal patterns might not satisfy all of today's readers, this narrative closure had a special significance for the novel's nineteenth-century readers. Order is restored in the conventional narrative closure of Jane's marriage to Rochester, but Jane is a protagonist for whom the system has never worked, and for whom this closure is never a realistic possibility. For readers who value these systems, conventional narrative, and pure survival, Jane's status at the end of the novel is a triumph (and no small one, given the rigidity and exclusivity of these systems, and the odds against real outsiders).

Victorian gender ideology located women in the private sphere, creating the ideal of the white, middle-class woman in domestic space, who neither worked outside the home nor received money for labor. Working women threatened contemporary gender ideology, which ascribed dependency, natural passivity, and sincerity to females, particularly middle-class women who were not supposed to work. Middle-class working women were thus an especial cause of ideological anxiety, as they defied not only gender assumptions, but also class expectations, and, within the context of Empire, racial expectations. Working women, then, as Rachel Brownstein, author of *Becoming a Heroine*: *Reading About Women in Novels*, writes, are "unsuitable for narrative, which is bound to conventional concepts of woman" (171). Jane Eyre, as a woman who must work, moves beyond the boundaries of conventional narrative, which relies on normative, patriarchal, and heterosexual institutions and their constructs of the ideal woman. Her inclusion in the novel is thus incredible on a narrative level, and her existence in liminal spaces throughout reminds us of this. Jane progresses from the curtained window seat, to the charity school in an uninhabitable clime, to a seat on the edge of the parlor during Rochester's house party, to the open moors, to the outskirts of Morton, ultimately to be wrenched into hetero-patriarchal systems of power to become the mistress of Ferndean. Jane Eyre achieves the narrative closure usually offered only to female characters of more promising social statuses. While her marriage to Rochester may seem like narrative capitulation, when read in the context of Jane's trajectory as a female who must fend for herself from the very first passage of the novel, and in light of contemporary anxieties regarding women and work, such closure is far from conventional.

The novel's first readers would have had the cultural context to recognize Jane as a woman who worked. While *Jane Eyre*, published in 1847, appeared before Barbara Bodichon's "Women and Work" of 1857 and W. R. Greg's "Why Are Women Redundant?" of 1862, its middle-class, British readership would have already been familiar with the plight of governesses and needlewomen. Relief efforts for genteel working women in distress, such as the founding of both the Governesses' Benevolent Institution in 1841 and the Association for the Aid of Milliners and Dressmakers in 1843, aimed to ameliorate the situation that resulted from the flooding of the market, a population imbalance, and the lack of education and training of women for any other occupations. Such relief efforts grew out of anxieties regarding middle-class women who had to work, and the threat that their circumstances posed to ideals of gender and class.

Concurrently, middle-class England was becoming aware of the deplorable working conditions of many working-class women. In 1840, Parliament deployed a committee to investigate working conditions for children in mines and collieries, workplaces which were not included in England's initial, earlier factory acts. The committee discovered conditions so shocking that they redefined the parameters of their study to include women (Johnson 19). The committee reports were published in Parliamentary Blue Books and later in the *Westminster Review*, with illustrations that depicted women partially-clad, crawling on all fours, and chained to heavy mining carts.

© *Bodleian Libraries/University of Oxford. Reprinted with permission.*

When the general public became aware of these working conditions, most notably reacting to the published images, responses to the slavish, animalistic, and downright "unnatural" positions that women had been forced into were volatile (Johnson 19). Working-class women, who, according to socioeconomic ideology were *supposed* to work, faced gendered degradation to an extent that the middle- and upper-classes found abhorrent. Consequently Parliament passed the Mines and Collieries Act of 1842, which forbade women from working below ground entirely. Other protective legislation was soon to follow: factory and mines acts became law in 1844, 1847, and 1850.

Part of *Jane Eyre*'s sensationalism lies, then, not only in the threat of bigamy, and in Bertha herself (see Queen Victoria's note, above), but also in the image of Jane reduced to all fours on the open moors. For readers who had seen the illustrations in the *Westminster Review*, Brontë's descriptions of Jane crawling on the open moors would have recalled those iconic images. Brontë is specific in noting that Jane falls repeatedly upon leaving Rochester's house, and that she is regularly on her hands and knees. Upon leaving Thornfield, Jane desperately crosses the moor to get to the road:

> I was weeping wildly as I walked along my solitary way: fast, fast I went, like one delirious. A weakness, beginning inwardly, extending to the limbs, seized me, and I fell: I lay on the ground some minutes, pressing my face to the wet turf. I had some fear – or hope – that here I should die: but I was soon up; crawling forwards on my hands and knees, and then again raised to my feet – as eager and as determined as ever to reach the road. (274)

Jane continually finds herself on her hands and knees. Thus she recalls that, after sleeping upon the heath, "Worn out with this torture of thought, I rose to my knees. [. . .] I had risen to my knees to pray for Mr. Rochester" (276). Ultimately, "I tried to walk again: I dragged my exhausted limbs slowly towards it. [. . .] Here I fell twice; but as often I rose and rallied my faculties" (282). Further, Brontë makes explicit the connection between Jane's physical circumstances here and her search for a job: "Human life and human labour were near. I must struggle on: strive to live and bend to toil like the rest" (279). In asking a Morton woman if she needs a servant, Jane tells her, "'I want some work: no matter what'" (279). Jane is on all fours while seeking work, and this image of a woman crawling on her hands and knees upon the ground would have suggested to some readers the then-iconic images from the Parliamentary Blue Books, which were published, like George Henry Lewes' glowing review of *Jane Eyre*, in the *Westminster Review*. These descriptions of Jane, destitute on the heath, could also recall the alarm aroused by the graphic representations of women workers. Memories of these iconic images could have helped readers transcend the class distinction between Jane and the mining women, and help them read Jane as a working woman without protection and resources. This connection to the illustrations of the mining women heightens the desperation, danger, and urgency Jane faces when she walks out of Rochester's home and into the wild. Granted, this action is probably less shocking than a wife with mental health issues burning down the house in the night, but it certainly underscores and contributes to anxiety concerning Jane's situation. *Jane Eyre* benefits from this cultural context. For Victorian readers, the narrative convention of marriage to an estate owner thus offers a welcome relief to this very real and often tragic plight of women having to become self-sufficient in a culture that trains them to be dependents.

If Jane Eyre's very existence as a working woman is "unsuitable for narrative," then this novel, Jane Eyre's experience in narrative form, is defiant. Jane's true rescue, however, comes at the moment of her inheritance, and not with her marriage to Rochester. She moves from a woman on all fours to mistress of Rochester's estate, but she walks into Ferndean as her own mistress, as the heir of the Madeira fortune. Brontë is careful to ensure that Jane does not need marriage as a rescue from her situation, but rather that she chooses to enter it as a self-sufficient woman. This is part of Brontë's narrative coup. Yes, it is extraordinary that Jane moves from orphan governess to Mrs. Rochester, but the bigger jump happens when Jane moves from orphan governess to heir of her Uncle Eyre's fortune. Jane's end position as mistress of Ferndean, as Rochester's wife, should be read not as her saving grace, but rather as a measure of how far she has come, and how she is able to enjoy the comforts of what her culture values. We can read her marriage as a narrative triumph for a woman whose experiences are unsuitable for conventional narrative, though, notably, the marriage is not Jane's rescue.

Jane Eyre and *Jane Eyre* are troubling. From the start, Jane is the trouble in Aunt Reed's family, and like Bertha, she cannot be contained. Similarly, we continue to wrestle with the novel's complications. We keep revisiting *Jane Eyre* because it is complex, and because there are contradictions and problematic elements. While it is Jane's feistiness and resilience that we may remember, along with her romantic ending, we also need to remember just what this happy ending signifies for her as a working woman, and how she gets there on her own. While there are readers, myself included, who are frustrated with the seemingly conventional narrative closure, we should remember what this convention means to a character like Jane. We read *Jane Eyre* against ourselves not only, as Radway argues, in the romantic sense, but also in the context of our own concerns and anxieties regarding gender, labor, class, and self-sufficiency. These vary, of course, from one reader to another, as do historical, cultural, and reading circumstances, but it is because, for so many of us, these issues are unresolved that we find *Jane Eyre* an intriguing read. Just as the novel may have resonated with its initial readers due to its connections with contemporary issues of gender and labor, in the United States, today at least, these are related issues that have yet to be resolved in mainstream discourse.

At the time of writing this essay, Sheryl Sandberg's controversial *Lean In: Women, Work, and the Will To Lead* has been at the top of the *New York Times* best-seller lists for weeks; a recent *New York Times Magazine* cover story featured women who left high-profile careers to be stay-at-home mothers who were feeling ambivalent and sometimes regretting their choices (Warner); and *The Chronicle of Higher Education* has published another essay about "The Superwoman Myth." Whether or not women "can have it all" is still the question we are asking. Furthermore, exactly one hundred fifty years after Currer Bell published *Jane Eyre*, J. K. Rowling, wary of readers who might be deterred by knowing that a certain kind of book had been written by a female author, published the first book of what would become one of the best-selling series of all time using her initials in order to disguise her gender. Although some of the specifics regarding the issues may have changed with time, our anxieties regarding gender and labor have not dissipated. We read *Jane Eyre* against ourselves, and in the context of our own lives and experiences, the feelings of relief, disgust, and ambivalence we experience when reading "Reader, I married him," are valid

---

responses. The will-she-or-won't-she romantic question that drives the novel for some readers is embedded in the context of concerns that we have yet to resolve as individuals and a culture, and this lack of resolution continues to affect our readings and appreciations of the novel.

So, while we may hope that Jane finds fulfillment in teaching at the girls' school in Morton, and although we may want her to resist running back to Rochester, reconsidering Jane's plight as a woman who works can help us to appreciate what it means for her to finish the narrative as the mistress of Ferndean. While the relationship between Jane and Rochester is what readers may remember most or first, it is Brontë's sophisticated and radical narrative moves that make *Jane Eyre* a novel we continue to revisit.

Works Cited

Adams, Jennifer. *Jane Eyre: A BabyLit Counting Primer*. Utah: Gibbs Smith, 2012.

Allott, Miriam, ed. *The Brontës: The Critical Heritage*. London: Routledge and Kegan Paul, 1974.

"Elizabeth Rigby, from an unsigned review, *Quarterly Review*: December 1848, xxxiv, 153-85."*The Brontës: The Critical Heritage*. Ed. Miriam Allott. London: Routledge and Kegan Paul, 1974. 105-112.

"From an unsigned review, *Christian Remembrancer*: April 1848, xv, 396-409." *The Brontës: The Critical Heritage*.Ed. Miriam Allott. London: Routledge and Kegan Paul, 1974. 88-92.

"Queen Victoria on Jane Eyre: 1858 and 1880." *The Brontës: The Critical Heritage*. Ed. Miriam Allott. London: Routledge and Kegan Paul, 1974. 389-90.

Bodichon, Barbara. *Women and Work*. New York: C. S. Francis and Co., 1859.

Bolt, David, Julia Miele Rodas, and Elizabeth J. Donaldson, eds. *The Madwoman and Blindman: Jane Eyre, Discourse, Disability*. Columbus: The Ohio State UP, 2012.

Brontë, Charlotte. *Jane Eyre*. Ed. Richard J. Dunn. New York: W. W. Norton, 2000.

Brownstein, Rachel M. *Becoming a Heroine: Reading About Women in Novels*. New York: Columbia UP, 1994.

Gilbert, Sandra M. and Susan Gubar. *The Madwoman in the Attic: The Woman Writer and the Nineteenth-Century Literary Imagination*. New Haven: Yale UP, 2000.

Greg, W. R. "Why Are Women Redundant?" *National Review 14* (April 1862): 434-460.

Jane Eyre. Dir. Cary Fukunaga. Perf. Mia Wasikowska, Michael Fassbender, and Jamie Bell. Focus Features, 2011. DVD.

Johnson, Patricia E. *Hidden Hands: Working-Class Women and Victorian Social-Problem Fiction*. Athens: Ohio UP, 2001.

"Paranoia." *Law and Order*. Season 6, Episode 6. 15 Nov 1995. Television.

Radway, Janice. *Reading the Romance: Women, Patriarchy, and Popular Literature*. Chapel Hill: U of North Carolina P, 1984.

Rich, Adrienne. "When We Dead Awaken: Writing as Re-vision." *College English* 34.1 (1972): 18-30.

Rubik, Margarete and Elke Mettinger-Schartmann, eds. *A Breath of Fresh Eyre: Intertextual and Intermedial Reworkings of Jane Eyre*. Amsterdam: Rodopi, 2007.

Sandberg, Sheryl. *Lean In: Women, Work, and the Will To Lead*. New York: Knopf, 2013.

Spar, Debora L. "The Superwoman Myth." *The Chronicle of Higher Education* 2 Sept. 2013 Web. 4 Sept 2013.

Warner, Judith. "The Opt-Out Generation Wants Back In." *The New York Times Magazine* 7 Aug. 2013.

Biography of Charlotte Brontë

Joanne Cordón

Charlotte Brontë was born on 21 April 1816, the third of six children born to Maria, née Branwell, and Patrick Brontë (né Brunty). When Charlotte was four, her family moved to Haworth in Yorkshire, the north of England. Here Patrick would serve as an Anglican minister for the rest of his career, quite a feat for the son of a poor Irish farmer, who managed to achieve a Cambridge education and marry an English wife during a posting in Cornwall.

The family was a close one, living together in the parsonage on the top of a hill on the main street of Haworth. Their location was one of contrasts, with the moors on one side and the mills and manufacturing on the other. According to Elizabeth Gaskell, the popular novelist and author of the first authorized biography, *The Life of Charlotte Brontë*, the town's setting had a raw beauty:

> All around the horizon there is this same line of sinuous wave-like hills; the scoops into which they fall only revealing other hills beyond, of similar color and shape, crowned with wild, bleak moors—grand, from the ideas of solitude and loneliness which they suggest, or oppressive from the feeling which they give of being pent-up by some monotonous and illimitable barriers, according to the mood of mind in which the spectator may be. (4)

The Brontë marriage was a happy one, and the couple had six children in seven years: Maria, Elizabeth, Charlotte, Branwell, the only son, Emily, and Anne. Maria's early death was a terrible loss to the family; Charlotte was five when her mother died. Widowed at forty-three, Patrick did not remarry, though he did propose to three different women before he realized that Elizabeth Branwell, Maria's unmarried sister, was his best hope for helping him to raise the family, while he performed his ministerial duties.

Charlotte had a small and slight figure, and her hazel eyes were her best and most often-remarked upon feature. Her brother

Branwell's portrait of her (1834) emphasizes her pale skin, light brown hair, and large, staring eyes. George Richmond's 1850 chalk sketch of her,commissioned by her publisher and now in the National Portrait Gallery, also suggests her intelligence, giving her a resolute countenance that defies her simple hairstyle and lacy collar. Gaskell describes her expression as transcending the plain face with its strong features:

> The usual expression was of quiet, listening intelligence; but now and then, on some just occasion for vivid interest or wholesome indignation, a light would shine out, as if some spiritual lamp had been kindled, which glowed behind those expressive orbs. (*Life of Charlotte Brontë* 65-66)

Her character was intricate. She could be shy with strangers or in large groups, but when roused she could be fierce, especially in defense of someone she loved. She was also honest, affectionate, direct, passionate and loyal; she had a great capacity for kindness and could be gentle and firm simultaneously. She was very religious, but her understanding was nuanced and thoughtful. She loved nature and drawing, and her favorite pastimes were those that allowed her liberty to read, write, and exercise her imagination.

Her education began at home, as all of the siblings seem to have had an early love for reading. They read widely in popular and classical texts—Sir Walter Scott's novels were in heavy rotation, as were *The Arabian Nights*, *The Pilgrim's Progress*, and *Paradise Lost*—books of geography or history, both national and natural, as well as in the newspaper and popular periodicals, the favorite being *Blackwood's Magazine*.

She had some formal education, and though she was a diligent and gifted student, her experiences at school varied wildly. At eight, she spent a year at the Clergy Daughters School at Cowan Bridge; she survived the demanding Victorian curriculum and the execrable nutrition provided, but her two older sisters, Maria and Elizabeth, who enrolled at the same time, were not so lucky. Both were dead within the year.

Back at home, Charlotte resumed her more informal studies. Years later, in a letter to a friend, sixteen-year-old Charlotte explained the happy repetition of her days as a sequence of studies, drawing, walking, reading, writing, or needlework, all in the company of her three siblings, observing that "an account of one day is an account of all" (*Letters of Charlotte Brontë* 21 July 1832).

When nearly fifteen, she returned to school at Miss Wooler's in Roe Head. Though her adjustment was slow, Charlotte's fierce drive and love for learning soon made her a top student; it took her only three terms to master the curriculum. Equally impressive was her progress at the Pensionnat Heger in Belgium a decade later. In both cases, after a short span of instruction—a year and a half at Roe Head, six month in Brussels—she was offered a teaching position at the school.

While often shy in social situations, Charlotte made the first real friends outside of her family, Mary Taylor and Ellen Nussey, as a teenager at Roe Head. Their connection with her would be lasting. Charlotte's social life revolved around the poles of her family and friends. She stayed with the Nussey and Taylor families, and her friends visited at Haworth. With Ellen, she made her first trip to the seaside, relishing her trip to the ocean. Mary's travels to the continent encouraged Charlotte to go to school in Brussels.

Though she often found it grueling, Charlotte made several forays into employment. At nineteen in July of 1835, Charlotte accepted a teaching job at Roe Head, where she stayed until May 1838. Her other employment was as a governess. She held a temporary position with the Sidgwick family during the summer of 1839, and she spent March to September of 1841 with the White family. She found the work oppressing: "I am sad, very sad, at the thoughts of leaving home but Duty—Necessity—these are stern Mistresses who will not be disobeyed" (*Letters of Charlotte Brontë* 2 July 1835).

Back at home, she relished the stimulating company of her siblings and the freedom to exercise her imagination, so when she lost three of her siblings in less than a year, her distress was extreme. In September of 1847 Branwell died after a rapid and alcohol-fueled decline. Emily died in December that same year of consumption; Anne died of the same cause the following May. In the aftermath of so much loss so soon, Charlotte describes home as a haunted place: "I am free to walk the moors—but when I go out there alone—everything reminds me of the times when the others were with me and then the moors seem a wilderness, featureless, solitary, saddening" (*Letters of Charlotte Brontë* 22 May 1850).

As her loyal circle of friends suggests, Charlotte was capable of strong attachments. She received proposals of marriage from four different men between 1839 and 1852, the first from Ellen's brother Henry and the last from Arthur Bell Nicholls, the man she married. Her letters to Constantin Heger after she left his Pensionnat suggest that she had a passionate attachment to her married tutor. Her courtship to her father's curate was unorthodox. Between his proposal in December 1852 and her wedding, Charlotte weathered not only her father's strong disapproval and her friend Ellen's severe condemnation, but also her own change of heart. Her marriage at the end of June 1854 seems to have been brief but happy.

Charlotte Brontë died 31 March 1855. The doctor listed the cause of her death as phthisis, a chronic pulmonary disease, but her severe pregnancy-induced nausea may have contributed to her decline (Barker 911).

Life's Work

As her juvenilia shows, the imagination of Charlotte Brontë fires early and rich. The Brontë siblings wrote and acted out their own plays, some inspired by contemporary accounts of political or military battles. A set of toy soldiers bought for Branwell sparked a saga of the imaginary realm. In collaboration with her brother, Charlotte created, over the course of many years, elaborate narratives full of battles, political maneuvering, love affairs, and acres of description. These incorporated illustrations, maps, a mix of poetry and fiction, and featured the exploits of the Duke of Wellington and his rivals in a land with various locales and exotic names that eventually became the land of Angria.

She describes how fully the stories absorbed her even as a teacher at Roe Head. One night, a fierce storm blowing outside shifts her from the school room to Angria:

> I sat by myself in the dining-room while all the rest were at tea the trance seemed to descend on a sudden, & verily this foot trod the war-shaken shores of the Calabar and these eyes saw the defiled & violated Adrianopolis shedding its lights on the river from lattices whence the invader looked out & was not darkened. (*Tales of Glass Town, Angria, and Gondal* 158)

The vividness of her imagination led Charlotte and her siblings to make their own little books, some so small that they measured less than two-by-three inches, lettering the pages in tiny script and sewing them together.

In 1845, she made a foray into publishing after she accidentally discovered a manuscript of Emily's recent poetry. Thrilled at their quality, Charlotte persuaded her sisters that their work should be published, plundered her Angrian manuscripts for her own contribution, and sent a fair copy off to the London publisher Aylott and Jones with a text of approximately twenty poems from each sister. Her sisters insisted on anonymity, so Charlotte's first book, a self-published volume using some of the money they had inherited from their aunt, bore her pseudonym Currer Bell. The poems were well reviewed in the *Critic* and the *Athenaeum* but sold only two copies.

Switching to fiction after the unprofitable experience of poetry, Charlotte soon wrote *The Professor* while her sisters worked on their own novels. Sending the work out to London publishers, Charlotte collected a number of rejections until lucking upon Smith, Elder. They also rejected the novel, but saw enough talent in the prose to want to see more and sent an encouragingly long reply indicating their willingness to read later work.

Charlotte had begun writing *Jane Eyre* while in Manchester, helping her father as he recovered from cataract surgery over five weeks. The composition proceeded very rapidly. By the time she got the encouragement from Smith, Elder, she was well into the story and within two weeks of her letter from London had finished with the manuscript. Smith, Elder accepted *Jane Eyre* immediately for publication, and the novel was such a success that its original print run in October 1847 of 2500 copies sold out in three months. The novel had two more reprintings in January and April 1848.

The composition of *Shirley*, her third novel, was slower. Branwell's illness interrupted her writing, and his death and the deaths of Emily and Anne in rapid succession plunged her into grief. She returned to the novel after Anne's death, and by August, she had a copy ready for the publisher. Recourse to literary composition served as healing. She wrote to her publisher, speculating on what she would do after the loss of her three remaining siblings without her literary work: "In that case I should have no world at all" (*Letters of Charlotte Brontë* 3 July 1849).

After the publication of *Shirley* (1849), Charlotte's circle of acquaintance included some notable additions as her anonymity eroded. William Thackeray and George Henry Lewes were early fans of her work, and Brontë met them on occasional trips to London. She came to know Harriet Martineau and Elizabeth Gaskell more intimately, visiting both of their homes, and she received a visit from Gaskell at the Parsonage.

Charlotte took a long break between *Shirley* and her fourth composition. She enjoyed some aspects of being the celebrated author of *Jane Eyre* and made several trips to London. In 1851, she visited the Crystal Palace to see the Great Exhibition five times, and she enjoyed looking at painting exhibitions, attending several of Thackeray's lectures on eighteenth-century English humorists, and travelling to Newgate Prison. The writing of *Villette* took much longer than the other novels. She finished her draft in November of 1852, and the published text appeared in January of 1853. The novel was a success.

The Professor appeared posthumously in 1857; it was the only one of the novels to bear Brontë's name on the title page. Her publisher carefully arranged that Brontë's final novel would appear after Gaskell's biography, a work he also published, hoping that Gaskell's sympathetic story of Charlotte's life would placate the harsh critics who complained about the coarse, vulgar, or enthusiastic elements of her fiction. It was a strategy that paid off completely, as the early and flawed work *The Professor*, had modest sales. Brontë's final piece of writing, "Last Sketch," a fragment of a novel she never finished, appeared in *Cornhill Magazine* in 1860.

Works Cited

Barker, Juliet. *The Brontës: Wild Genius on the Moors: The Story of A Literary Family*. New York: Pegasus, 2012.

Brontë, Charlotte et. al. and Christine Alexander, ed. *Tales of Glass Town, Angria, and Gondal:Selected Writings*. Oxford: Oxford UP, 2010.

Gaskell, Elizabeth Cleghorn. *The Life of Charlotte Brontë*. Vol. 1. London: Smith, Elder, 1857.

Margaret Smith, ed. *The Letters of Charlotte Brontë*. 3 vols. Clarendon, Oxford UP, 1995-2004.

CRITICAL
CONTEXTS

Souvenirs of Sadism: Mahogany Furniture, Deforestation, and Slavery in *Jane Eyre*

Elaine Freedgood

"The form of wood, for instance, is altered, by making a table out of it. Yet, for all that, the table continues to be that common, every-day thing, wood. But, so soon as it steps forth as a commodity, it is changed into something transcendent. It not only stands with its feet on the ground, but, relation to all other commodities, it stands on its head, and evolves out of its wooden brain grotesque ideas, far more wonderful than "table-turning" ever was."

– KARL MARX, *Capital*, vol. 1

"Thinking guides and sustains every gesture of the hand. . . .We chose the cabinetmaker's craft as our example, assuming it would not occur to anybody that this choice indicated any expectation that the state of our planet could in the foreseeable future, or indeed ever, be changed back into a rustic idyll. The cabinetmaker's craft was proposed as an example of our thinking because the common usage of the word "craft" is restricted to human activities of that sort. However—it was specifically noted that what maintains and sustains even this handicraft is not the mere manipulation of tools, but the relatedness to wood. But where in the manipulations of the industrial worker is there any relatedness to such things as the shapes slumbering within wood?"

–MARTIN HEIDEGGER, "WHAT IS CALLED THINKING"

"From today's perspective, the subject of timber may seem a bit obscure, but to generations past it was exceedingly mundane. No contemporary resource can match timber's preeminent ranking in the pre-industrial world. Timber was not only the steel, aluminum, plastic and fiberglass of past ages, but oil, coal, and gas as well. . . . From the cradle to the coffin, the largest percentage of all past material culture has been wooden."

–Mills and Boon, *Fruitless Trees: Portuguese Conservation and Brazil's Colonial Timber*

I. Furniture

Jane Eyre has been widely discussed as a text of empire; it has less often been commented on as a work about interior decoration. Yet this is a novel that is flush with the details of furniture and drapery; in particular, Charlotte Brontë seems to have been something of an aficionado of wood, and we would do well to note whose furniture is made of what. At Gateshead, the residence of the despicable Reed family, there is massive mahogany furniture. At Lowood School, the teacher's room is furnished in mahogany—undoubtedly in a plainer style and probably in a cheaper variety than that of Gateshead—but the students' dining room has long "deal tables." Deal—planks of pine or fir—was the lowliest Victorian wood.

Indeed, mahogany and deal are two of the great class markers in Victorian fiction: mahogany, which is always being polished or burnished, represents tasteful opulence or nouveau riche groping for the trappings of bourgeois arrival; deal, which we usually find being scrubbed, can't approximate the luster of the much more expensive wood, but if it's clean it connotes honesty and employment in some form of hard work that doesn't pay well. A third kind of wood gets special mention in *Jane Eyre*: Thornfield has walnut-paneled walls, and the Rivers siblings have several pieces of walnut furniture. The "age of walnut" in English furniture history runs from 1660–1720, so that possession of walnut furniture in a novel in which empire has spawned much new richness indicates the relatively long duration of a family's gentility and lineage. The Rivers are cash poor now, but their walnut dresser suggests they've got good blood (as does Jane, their first cousin, as it miraculously turns out in this most improbably plotted of realist novels).

Jane redecorates two residences in the last third of the novel: Moor House, the home of the Rivers siblings, where she is taken in by chance (no one knows yet that they are cousins) after she leaves Thornfield upon learning that Rochester is already married, and Ferndean, to which Rochester decamps when Thornfield conveniently burns to the ground, taking Bertha Mason with it. Jane avoids refurnishing Moor House too extensively; she allows this rural cottage to retain its own history and culture in the fact of its plain, but old and elegant, furnishings. She most aggressively tackles a few rooms that are only minimally furnished. Turning them, oddly enough, into replicas of the infamous red room at Gateshead, she fills them with the "old mahogany" furniture and crimson drapery that contributed to her terror during her imprisonment in the room where her kindly uncle died, taking all of her immediate prospects of happiness with him. She thus creates for herself a souvenir of the sadism she endured at the hands of her cousins and her Aunt Reed at Gateshead; she makes it her own. Jane also buys souvenirs of what might be described as another form of sadism: the deforestation, colonization, and implementation of plantation slavery in the two critical sources of wealth in the novel, Madeira and the Caribbean. "Old" mahogany is probably, in the early decades of the nineteenth century, furniture made in the age of mahogany, 1720–60, when this wood, and furniture made from it, was still being imported in large quantities from those islands.[1]

When Jane returns to the environs of Thornfield at the end of the novel (after the famous Gothic eruption in which she "hears" Rochester calling her name), an innkeeper tells her about the fire that has burned down the house: "Thornfield Hall is quite a ruin;" he says, "it was burnt down just about harvest time. A dreadful calamity! Such an immense quantity of valuable property destroyed. Hardly any of the furniture could be saved."[2] It is worth remarking that furniture is of paramount importance; it takes about five more pages for the innkeeper to mention Bertha Mason's suicide during the fire. And at the end of the novel, the first thing we learn about Ferndean is that it "has been uninhabited and unfurnished" (455). We can only speculate about Jane's designs on this new residence—no specific plans or purchases are mentioned—but the most important point for now is to notice the benefit of unfurnished space in this novel. Like the fictitious but still convincing "blank" spaces on the map of empire, the idea of empty space invites the exercise of habitation as a demonstration of power.[3] The disposition of things in space is also a way of externalizing an internal arrangement of objects and of enacting, however unconsciously, a strict control over them.

And it is no mistake that a character like Jane—tough, practical and resilient as she is—would choose mahogany furniture.

Because mahogany, according to a handy little book called *Wood*,[4] is termite resistant; it is not subject to dry rot; it has little tendency to warp or twist; it is hard-hearted, which is a good thing for wood, making it dense and heavy; it has a fine straight grain and it polishes up beautifully to a reddish brown hue. It also takes glue exceedingly well, an important characteristic for Victorian furniture making. The great size of mahogany logs and the strength of the wood changed furniture design in the eighteenth century: very large and yet still delicate pieces could be made; the intricate carving and fretwork, skinny legs, and wafer-thin splats, seats, and table tops that characterize much eighteenth-century mahogany furniture might be imagined as attempting to ornately reverse, in the light airy quality they produce, the literally and figuratively heavy legacy of this wood's arrival in England.

R. W. Symonds, in *English Furniture from Charles II to George II*, recounts a curious anecdote about the advent of mahogany in England; he cites *A Book of English Trades* (1823) as his source.[5] In the late seventeenth century, one Dr. Gibbons had a brother who was a "West India captain." This brother brought some planks of mahogany back from the Caribbean because he needed ballast on his return journey to make up for the weight of the slaves he had delivered. On his return to England, he gave the planks to his brother Dr. Gibbons, who was in the midst of building a house. Initially the builders employed by Dr. Gibbons found the wood too hard to work with, but eventually he prevailed on them to make a candle box. The beauty of the wood was so striking that he commissioned a chest of drawers, which visitors admired immensely, and from this humble start, according to Symonds, mahogany as a furniture wood began to be imported into England in large quantities.

Jane can afford to refurnish and refurbish Moor House and Ferndean because she inherits a large sum from her uncle, an agent in Madeira of a trading company owned, in another almost unbelievable coincidence of connection, by the Mason family in Jamaica. During this period, Jane's uncle, John Eyre, was probably exporting the very popular madeira wine to the West Indies and Britain. Thornfield and Ferndean can be maintained because of the proceeds of this trading company in Madeira and because of the profits from a sugar plantation, also owned by the Mason family, in Jamaica. Curiously enough, some of the finest mahogany once came from Madeira and the Caribbean; indeed, in the Caribbean the word "madeira" meant mahogany (as well as wine) well into the nineteenth century. The world of *Jane Eyre* is decorated with the literal and figural proceeds of Atlantic trade in these two crucial locations. Both places were deforested of mahogany and planted with the cash crops that allow Jane Eyre to furnish her world with souvenirs, in the form of mahogany furniture, of the original material source of her wealth. I'm going to argue in this chapter that Jane's purchase and placement of mahogany furniture symbolizes, naturalizes, domesticates, and internalizes the violent histories of deforestation, slavery, and the ecologically and socially devastating cultivation of cash crops in Madeira and Jamaica.

In a recent book on consumer protest in the eighteenth century, Charlotte Sussman has argued that colonial products like tea and sugar made consumers anxious because they threatened to bring home the violence that attended their production.[6] This anxiety suggests the ways in which acts of consumption were regarded as moral choices at a moment that seems to be prior to the development of the consciousness Marx called commodity fetishism. Rather than being disavowed in the form of fetishes, the social relations of production that inhere in commodities were still all *too* present to protesting eighteenth-century consumers: an anxiety-reducing containment system for such cultural knowledge had not yet been developed. And for at least some consumers in the following century, the social relations of production also remained available to consciousness, but quite happily in many cases. The symbolic compression of violence in mahogany furniture was not a source of anxiety for a character like Jane—a poor, small, female person—but a source from which to draw consolation and a sense of power. Jane's ability to buy this fetish means that she can avow and disavow its history, and so can we: it will hide in plain sight in the rooms of her home and it will hide interpretively as a reality effect for the very readers of the novel who would otherwise have made this connection long ago, especially feminist and postcolonial critics who have been confined, by critical canons, to allegorical modes of reading.[7]

The ability to read fables of gender into the nineteenth-century novel, or to historicize the stories of poor governesses and creole madwomen, has revolutionized the criticism of the novel, and without it, the reading I do here would be impossible. But the intransigently allegorical mode of criticism blocks the reading of the *material* properties and relations of objects that don't give us immediate clues that will help us construct what we have come to understand as literary, rather than literal, meaning. For "the allegorist," Benjamin reminds us, "objects represent only keywords in a secret dictionary."[8] In the secret dictionary of novel criticism—the dictionary about which initiates must prove their knowledge—objects are weak metonyms for the subjects they adorn or generic markers of the real they indicate. The method of this book, that of the collector, requires a moment of forestalling allegory and of taking things literally. My project here is to imagine, like Benjamin's collector, that "the world is present, and indeed ordered" in certain objects.[9] That ordering is not an allegory, but a history. And it is not the history that the novel narrates, but the history that the novel secretes: the history it hides and emits, the one it conceals and produces as it calls to mind the locations of deforestation and slavery for which mahogany is a metaphor, a metonym, and a literal representation.

II. Forests

The geographical coordinates of *Jane Eyre*—Britain, Madeira, and Jamaica—allow the novel to revisit and remember the violence that inheres in the history and geography of British colonization, slavery, and trade. The first step in these processes, wherever they take place, is to clear land. If, as ecology and now ecocriticism have taught us, civilization and forests have been historically at odds with one another, empires and forests are particularly and chronically in conflict. Robert Pogue Harrison points out that "Rome . . . triumph[ed] over the great forest mass of the ancient world. The forests were literally everywhere: Italy, Gaul, Spain, Britain, the ancient Mediterranean basin as a whole. The prohibitive density of these forests had once safeguarded the relative autonomy and diversity of the family- and city-states of antiquity, precisely because they offered a margin of cultural privacy. . . . The forests were obstacles—to conquest, hegemony, homogenization. . . . [T]hey enabled communities to develop indigenously, hence they served to localize the spirit of place."[10] Deforestation had already become a serious problem in England by the sixteenth century. Measures were being taken for conservation, and books were being written on what would come to be called sustainable forestry. In 1598, for example, John Manwood (a person obviously destined to do such scholarship) wrote *A Treatise of the Laws of the Forest*, a work that anticipates descriptions of contemporary ecology: "Before this nation was replenished with inhabitants, there were many great woods full of all sorts of wild beasts then known in England; and after the same came to be inhabited, the woods were, by degrees, destroyed, especially near the houses; and as the land increased in people, so the woods and coverts were daily destroyed, and by that means, the wild beasts retired to those woods which were left standing, and which were remote from their habitations."[11] Acts for the preservation of woods were passed to "safeguard future timber supplies" even before Manwood's work appeared.[12] The aptly named Manwood, in other words, is reflecting an environmental consciousness that is already well formed by the late sixteenth century.

Jane Eyre remembers the deforestation of England: Jane comes to understand, as a child reading *Gulliver's Travels*, that there are no elves left in England, because they have all gone "to some savage country where the woods were wilder and thicker, and the population more scant" (53). The deforestation of England was initially the result of imperial aggression visited on Britain by Rome; it was extended by the need for firewood and building materials—especially for the ships of the Royal Navy, and by the aggression against the landscape produced by enclosure—a process that was reaching the culmination of its official, that is to say, parliamentary phase at the same time that *Jane Eyre* was being written and published.

The enclosure of common or unowned land seals the gate against one of the final vestiges of feudalism in England: "the commoning economy." Commoners, the historian J. M. Neeson tells us, were the last of the English peasantry; enclosure made them into a working class.[13] The "closing of the countryside"[14] begets a new class that must figure out how to get its living within an economy that is unforgivingly modern *and* grossly underdeveloped, especially for women, especially in rural areas. When Jane leaves Thornfield on learning that Rochester is married, she arrives in the town of Whitcross, asks what the "chief trade" of the place is, and learns that some are "farm labourers; a good dealwork. . . at Mr. Oliver's needle-factory, and at the foundry." Mr. Oliver does not employ women, it turns out. Jane then asks, "[W]hat do the women do?" She gets the vague but nonetheless accurate answer for much of rural England at this time: "Some does one thing, and some another. Poor folk mun get on as they can" (353).

In *Jane Eyre*, enclosure is imagined twice. First, at Lowood School, where the whole system is writ small: "The garden was a wide enclosure, surrounded with walls so high as to exclude every glimpse of prospect; a covered veranda ran down one side, and broad walks bordered a middle space divided into scores of little beds; these beds were assigned as gardens for the pupils to cultivate, and each bed had an owner" (80). Part of the making of the modern individual, a process to which *Jane Eyre* the novel and Jane Eyre the character made, and continue to make, a powerful contribution, is this kind of competitive individuation: one girl, one plot of land, one set of results accruing to each owner.

In this school and in its garden, Jane learns how to perform another kind of enclosure, the enclosure of the self. When she believes that Rochester and Blanche Ingram are going to be married, she forcefully reins herself in: "When I was once more alone, I reviewed the information I had got; I looked into my heart, examined its thoughts and feelings, and endeavored to bring back with a strict hand such as had been straying through imagination's boundless and tractless waste, into the safe fold of common sense" (190). Subjectivity has no limits or boundaries: it is a wasteland, a wilderness that must be enclosed by a strict "hand" reaching inside the self, ordering its contents, and closing its borders.

Enclosure requires deforestation; deforestation in turn guarantees the legible demarcation of space—its visibility and its representability. And yet the ugly remains of deforestation haunt *Jane Eyre* just as surely as its benefits underwrite crucial ideas and practices concerning the organization of subjective, domestic, and national space. In a desperate moment, after Bertha Mason attacks her brother and he is treated and removed from Thornfield, Rochester figures his home as a collection of the waste products of the deforestation process. He tells Jane that she cannot discern that the "polished woods" are mere "refuse chips and scaly bark." Pointing to the "leafy enclosure" they have entered, Rochester continues, "Now *here* . . . all is real, sweet and pure" (244). This bit of artificial wilderness on the grounds of Thornfield promises a form of wildness that can be strictly controlled: arbors, hedges, gardens, and enclosures seem to offer protection from both civilization and nature.[15] Or perhaps such cultivations promise a respite from attempts to balance what have long been imagined as the competing claims of the structures imagined oppositionally as "civilization" and "nature." A novel haunted by the ecological devastation of two far-flung archipelagoes, by the advent of a particularly horrific system of plantation slavery, by an inability to properly—which is to say spontaneously—domesticate national space might well need such a respite.

III. Trading Places

The Madeira Islands, an archipelago some four hundred miles off the coast of Africa between the Azores and the Canary Islands, were colonized by the Portuguese in the early fifteenth century, or more accurately, peopled by them, since the islands were uninhabited.[16] Madeira, the largest island of the group, means "wood" in Portuguese, and indeed, when it was discovered, the lower reaches of this very mountainous island were thickly timbered with a variety of fine wood-producing trees, including mahogany. Colonists burned off much of this wood in legendary conflagrations that lasted between seven and ten years and that, perhaps apocryphally, sometimes sent colonists fleeing into the ocean to prevent themselves from being devoured by flames along with Madeira's trees. Once the island was adequately deforested, cash crops were brought in. Sugar cane came from Sicily, and it thrived (as sick Britons would later) in Madeira's mild climate, and by 1500, most of the sugar consumed in Europe came from Madeira.[17] Grapes were also imported, from Crete and Cyprus, and by 1700, wine replaced sugar as the chief export, and this wine was largely exported to the West Indian and North American colonies, often in exchange for, ironically, timber—the resource Madeira had once had in abundance. The export of wine was facilitated by Madeira's critical position in Atlantic trading routes: ships from England headed to the east or the west often stopped at Madeira for revictualling.

Both the sugar and the grapes of Madeira were harvested by slaves. The first slaves in Madeira were Guanches, the indigenous people of the Canary Islands, who were taken as prisoners of war during Portuguese raids on the Spanish colony. In *Ecological Imperialism*, Alfred Crosby notes that only the Arawak Indians of the Caribbean compare to the Guanches in the earliness of their extinction due to the depredations of European colonization.[18] Once the Guanches had been entirely killed off, Madeirans turned to Africa for their slaves, and Madeira became one of the first places in which African slaves were used exclusively in a plantation system, marking an epoch in the history of slavery, forming "the pattern" that was then "to dominate the New World."[19]

In an 1890 memoir that surveys much of the Victorian period, *Leaves from a Madeira Garden*, Charles Thomas-Stanford notes that "Madeira has indeed been long a household word in Great Britain. Its generous wine has played an important part in producing the hereditary goutiness of the nation; and its genial climate is remembered in many families as having mitigated the sufferings of an invalid relation."[20] Less happily, the Madeira diary of Fanny Burney's great niece, Fanny Anne Burney, is punctuated by a death count of Britons from tuberculosis: she notes how difficult it can be to procure traditional British mourning clothes in Funchal when "several invalids have died in a short space of time."[21] Such descriptions alternate with more typical travel writing, including enthusiastic descriptions of the "extremely picturesque" *Vinhatico*, or "island mahogany," and minute detailing of the varieties of grape used in making madeira wine.[22] The familiarity of Madeira to nineteenth-century Britons is also suggested by Jane herself: when Bessie tells Jane about her uncle, John Eyre, Bessie can't remember the name of the island where he lives, but Jane guesses it immediately based on the single fact that Bessie can recall: that it produces wine.

Two hundred years after the deforestation and colonization of Madeira, that is, in the seventeenth century, Jamaica and other Caribbean islands were also heavily deforested and colonized for the purpose of producing cash crops, chiefly sugar. Just as Madeira had been the principle supplier of sugar to Europe until the seventeenth century, the Caribbean colonies became the principle supplier of sugar in the eighteenth. As it was in Madeira, and in Thornfield, I might add, much of the wood was cleared through burning, but fine furniture woods like mahogany were also exported in large quantities, causing what *A World Geography of Forest Resources* describes as a "heavy drain in precious woods," which combined with "clearing for plantations and subsistence crops . . . led to the destruction of most of the accessible forests [not only in Jamaica but throughout] the West Indies."[23] Jamaica, like Madeira, was also a major port of call in Atlantic trade and functioned as a distribution point for both slaves and sugar, so that it had a critical imperial role as both a trading and a plantation colony.[24]

One crucial difference between the two islands is that although Madeira's economy was unofficially but for all intents and purposes run by the British from the seventeenth century until the 1970s, it was not a colony.[25] It was and is a province of Portugal. Madeira, politically (or theoretically) speaking, was free to trade with Europe and European colonies without protection or impediment from a home government. Jamaica was, of course, a colony of Britain, and like all the West Indian colonies, heavily protected until the beginning of the nineteenth century. The British government kept the price of Caribbean sugar high by barring imports of sugar into

Britain (and British colonies) from other places. In other words, the West Indian plantocracy did not have to compete in an open or "free" market either in terms of production (since they relied on slave labor) or distribution (since their monopoly on British and colonial markets was government protected). *Jane Eyre*, in an implicit brief for free trade, suggests the result of this protection in the characterization of Richard Mason, Bertha's brother. He is weak, effeminate, and unable to tolerate the lack of central heating in Thornfield. The contempt with which Mason is treated in *Jane Eyre* by Jane—who knows nothing of "creole" stereotypes, and by Rochester, who finds them confirmed in this sickly and ineffectual man—suggests the extent to which the planter class became despised by many metropolitan Britons both for its wealth and for the fact that it was not earned competitively—even if those critical souls had not themselves earned their own wealth on a particularly level playing field.

Jane Eyre was written and published at the height of the free trade debates that raged throughout the first four decades of the nineteenth century; the Corn Laws were repealed finally in 1846, one year before the novel's publication. Free trade produced, according to its advocates, a kind of wealth any Briton could be proud of because the competition involved in it was imagined as fair. And it is no mistake that it is wealth from the informal, or what some historians have called, often with intended irony, the "free trade empire,"[26] that saves the day (and provides new furniture) in *Jane Eyre*. In the pro-free-trade argument, the noncolonizing form of imperialism is a far less expensive and less politically arduous way to get the stuff—the natural resources and the cash crops—out of various places in exchange for British manufactures.

The case of wood reveals starkly the uneven playing field of so-called free trade. Places that are deforested are put in the paradoxical position of then having to get their timber elsewhere. Either they can consider places in the north where conservation and property laws disallow the kind of ransacking that makes natural resources cheap in the south, or they can look to other parts of the south that are currently undergoing the ransacking of *their* natural resources by the north—Madeira, for example, turned to Jamaica for lumber in the eighteenth and nineteenth centuries. An ecological economist points out that "the environment, which is one of the factors of production, is owned as unregulated common property in the South, and as private property in the North." She goes on to argue that "the south produces and exports environmentally intensive goods to a greater degree than is efficient, and at prices that are below social costs."[27] Adam Thorpe argues that although "the richest long-term resource of equatorial Africa is the forest . . . known officially as the Congo Basin Rainforest. . . . [W]e Europeans are busy getting rid of it. Most of the damage is done by European mining and logging companies, and most of the clientele are European—lovers of mahogany wardrobes." He points out that "Nigeria, once a major exporter of timber, now has to import the stuff." A "mature mahogany," he continues, "is worth about $30,000, of which some $30 goes to its country of origin."[28] Compare this statement to a report in the *London Times* in 1823 of "the largest and finest log of mahogany ever imported into this country." It is purchased by one James Hodgson for 378 pounds, and afterwards sold by him for 525 pounds, "and if it open well, is supposed to be worth a thousand." In free trade, practice seems to make for ever more perfect profits.

IV. Souvenirs and Selfhood

John Maynard Keynes described free trade as the "most fervent expression of laissez faire," and we might imagine that, as such, it forms the global analogue for the nineteenth-century fantasy of an intensely self-determining individualism—a fantasy that arises, as Marx notes in the *Grundrisse*, at the moment of the "most developed social relations."[29] Gayatri Spivak has famously argued that in *Jane Eyre*, "[w]hat is at stake, for feminist individualism in the age of imperialism is precisely the making of human beings, the construction and 'interpellation' of the subject not as individual, but as 'individualist.'"[30] In this highly compressed formulation, Spivak links feminism, liberal individualism, and imperialism and suggests that the master narrative is imperialism. Imperialism dictates or requires a certain narrative of liberal individualism, and that becomes the narrative available to both nineteenth- and twentieth-century liberal feminists. She later calls this narrative "abject." I agree to the extent that it is essentially contradictory for a nineteenth-century British woman to think of herself as an individual, although she can be an individualist. By this I mean that although socially, legally, politically, and economically women were not recognizably individuals throughout most the nineteenth century, they were still free to subscribe to the ideology of individualism and therefore could be individualists. They could be individualists without being able to be individuals themselves; they could aspire—like the poor, the colonized, the racially, ethnically or religiously disenfranchised—to a condition that they could not attain.

Imperialism, ever productive of ideological bounty, offers Jane a *second* narrative, and this one is not abject, but instead usefully sadistic. In this narrative, subjection, first of the self and then of others, makes for subjecthood.[31] This narrative runs counter to Freud's trajectory of sadomasochism, in which sadism precedes and evolves into masochism. In Freud's account, aggressive impulses are initially directed at objects *outside* the self; only then are these impulses turned *inward*, against the self.[32] But in the imperial narrative of sadism, the narrative that forms the structure of *Jane Eyre* as bildungsroman, and that suggests a template for female individualism, masochism comes at the *beginning* of the story. In this narrative, the psychoanalytic progression of sadism to masochism is reversed, destructive impulses are usefully remembered as originating in a relationship with the self, and, in a movement we think of as characteristic of empire, such impulses are then directed outward, in an ever-expanding scope, to objects outside the self.

I would argue that selves and empires are imagined to work from the inside out in order to provide fantasies of a tradition or a history of mastery. Nationalism is often imagined as *prior* to empire; this precedence is often referred to casually, as though it were self-evident that it is the originary, motivating and sustaining ideology of imperial expansion. But there is much evidence to suggest that nationalism comes after empire,[33] in the same way that the word (and to some extent the concept) "heterosexuality" postdates the word "homosexuality." In other words, a "normative" identity is often constructed on the run, after the need for it is realized because of the presence of something alien or something that needs to be *made* alien. In the early colonization of the Caribbean and South Asia, Britons initially formed new and hybrid cultures, however problematically, with indigenous people and with slaves—the terms "creole" and "Anglo-Indian" suggest such cultural mingling. It was not until the nineteenth century that a national identity took shape in a form we now recognize, and some historians have argued that what we regard as a nearly antediluvian "Englishness" is largely a late nineteenthcentury invention.[34]

Jane, like the small island of England at the heart of a largely overseas empire, needs to remember herself as master of herself. Jane the adult recounts Jane the child executing extraordinary feats of self-discipline and control.[35] Jane the child, for example, finds out how to tell her story to her beloved teacher Miss Temple in a way that will give it credibility. She learns (from no less of an authority on masochism than her tubercular schoolmate and romantic friend Helen Burns) that if she withholds the "wormwood and gaul" from her narrative, even though she genuinely feels the bitterness they evoke, she is more likely to be believed. Jane alienates her story from her self and imagines it as the object of another's attention. It becomes a souvenir of her self, an object through which she can remember her own mastery. She becomes the kind of first-person narrator of a realist novel that we now immediately recognize as somehow normative, as is the fact that this novel can be subtitled "an autobiography."

In the process, Jane delimits a space for her own subjectivity; she sets the boundaries across which the self cannot venture, because she knows that selves, when left to themselves, tend toward an infinite vagrancy. The enclosure of the self makes a clearing, a space around the edges of which disorder is kept at bay. One of the lessons of *Jane Eyre*, and one of the reasons it is something of an owner's manual for the modern self, is that it imagines subjective interiority in terms of space: space that can be enclosed. Like the modern nation-state, the self has borders beyond which it will no longer be itself. But if the modern self follows the logic and ideology of enclosure in this novel, it also follows the logic and ideology of free trade. The bounds of the self must be strong and yet permeable, able to open up to exchange with others; subjectivity thrives when it can get from others that which it cannot produce for itself.

The subjective analogue to free trade occurs in the novel at the level of metonymy: its details are drawn from a truly international frame. The claustrophobic spatial limitations of Jane's life stand in remarkable contrast to the extraordinary range of reference her intellect and imagination produce. Jane conjures up seraglios, harems, suttee, and slavery, and critics have responded with a usefully complex set of arguments about Brontë's alignments and nonalignments of Jane with "Oriental," colonized, and enslaved peoples.[36] What I want to point out here is that Jane marshals experiences of abjection to build her own sense of subjectivity and a sense of control over it. She transforms the practices of domination she has experienced and those she imagines into material out of which to construct and understand her self; there can be no limits placed on her use of this material and in this sense she is free to trade in that which she has discovered about the world and the conditions of oppression in it.

Jane's experiences of mastery are very specifically built on her knowledge of oppression in general and slavery in particular. She feels herself to be held unjustly captive by her cousin John Reed early in the novel and declares herself a rebel slave; she claims this identity again in the face of what she experiences as Rochester's oppressively intense affection. Jenny Sharpe and Susan Meyer have pointed out that Jane threatens to organize precisely the kind of uprisings that rocked the Caribbean throughout the seventeenth, eighteenth, and nineteenth centuries.[37] The novel invokes a metaphorical slavery to enact its metaphorical overthrow in a risky allegorical gambit: the rebellions of slaves have only recently overthrown French domination in Haiti (in 1803) and have very nearly overthrown European hegemony time and again throughout the Caribbean. And former slaves are still rebelling in the region when *Jane Eyre* is being written: the historian Woodville Marshall points out that "[r]iots were a commonplace of the post-slavery British Caribbean in much the same way that slave revolts were a feature of slavery."[38] In *Jane Eyre*, Brontë dares to use a pressing historical issue for secondary symbolic gain, and although women and workers have "harnessed" the language of the antislavery movement "for articulating their own struggles for equality,"[39] the particulars of a very recent form of slavery come into scandalous analogy with the workings of domination and submission in one of the emblematically heterosexual relationships of nineteenth-century British literature, that of Rochester and Jane.

V. The Politics of Shopping

Jane decorates, but she refuses to be decorated. On the prenuptial shopping trip to Milcote, she refuses to buy much of anything, she will not be "tricked out in stage trappings" to become one of the many characters in Rochester's busy imagination: "I will be myself," she says flatly (288). But of course she knows that is not enough. Acutely aware of the fine-tuning that must be continually performed on the dynamics of power relations, Jane learns quickly how to maintain the upper hand with Rochester, teasing and torturing him to just the right distance from the edge of the brink: "[Y]ou master me," Rochester says, "[Y]ou seem to submit, and I like the sense of pliancy you impart; and while I am twining the soft, silken skein, round my finger, it sends a thrill up my arm to my heart. I am influenced—conquered; and the influence is sweeter than I can express; and the conquest I undergo has a witchery beyond any triumph I can win" (289). In what might be described as a high-speed Hegelian master/slave dialectic, Jane and Rochester change places every other paragraph or so. Readers, like onlookers at a shell game, are never sure who is master at what moment, or if the apparent master is really the slave of a canny and *apparently* powerless master. Perhaps power is best held on to by someone like Jane, who can disavow and thereby maintain mastery behind a screen of cunningly convincing abjection.

When Rochester asks Jane to give up what he calls her "governessing slavery" once they decide to get married, Jane insists on continuing it. In this exchange, *Jane Eyre* and Jane Eyre do a quintessentially Victorian ideological thing: the novel and its narrator-heroine begin to make an actual historical problem into a part of a newly constructed unchanging human condition.[40] In rendering a problem transhistorical, and thereby spiritual and psychological and above all, individual, its solution lies also in the realm of the spiritual and what will become the psychological—in the realm of individual interiority. You don't have to be a slave if you don't want to be one; if you think of yourself as free, you are free. This is the language and ideology of much of the self-help movement, from Samuel Smiles's *Self-Help* of 1859 to the current crop of works that would teach us to how to live happily in the world no matter how terrible it is.

These radically individualist ideas were the paradoxical lot of smart women in the nineteenth century, some of whom refused feminism in any of its early forms because they did not want to be identified with or reduced to the limitations of their gender.[41] Being a woman first and foremost and part of a group of women would be incompatible with being an individual. So returning to Spivak's idea of the centrality of *Jane Eyre* in the imagining of the female individualist, women are abject as women, but they are subjects as genderless individuals—a condition women can attain only in the privacy of their own minds, the place where novel reading goes on.

VI. Metonyms of Mastery

The curious thing about madeira wine is that like mahogany, like Jane, and like the individualist that Jane would teach us to become, it is almost preternaturally rugged and resilient. The wine of Madeira actually gets better during its passage across the Atlantic: "Madeiras do not spoil in hot weather; heat actually ripens and improves them, and a passage in the hold of a sailing ship, through burning tropical waters, results in a better wine. Madeiras do not mind being moved about, transported by ship or cart, and no amount of rough handling will damage them; quite the contrary, the more madeira is banged about, the better it tastes. Thus it was that the nineteenth-century Englishman demanded that his madeira be imported, not directly from the island, but by way of the West Indies or Brazil, where it would benefit from the hot and agitated voyage."[42] Madeira wine is thus a poster child for Atlantic trade, perhaps the only "commodity" that actually benefited from the rigors of its journey. Some of the cost of the millions of African people who died in the same passage is literally, symbolically, and horrifically recuperated by the extraordinary profits made on this peripatetic aperitif (or digestif).

These profits allow Jane to buy the furniture that remembers, as it were, the ubiquity of slavery in the geography and the history of Atlantic trade. Slaves—despite their problematic propensity to die in transit, to commit suicide from ships or once landed, to escape to what was left of the Caribbean forests and live as Maroons— are remembered, along with the mahogany that they cleared and to which brown and black people have since been likened endlessly, in the furniture that Jane buys as the sign of her own independence and financial freedom.[43] They are remembered in this symbolic reification, despite the extent and near success of their rebellions, as permanently subject to British control. And the bad news continues: someone like Jane needs souvenirs of this kind of sadism. They are the coordinates on the map of selfhood drawn by a small, poor, plain girl who would be a rebel slave. She becomes instead a master, and a master of Atlantic metonyms of mastery. And this is not a paradox: it is the logical narrative trajectory in an individualist meritocracy.

Victorian novels would seem to proffer a limited set of narrative possibilities, tricked out, to borrow Brontë's phrase, in an infinite wardrobe of significant and insignificant detail. Our endless task is to undo what Susan Stewart has called "the hierarchy of detail," the structure that generates various ideologies of the real, invisibly and insidiously: "Realistic genres do not mirror everyday life," she writes, "they mirror its hierarchization of information. They are mimetic in the stance they take toward this organization and hence are mimetic of values, not of the material world."[44] What we "figure out" about a novel and its meanings has been prefigured by the order of detail, as well as by the history of the literary novel and of novel criticism and the directions that criticism gives us about how to read, or more importantly how *not* read, those details. To fasten on certain details—and undoubtedly mahogany furniture is one such detail—is to risk making an incredibly goofy interpretive blunder. It cannot be a symbol, or fetish, or symptom: furniture, after all, is not "the superfluous, perplexing, derailing detail" Emily Apter describes as the fetish in fiction.[45] There is nothing particularly confusing, alarming, or notable about the presence of wooden furniture in a Victorian novel: it doesn't stand out, it just stands.

I am trying to make the furniture of *Jane Eyre* into what Marx would call a "social hieroglyphic": to treat it as a complex and partly legible sign, to help us get "behind the secret of our own social products."[46] The fact that furniture is not generally interpreted in all its woody splendor means that it can do lots of unapprehended symbolic work in the novel. An apparently innocent object like a mahogany dresser or a walnut panel decorates the moral and moralized space of the novel's winners, while sneaking in the true extent of their morally precarious triumph and evoking useful and self-protective memories of imperial mastery. Britons knew where their wood was coming from, especially that tropical treasure, mahogany. Even the slightest end table, the most unassuming side chair, could be a souvenir of sadism for Victorian readers of the novel. But like the hieroglyphic, or the fetish, it can also remain illegible, its knowledge disavowed. In literary criticism, this second option has seemed the most reasonable one for a long time in the reading of prose fiction: it is the one I am trying to make strange.

Because we contemporary readers of Victorian fiction have lost many of the possible meanings of the things of those bulky, item-ful novels, what might be called the social destruction of meaning[47] in the novel has unwittingly been abetted by practices of reading that ignore the literal or material qualities of objects, the very qualities that might take us back in time to the meanings and resonances these objects may have had for earlier readers. What we take to be our interpretive and theoretical canniness becomes a kind of disability: the long standing, and largely unnoticed, degradation of metonymy has moved "things" further and further away from the possibility of meaning anything. To interpret most of the things of realism means performing a kind of broad-based recovery effort: scouring archives of all kinds; following the things of the novel as if they might be significantly, rather than weakly, meaningful, as if they might have ideas about history in them that the novel does not and perhaps could not narrate explicitly. Eventually, metonymy might be removed from its place as the figure of hopelessly flighty contingency[48] and reread as a figure of compellingly significant contiguity.

VII. Tourism and the Pastoral

At the end of *Jane Eyre*, Ferndean must be transformed from its former status as a hunting lodge into a haven of domesticity. Its wooded surroundings are initially described as "ineligible and insalubrious" (455), but in just a few pages it becomes a paradise found. Jane and Rochester, after deciding (again) to get married, "entered the wood, and wended homeward" (473). The novel seems to slip its generic constraints and enter the pastoral, symbolically undoing the violence to various landscapes and peoples that it has so faithfully recorded. Jane and Rochester, who have long described one another as various kinds of woodland creatures—fairies, sprites, elves, and brownies—return to what has been rhetorically invoked and evoked as their natural habitat. Their naturalization in this environment reaches its apex when they both agree that Rochester himself is something of a tree: not the "old lightning-struck chestnut-tree at Thornfield" (469), as he describes himself, but rather, as Jane has it, a "green and vigorous" tree around which plants will grow with the "safe prop" of his strength. And sure enough, some sketchily narrated reproduction follows.

Like Jane and Rochester, Madeira and Jamaica are returned to a pastoral condition in the second half of the nineteenth century, even as they continue to be bound in relations of domination with the North Atlantic: both islands become, from the mid-nineteenth century, increasingly reliant on the tourist industry, which is, in the description of the historian Frank Taylor, "a South Atlantic system . . . of hotel chains and of profiteering based on a new kind of trade in human beings."[49] Indeed, in the nineteenth century, the two islands begin to compete for visitors. Both become places where invalids can regain their health, even though Jamaica had long been associated with yellow fever in particular and broken health generally. It becomes suddenly safe: Robert Baird, in his memoir, *Impressions and Experiences of the West Indies and North America in 1849*, observes that "Jamaica as a place of sanitary resort" is likely "if not to supersede, at least greatly to interfere with the island of Madeira in that respect, and certainly truth compels me to admit that there are few places to which an invalid from Europe could go with better hope or benefit than the salubrious island of Jamaica."[50] Visitors from the North Atlantic return to the scene of their collective historical crime, to enjoy and to benefit from that which they very nearly wiped out—the natural habitat. The habitat they find, and the one we find in tourist brochures, is of course a recent habitat, one created by heavy deforestation, cash crops, and an enrichment of the soil produced by literally working people—in all their nitrogenous richness—into the ground.

The social relations of these people, the nameless inhabitants of the Caribbean who do not find subjecthood in the Victorian novel or in histories of the "first world," are recovered through reading the properties and relations of objects like mahogany furniture.

Through such readings, we can move beyond the impasses that are soon reached in discussions of the identity and meaning that can or should be assigned to the mad creole woman in the attic. The explicit subjects of fiction are not the only subjects of fiction. The idea of reification as we have long understood it ought to have indicated this to us before now: social relations hide in things. When we start looking into them, the long violence of empire reaches home, not only to Moor House and Ferndean, but also to the home in which we read *Jane Eyre*, the novel that teaches us how to be at home in a place as uncanny as the world it describes.

From The Ideas in Things: Fugitive Meaning in the Victorian Novel *by Elaine Freedgood* ©2006 *by The University of Chicago Press. All rights reserved. Reprinted with permission.

Notes

1. Mahogany was exported to Europe from Jamaica in the form of logs; Madeira, on the other hand, had a furniture trade: "Furniture shops are plentiful, and in some of these excellent wardrobes, chairs, and tables may

be found of . . . Vinhatico [*Persea indica*, the Madeiran mahogany], walnut or plane. . . . The manufacture of many articles in wickerwork has increased enormously within the last ten years. Sofas, tables, chairs, and baskets of all shapes are made, and shipped by thousands every year" (Ellen M. Taylor, *Madeira: Its Scenery, and How to See It* [London: Edward Stanford, 1889], 77–78).

2. Charlotte Brontë, *Jane Eyre* (Harmondsworth: Penguin, 1985), 451. All references will be to this edition and will be cited parenthetically in the text hereafter.

3. See Henri Lefebvre, *The Production of Space*, trans. Donald Nicholson-Smith (Oxford: Blackwell, 1991), 97.

4. G. S. Boulger, *Wood: A Manual of the Natural History and Industrial Applications of the Timbers of Commerce* (London: Edward Arnold, 1902).

5. R. W. Symonds, *English Furniture from Charles II to George II* (New York: International Studio, 1929), 167.

6. Charlotte Sussman, *Consuming Anxieties: Consumer Protest, Gender and British Slavery, 1713–1833* (Stanford: Stanford Univ. Press, 2000), 13–14.

7. Susan Meyer comes close to breaking out of this pattern and actually reading things near the end of her essay on *Jane Eyre* when she notes that "St. John announces Jane's accession to fortune by pulling the letter out of a 'morocco pocket-book' and he is able to identify Jane as the heiress because she has written her name, on a white sheet of paper, in 'Indian ink'" ("Colonialism and the Figurative Strategy of *Jane Eyre*," in *The Macropolitics of Nineteenth-Century Literature: Nationalism, Exoticism, Imperialism*, ed. Jonathan Arac and Harriet Ritvo [Philadelphia: Univ. of Pennsylvania Press, 1991], 180).

8. Walter Benjamin, *The Arcades Project*, ed. Rolf Tiedemann, trans. Howard Eiland and Kevin McLaughlin (Cambridge, Mass.: Harvard University Press, Belknap Press, 1999), 211.

9. Ibid., 207.

10. Robert Pogue Harrison, *Forests: The Shadow of Civilization* (Chicago: Univ. of Chicago Press, 1992), 51.

11. Quoted in Harrison, *Forests*, 71.

12. N. D. G. James, *A History of English Forestry* (Oxford: Basil Blackwell, 1981), 161.

13. J. M. Neeson, *Commoners: Common Right, Enclosure and Social Change in England, 1700–1820* (Cambridge: Cambridge Univ. Press, 1993), 12.

14. Ibid., 12.

15. Susan Stewart has pointed out to me that the gardening nationalism of the English centered on the idea that their gardens were more "natural" than those

of the French. Lancelot "Capability" Brown pioneered designs that famously made use of "wildness"; this ideology obscures the fact that landscaping did cause deforestation, albeit selectively (personal communication).

16. For the history of Madeira, see T. Bentley Duncan, *The Atlantic Islands: Madeira, the Azores, and the Cape Verdes in Seventeenth-Century Commerce and Navigation* (Chicago: Univ. of Chicago Press, 1972); Desmond Gregory, *The Beneficent Usurpers: A History of the British in Madeira* (London: Associated Univ. Presses, 1988); and also the Victorian memoirs of Madeira, including Anothony J. Drexel Biddle, *The Madeira Islands* (London: Hurst and Blackout, 1900); Charles Thomas-Stanford, *Leaves from a Madeira Garden,* 2nd ed. (London: John Lane, 1910); and Ellen Taylor, *Madeira.*

17. Sugar was also grown in Sicily, North Africa, and the southern Mediterranean.

18. Alfred W. Crosby, *Ecological Imperialism: The Biological Expansion of Europe, 900–1900* (Cambridge: Cambridge Univ. Press, 1986), 70–103.

19. Sidney Greenfield, "Madeira and the Beginnings of New World Sugar Cane Cultivation and Plantation Slavery: A Study in Institution Building," in *Comparative Perspectives on Slavery in New World Plantation Societies,* ed. Vera Rubin and Arthur Tuden (New York: New York Academy of Arts and Sciences, 1977), 537. Slavery was abolished in Madeira quite early—1755—and replaced by a sharecropping system.

20. 20. Thomas-Stanford, *Leaves from a Madeira Garden,* vii. A nice Lamarckian joke reveals more than it means to, I think, in this description of the effect of madeira wine on Britons: once it enters the nation's bloodstream it seems also to alter it genetically, attributing a power to tropical colonies and their products that also manifests itself in fears about racial change, including the apparent racial contamination or transformation of Bertha Mason and her sickly brother.

21. Fanny Anne Burney, *A Great-Niece's Journals*, ed. Margaret S. Rolt (London: Constable and Company, 1926), 209.

22. Ibid., 189, 193.

23. Leslie R. Holdridge, "Middle America," in *A World Geography of Forest Resources*, ed. Stephen Haden-Guest, John K. Wright, and Eileen M. Teclaff (New York: Ronald Press), 189. See also G. F. Asprey and R. G. Robbins, "The Vegetation of Jamaica," *Ecological Monographs* 23, no. 4 (Oct. 1953): 359–412.

24. My discussion of Madeira and Jamaica admittedly ranges across not only long geographical distances but also across several hundred years: this is a self-conscious attempt to meet the challenges set out in the recent work of the medievalist David Wallace, who has charged that literary historicism has been too cramped both in its temporal and spatial parameters (see *Chaucerian*

Polity: Absolutist Lineages and Associational Forms in England and Italy [Stanford: Stanford Univ. Press, 1997] and *Premodern Places: Calais to Surinam, Chaucer to Aphra Behn* [Malden, Mass.: Blackwell Publishers, 2004]). It is only through taking a very long historical view, by engaging in what Wallace calls "diachronic historicism," that we can begin to adequately appreciate the ways in which mahogany furniture haunts this novel.

25. See Gregory, *The Beneficent Usurpers*, for a description of the British economic domination of Madeira.

26. See John Gallagher and Ronald Robinson, "The Imperialism of Free Trade," *Economic History Review* 6, no. 1 (1953): 1–15. See also Bernard Semmel, *The Rise of Free Trade Imperialism: Classical Political Economy, the Empire of Free Trade and Imperialism, 1750–1850* (Cambridge: Cambridge Univ. Press, 1970).

27. Graciela Chichilnisky, "North-South Trade and the Global Environment." *American Economic Review* 84, no. 4 (Sept. 1994): 851, 852.

28. Adam Thorpe, letter to the editor, *London Review of Books*, 25 Jan. 2001.

29. Karl Marx, *Grundrisse*, trans. Martin Nicolaus (Harmondsworth: Penguin, 1993), 84.

30. Gayatri Chakravorty Spivak, "Three Women's Texts and a Critique of Imperialism," in *Feminisms: An Anthology of Literary Theory and Criticism*, ed. Robyn R. Warhol and Diane Price Herndl (New Brunswick, N.J.: Rutgers Univ. Press, 1991), 897.

31. Judith Butler describes this narrative in *The Psychic Life of Power: Theories in Subjection* (Stanford: Stanford Univ. Press, 1997.

32. *The Standard Edition of the Complete Psychological Works of Sigmund Freud*, trans. James Strachey (London: Hogarth Press, 1953), 7:157, 14:137–139.

33. See Gauri Viswanathan, "Raymond Williams and Colonialism," in *Cultural Materialism: On Raymond Williams*, ed. Christopher Prendergast (Minneapolis: Univ. of Minnesota Press, 1995): 188–210.

34. See for example, Robert Colls and Philip Dodd, *Englishness: Politics and Culture, 1880–1920* (London: Croom Helm, 1986).

35. Bette London reads *Jane Eyre* not as a "manifesto of self-creation but as [a] textbook of self-discipline" ("The Pleasures of Submission: *Jane Eyre* and the Production of the Text," *ELH* 58 [1991]: 209).

36. In addition to the texts by Meyer, Sharpe, and Spivak cited in this chapter (see nn. 7, 30, and 37), see Mary Poovey, "The Anathematized Race: The Governess and Jane Eyre," in *Uneven Developments: The Ideological Work of Gender in Mid-Victorian England* (Chicago: Univ. of Chicago Press, 1988); Sue Thomas, "The Tropical Extravagance of Bertha Mason,"

Victorian Literature and Culture 27, no. 1 (1999): 1–17; and Joyce Zonana, "The Sultan and the Slave: Feminist Orientalism and the Structures of *Jane Eyre*," *Signs: Journal of Women in Culture and Society* 18, no. 3 (Spring 1993): 592–617.

37. See the chapters on *Jane Eyre* in Susan Meyer, *Imperialism at Home: Race and Victorian Women's Fiction* (Ithaca: Cornell Univ. Press, 1996); and Jenny Sharpe, *Allegories of Empire: The Figure of Woman in the Colonial Text* (Minneapolis: Univ. of Minnesota Press, 1993).

38. Woodville K. Marshall, "'Vox Populi': The St. Vincent Riots and Disturbances of 1862," in *Trade, Government and Society in Caribbean History, 1700–1920*, ed. B. W. Higman (Kingston, Jamaica: Heinemann Education Books Caribbean, 1983), 85.

39. Sharpe, *Allegories of Empire*, 40.

40. See Catherine Gallagher, *The Industrial Reformation of English Fiction: Social Discourse and Narrative Form, 1832–1867* (Chicago: Univ. of Chicago Press, 1985), esp. 113–186.

41. See Poovey, *Uneven Developments*, esp. 164–201.

42. Duncan, *The Atlantic Islands*, 38.

43. The wood has stood for dark skin from W. M. Thackeray's frequent description of the "mahogany" faces of the Schwartz family in *Vanity Fair* (1848) to Diana Ross's 1975 film *Mahogany*.

44. Susan Stewart, *On Longing: Narratives of the Miniature, the Gigantic, the Souvenir, and the Collection* (Durham: Duke Univ. Press, 1993), 26.

45. Emily Apter, *Feminizing the Fetish: Psychoanalysis and Narrative Obsession in Turn-of-the-Century France* (Ithaca: Cornell Univ. Press, 1991), xi.

46. Cited in Apter, *Feminizing the Fetish*, 1.

47. Thanks to Mary Poovey for this phrase.

48. See the first chapter, "Semiology and Rhetoric," in Paul de Man's *Allegories of Reading: Figural Language in Rousseau, Nietzsche, Rilke, and Proust* (New Haven: Yale Univ. Press, 1979), for an extraordinary deconstruction of metaphor's aesthetic and epistemological precedence over metonymy in Proust's descriptions of summer. From his bedroom, Marcel hears flies buzzing and describes this "chamber music" of summer as linked to the essence of that season. De Man points out that the buzzing flies are a synecdoche of summer that Proust renders as a metaphor. Metaphor is thereby constructed out of metonymy, and metonymy wins a kind of grammatical and semiotic precedence in de Man's argument, but it remains a figure of chance for de Man as for Proust and therefore is always subject to meaninglessness or a random and nonessential particularity.

49. Frank F. Taylor, "From Hellshire to Healthshire: The Genesis of the Tourist Industry in Jamaica," in Higman, *Trade, Government and Society*, 139.

50. Quoted in Frank F. Taylor, "From Hellshire to Healthshire," 142.

From Myth to Materiality: Critical Reception of Charlotte Brontë's *Jane Eyre* from the 1840s to the 2010s _____

John O'Hara

Jane Eyre astonished critics upon its publication in October of 1847. It was an exceptional artistic achievement during a tumultuous decade that saw the exposure of child labor and poor working conditions, revelations that lead to the Mines and Collieries Act of 1842 and the Chartist demonstrations of 1848. The mythic *Jane Eyre* seems to stand apart from this troubled political climate, yet it is very much a product of its revolutionary time: it is, at once, one of the last expressions of Romanticism and one of the first Victorian explorations of psychological depth; it imbues worn Gothic figures with new significance and it deploys the narrative of Christian redemption for secular, proto-feminist ends; it prefigures the sensation novel and anticipates themes women writers would return to for the next century and a half. In short, it fashions, out of the past, a language for the future. The novel has remained in print continuously since its original publication, a testament to its enduring relevance to both critics and readers alike. It has been adapted numerous times for film, television, radio, and the stage; other writers have penned prequels, sequels, and revisions through the eyes of other characters and writers of romance. Young adult literature has offered readers thousands of permutations of the Jane/Rochester dynamic, from Daphne du Maurier's *Rebecca* to Stephenie Meyer's *Twilight*.

Brontë published only three novels in her lifetime—*Jane Eyre*, *Villette*, and *Shirley*—but those three novels (along with her juvenilia, poetry, and a fourth novel, *The Professor*, written before the others but published posthumously) have elicited thousands of pages of criticism and analysis. The deluge of *Jane Eyre* reviews relented in the years following the novel's publication, but since scholars of the 1960s and 1970s made *Jane Eyre* an iconic feminist text—finally matching in popularity and stature Emily Brontë's well-regarded *Wuthering Heights*— there has been a swelling tide of *Jane Eyre* criticism from scholars of feminism, postcolonialism, gender studies, and cultural studies.

Initial Reception

Though the Brontës had already published a collection of poetry as the brothers Currer, Ellis, and Acton Bell, the brilliance of *Jane Eyre*— the first novel to be published by one of the Bells—took reviewers by surprise in the winter of 1847-48. Even among the crowded field of 1847 publications, which included novels by both Anne and Emily Brontë—*Agnes Grey* and *Wuthering Heights* respectively—as well as William Makepeace Thackeray's *Vanity Fair*, *Jane Eyre* received considerable attention. These initial reviews of the novel fall into three camps: praise for first-time novelist's originality, power, and control; speculation about the true identity of the mysterious Currer Bell; and objections to the novel's perceived immorality and anti-Christian attitudes.

Very few were fooled by the author's ambiguous pseudonym and the presentation of the novel as the autobiography of Jane Eyre, edited by Currer Bell. Thackeray, for one, ventured that the writing was that of an educated woman (70). Likewise, a review in the *Christian Remembrancer* asserted unequivocally that "we cannot doubt that the book is written by a female" (89). A.W. Fonblanque, writing for the *Examiner*, also praised the originality of the story while weighing in on the identity of Currer Bell, pointing out that although the novel is presented as the autobiography of a woman, "we do not believe [*Jane Eyre*] to have been written by a woman" (77). The review published in *Era* agreed with the *Examiner's* erroneous assessment, determining that "no woman *could have* penned 'The Autobiography of Jane Eyre'" (79). George Henry Lewes, on the other hand, took the novel's presentation as an autobiography at face value: "The writer is evidently a woman, and unless we are deceived, new in the world of literature" (84). His acceptance of the device may not have been so straightforward, however, as he notes that the book is an autobiography "not, perhaps, in the naked facts and circumstances, but in the actual suffering and experience"

(84). Contrary to the *Era*'s opinion, Lewes seems to believe that *only* a woman could have written *Jane Eyre*. The question would preoccupy reviewers until Charlotte Brontë herself revealed her and her sisters' identities in her preface to the 1850 editions of *Wuthering Heights* and *Agnes Grey*.

The initial reviews, concerned though they were with the identity of the author and his brothers, were overwhelmingly positive. The *Atlas* admired the novel's "youthful vigor" and "freshness and originality" (68). The author of this unsigned review attributed the novel's power to the "deep insight into human character" possessed by its mysterious author. Lewes as well praised Brontë's skill in believably rendering powerful emotions. He published at least two glowing reviews of the novel, one in *Fraser's Magazine* in December 1847 and the other in *Westminster Review* in January 1848. Like many other contemporary reviewers, Lewes's notice in *Fraser's* regards Brontë's ability to sketch realistic characters as her greatest asset, noting that even minor characters are vividly drawn (85). His much shorter notice in the *Westminster Review* echoed his lengthier earlier statements, calling *Jane Eyre* "the best novel of the season" (87). Eugene Forcade, in a review wrapped in a diatribe against French socialism and the metaphysical orientation of French writers, lauds not only *Jane Eyre* but the entire Anglo-Saxon "spirit of enterprise" (102).

There were, however, a few dissenters to this critical consensus. The *Spectator* found the story too contrived, the characters too rigidly consistent in their actions, and the dialogue too heavy on exposition to be taken seriously (74). For most of these early reviewers, the originality of the story and the strength of the prose outweighed these faults. Overall it was not the quality of the writing but the immorality of the subject matter that vexed most of the novel's detractors.

Jane's "unfeminine" behavior shocked moralistic readers across Britain. The *Christian Rembrancer* took particular umbrage at the novel's representations of Christianity, citing Brontë's characterization of clergyman St. John Rivers as selfish, proud, and ambitious as indicative of an almost anti-Christian attitude apparent in the novel (91). Elizabeth Rigby, writing for the *Quarterly Review*, penned perhaps the most damning indictment of the novel, calling it a "pre-eminently anti-Christian composition" full of "murmuring against the comforts of the rich…which…is a murmuring against God's appointment" (109). In a more tongue-in-cheek vein, Edwin Percy Whipple wrote of "a distressing mental epidemic" called "Jane Eyre fever" that seized the New England states in 1848 (97). For Whipple, the book's popularity rested solely on its reputation as something that had no place in a respectable household (97).

Jane Eyre's Reputation
Despite the sensation the novel caused upon its publication and its enduring popularity with readers, *Jane Eyre* received little critical attention in the second half of the nineteenth century. The myth surrounding the Brontë sisters, however, grew larger, encouraged in part by Elizabeth Gaskell's biography of Charlotte Brontë. Algernon Charles Swinburne's pamphlet *A Note on Charlotte Brontë* is indicative of the reputation of the novel in the decades following its publication, Swinburne calling Brontë "one of the greatest among women" (1) and extolling her literary prowess above that of Elizabeth Gaskell, George Eliot, and George Sand. Margaret Oliphant, on the other hand, lamented that the protest against convention voiced by the sensation novel—a melodramatic type of fiction popular in the late Victorian era—was due to the negative influence of *Jane Eyre* (390-391). This review, published in 1867, echoes her 1855 review of *Jane Eyre*, in which she railed against the rudeness of Jane and Rochester alike (312).

Writing at the end of the Victorian era, Henry James compared the novels of Charlotte Brontë unfavorably to those of Jane Austen, attributing the popularity of the works of Charlotte and Emily to "a force independent of any one of their applied faculties—by the attendant image of…their tragic history, their loneliness and poverty of life" (118). Austen, by contrast, labored in secrecy, stitching together "little touches of human truth" (118). Virginia Woolf presented a similar argument twenty-five years later, arguing that while Brontë may have been more worldly and intelligent than

Austen, she was a less-talented writer than her predecessor: Brontë wrote with rage and about herself, while Austen wrote calmly, with a focus on her characters (50). The sentiment expressed by both James and Woolf is indicative of the modernist attitude toward the role of the artist voiced by both Gustave Flaubert and James Joyce: an artist's creation may point to the artist, but must not be about the artist.

Postwar Resurgence

As a result of the dominance of New Criticism, twentieth-century scholarship on *Jane Eyre* was dominated until the 1960s by formalist and structuralist methods that eschewed biographical readings in favor of close textual analysis. These critics of *Jane Eyre* tended to read Brontë's characters as symbolic representations of universal archetypes. Melvin R. Watson's critique of the novel, representative of New Criticism's approach, argues that Charlotte Brontë's extensive juvenilia, including the chronicles of a fantastic realm she called Angria, can only go so far in helping a reader understand Brontë's adult novels, which must "be studied as self-contained units of artistic expression" (106). Watson determines that *Jane Eyre* is not as lofty an artistic achievement as Emily Brontë's *Wuthering Heights*, concluding that anyone of the opinion that *Jane Eyre* or *Villette* is of greater importance than *Wuthering Heights* is laboring under "a distortion of critical values" (117). Q.D. Leavis, in her introduction to the 1966 edition of *Jane Eyre*, dismisses both Lord David Cecil's opinion that *Jane Eyre* lacked artistry entirely and Henry James's classification of the novel as a typical Victorian "loose baggy monster," suggesting instead that Emily's and Charlotte's poetic sensibilities led them to develop innovative prose techniques that "led to the novel's becoming the major art form of the nineteenth century" (176).

In Richard Chase's view, "*Jane Eyre* and *Wuthering Heights* now seem the most exciting of Victorian novels" because unlike other Victorian novels, "these novels translated the social customs of the time into the form of mythical art" (103). Rochester is the "symbolic embodiment of the masculine *élan*" (107), Bertha symbolizes "what happens to the woman who gives herself to the Romantic Hero, who in her insane suffragettism tries herself to play the Hero" (108), and Jane herself is a "culture heroine....the solitary virgin of the folk tales who goes to the castle of the ogre" (111). Helene Moglen also focuses on the novel's mythic structure, though through a feminist lens, observing that "The truth of [Brontë's] fantasy" lies in its use of myth to "[dramatize] the conflict of larger social and psychological forces" (145). For these critics, this mythic aspect, in which Jane Eyre represents a transformative archetype, makes *Jane Eyre* one of the most important Victorian novels. In her introduction to a 1974 edition, Margaret Smith agrees that *Jane Eyre* "is less complex and challenging than *Wuthering Heights*," but admits that the former novel's "lasting popularity seems proof that Charlotte Brontë was right in appealing to the secret stores of 'romance and sensibility' hidden beneath the 'calm and sober' exterior of publishers and readers alike" (xx).

One standout formalist reading of *Jane Eyre* from this period is Robert B. Heilman's "Charlotte Brontë's 'New' Gothic." In this 1958 essay, Heilman argues that throughout *Jane Eyre*, Brontë evokes and then undermines Gothic situations and figures by deploying them in a symbolic sense, chasing not "the relatively simple thrill" of Gothic literature but a "more mature and complicated response" (120). Such rationalist evocations of the supernatural constitute a "plunging into feeling" (121), a movement toward psychological depth, expressions of psychological states, symbolic gestures that give "dramatic form to impulses or feelings" (131).

Marxist Interpretations

Terry Eagleton's *Myths of Power: A Marxist Study of the Brontës* (1975), with its challenge to New Critical evaluations and symbolic or archetypal interpretations, marks a turning point in *Jane Eyre* scholarship. His Marxist approach to the Brontës involves "identify[ing] the inner ideological structure of a work and... expos[ing] its relations both to what we call literary 'form' and actual history" (4). In *Jane Eyre*, in particular, Eagleton identifies the doubling motif so central to *Jane Eyre* criticism as a reflection of an ambiguity indicative of Brontë's historical moment: the fluid relationships between the landed aristocracy and the upstart middle class in general and the Brontës' class position as the daughters of a clergyman in particular. Other critics have followed in this manner. Nancy Pell notes that "Charlotte Brontë's romantic individualism and rebellion of feeling are controlled and structured by an underlying social and economic critique of bourgeois patriarchal authority" (399), and Esther Godfrey considers "the larger gender anxieties raised by Jane's class position" (853). Mary Poovey's book *Uneven Developments: The Ideological Work of Gender in Mid-Victorian England* exemplifies the depth of historical research of New Historicist critics, reading the role of the governess in *Jane Eyre* through the political and economic anxieties surrounding the profession in the mid-nineteenth century.

The Feminist Revolution
Though initial reviewers criticized the novel for being insufficiently feminine, *Jane Eyre* had long been seen as a novel addressing specifically female or feminine problems—"the Brontë novels are concerned with the neuroses of women in a man's society," as Chase put it (110)—but what is new in the explicitly feminist approach taken by Elaine Showalter in *A Literature of Their Own* (1977) and Sandra M. Gilbert and Susan Gubar in *The Madwoman in the Attic* (1979) is the placement of *Jane Eyre* within a tradition, an alternative canon of female writers that mirrors and subverts Harold Bloom's implicitly masculine Oedipal concept of the anxiety of influence. Showalter's primary concern is unearthing the neglected works of literature by women, texts that had been buried under an androcentric canon, though she also lays the groundwork for later feminist critics of *Jane Eyre*, particularly in her focus on the concept of the double as a central motif in feminist theory. Another important feminist reading of *Jane Eyre* is Adrienne Rich's "*Jane Eyre*: The Temptations of a Motherless Woman." Rich's essay, which originally appeared in the October 1973 issue of *Ms.*, argues that the novel's position "between realism and poetry" (90) allows Jane to reject romance and create her own identity; her marriage to

Rochester is not a surrender to patriarchy but "a continuation of this woman's creation of herself" (106).

For Gilbert and Gubar, the anti-Christian and individualistic attitudes that so vexed Victorian reviewers is actually the rebellious spirit of feminism (337). Jane's nascent feminism involves "fantasies of escape-into-wholeness" (336), the novel comprising a "feminine bildungsroman" of "enclosure and escape" (339). Gilbert and Gubar see the tension between enclosure and escape as a prevailing theme in literature by women from disparate historical periods and geographic locations.

As the book's title suggests, Gilbert and Gubar's reading of *Jane Eyre* transforms Bertha Mason from simply a symbol of Jane's repressed sexuality to a unifying figure for literature by women from the eighteenth to the twentieth centuries. Gilbert and Gubar depart from their predecessors by fitting Bertha within an explicitly feminist politics. Bertha, they argue, is "Jane's truest and darkest double... the angry aspect of the orphan child, the ferocious secret self" (360). Furthermore, she functions doubly for Rochester as both a symbol of "the secret of male sexual guilt" (354) and a mark of inferiority, a barrier preventing Rochester and Jane from meeting as equals (356). *The Madwoman in the Attic*, then, is just as much an aspect of the everywoman as Jane is, and it is the death of the Madwoman that "frees [Jane] rom the furies that torment her and makes possible a marriage of equality" and "wholeness within herself" (362).

In the wake of Gilbert and Gubar's massive—and massively influential—undertaking, critics focused further on Bertha. Morteza Jafari reads the function of Bertha as Jane's double or doppelgänger using the tools of Freudian psychoanalysis, Nicole A. Diederich focuses on the concept of the double as it pertains to the double role of Bertha as both a wife and a commodity, and Robyn Warhol returns to structuralist narratology to explore a "feminist narratology" that "revises the structuralist origins of this analytical method by placing observations about narration in a specific historical and cultural context and by considering the impact gender can have upon narrative structures" (858). Critiquing earlier readings that focus on the love story at the expense of other aspects of the novel, Jean

Wyatt argues that the near uniformity of women readers' response to it, since the time of its publication, is due to its ability to address both their unconscious psychological desires and their conscious political desires.

Against feminist psychoanalytical interpretations typified by Gilbert and Gubar, Laurence Lerner proposes interpreting *Jane Eyre* in terms of only what is explicitly stated in the text. Reducing the character of Bertha to a symbol of Jane's repressed sexuality, he claims, places the emphasis on sexual psychology rather than on the "social institutions and power structures that may be responsible for the hostile and dangerous impulses in the first place" (286). Lerner's essay is a caustic attempt to chasten the purveyors of the type of psychoanalytic feminism epitomized by *The Madwoman in the Attic.*

Later feminist and gender studies scholars also challenged what they saw as Gilbert and Gubar's essentialism and complicity with imperialism as well as the pair's uncritical acceptance of Jane as an avatar of feminism, while others further developed the ideas first expressed in *The Madwoman in the Attic*, using ever more sophisticated theoretical tools. Indeed, much *Jane Eyre* criticism of the past thirty years has sought to either correct perceived misreadings by Gilbert and Gubar or revise their ideas through poststructuralist theories ranging from text-centered deconstructive approaches, to historical and cultural critiques, to Lacanian psychoanalysis.

Ashly Bennett, for example, argues, in an essay reprinted in this volume, against a "sentimental identification" with Jane by focusing on the novel's conception of shame. Julia Miele Rodas is concerned with Jane's unusually withdrawn and reticent affect, going so far as to read Jane as being affected by autism. Rosemarie Bodenheimer chronicles Jane's quest to find her voice, moving through various conventional narratives such as the Gothic and the governess tale to find it (387), while Carla Kaplan, without denying that "Jane does move from silence to speech, thus proving a model of feminist resistance and liberation," suggests that critics have taken "the novel's own romance for granted" (6). Faced with this realization, Kaplan posits an "erotics of talk" that locates sexual relationships in the act of conversation. Kathleen Williams Renk, meanwhile, further develops Gilbert and Gubar's idea of *Jane Eyre* as a secular revision of the religious quest by casting Jane as a "female hunger artist" whose narration of hunger and privation reflects not an "intense personal relationship with a God" but "denotes a need for earthly justice" (3).

Along with these new psychoanalytical and psychological readings have come increasingly sophisticated textual analyses of the novel. Nina Schwartz, building on the deconstructive theory of Jacques Derrida, exemplifies the challenge to the essentialism inherent in earlier criticism of the novel: Schwatrz first frames, in opposition, two types of explanations for Jane's unfortunate childhood and then demonstrates how Jane's understanding of herself undermines both. Katharine Bubel reads *Jane Eyre*'s treatment of marriage as transcending the traditional model of desire that places subject, object, and mediator of desire in a triangulated relationship. Bette London sees in the form of the autobiography and in Jane's self-description a "reproduc[tion of] contradictions that structure the dominant domestic ideologies" (197). All of these readings add to critics' understanding of gender constructions by destabilizing the binaries that the ideologies of gender are constructed upon.

Postcolonial Approaches

With its repeated references to Turks, Gypsies, the Ottoman Empire, and Britain's own colonies, it makes sense that *Jane Eyre* would come under the scrutiny of postcolonial critics. Following Gayatri Spivak's argument that it "should not be possible to read nineteenth-century British literature without remembering that imperialism" was central to Britain's understanding of itself (243), many of these critics have drawn attention to the attitudes of British colonialist ideology reproduced in *Jane Eyre*. Joyce Zonana, for instance, critiques British imperial ideology from a passage in the novel, in which Jane compares her relationship to Rochester as that of a slave to a sultan. The passage is a point of irruption of the "feminist orientalist discourse that permeates *Jane Eyre*" (593).

Some critics read the colonialist themes in *Jane Eyre* through Jean Rhys's 1966 prequel to *Jane Eyre*, *Wide Sargasso Sea*, itself a postcolonial critique of Brontë's novel. Trevor Hope, for example, deconstructs the theme of the archive in both novels using the texts to reveal how "the workings of monumental inscription do at some level work to consolidate fragmentary signs into an account of national identity that appears 'permanent and standardized'" (59) while also undermining that function.

Lasting Influence

As interest in literature for young adults exploded in the 1970s and 80s, critics began to consider *Jane Eyre*'s influence on young adult literature and its place in the young adult canon, as in articles by Bachelder, et al. (1980) and Nelms, Nelms, and Vogel (1986). More recently, Katie Kapurch explores the similar uses of interiority and melodrama in *Jane Eyre* and *Twilight*, while Erica Hateley reads *Jane Eyre* through the lens of Jasper Fforde's novel *The Eyre Affair*, a novel that, Hateley argues, raises the question of the construction of not only the character of Jane Eyre but also of the author herself through the dual narratives of "gender/feminism and love/romance" (1023). Considering the popularity in young adult literature of heroines in search of an identity, who must navigate the bonds of femininity and their brooding Byronic love interests, this remains a rewarding area of study for *Jane Eyre* scholars.

Works Cited

Allott, Miriam, ed. *The Brontës: The Critical Heritage.* Boston, MA: Routlege and Kegan Paul, 1974.

Bachelder, Linda, et al. "Looking Backward: Trying to Find the Classic Young Adult Novel." *The English Journal* 69.6 (1980): 86-89.

Bennett, Ashly. "Shameful Signification: Narrative and Feeling in *Jane Eyre*." *Narrative* 18.3 (2010): 300-323.

Bodenheimer, Rosemarie. "Jane Eyre in Search of Her Story." *Papers on Language and Literature* 16.3 (1980): 387-102.

Bubel, Katharine. "Transcending the Triangle of Desire: Eros and 'The Fulfillment of Love' in *Middlemarch* and *Jane Eyre*." *Renaissance* 60.4 (2008): 295-308.

Chase, Richard. "The Brontës, or Myth Domesticated." *Forms of Modern Fiction.* Ed. William Vann O'Connor. Bloomington, IN: Indiana UP, 1962. 102-119.

Diederich, Nicole A. "Gothic Doppelgangers and Discourse: Examining the Doubling Practice of (Re)marriage in *Jane Eyre*." *Nineteenth-Century Gender Studies* 6.3 (2010): n. pag. Web. 18 Oct. 2013.

Eagleton, Terry. *Myths of Power: A Marxist Study of the Brontës.* New York: Harper and Row, 1975.

Fonblanque, A.W. Rev. of *Jane Eyre. Examiner.* 27 Nov. 1847. *The Brontës: The Critical Heritage.* Ed. Miriam Allott. Boston, MA: Routlege and Kegan Paul, 1974. 76-78.

Forçade, Eugène. Rev. of *Jane Eyre. Revue des deux mondes.* 31 Oct. 1848. *The Brontës: The Critical Heritage.* Ed. Miriam Allott. Boston, MA: Routlege and Kegan Paul, 1974. 100-104.

Gaskell, Elizabeth Cleghorn. *The Life of Charlotte Brontë.* New York: Oxford UP, 1919.

Gibson, Mary Ellis. "The Seraglio or Suttee: Brontë's Jane Eyre." *Postscript* 4 (1987): 1-8.

Gilbert, Sandra M. and Susan Gubar. *The Madwoman in the Attic: The Woman Writer and the Nineteenth Century Literary Imagination.* 2nd ed. New Haven, CT: Yale UP, 2000.

Godfrey, Esther. "*Jane Eyre*, from Governess to Girl Bride." *Studies in English Literature 1500-1900* (2005): 45.4. 853-871.

Hateley, Erica. "The End of *The Eyre Affair: Jane Eyre*, Parody, and Popular Culture." *The Journal of Popular Culture* 38.6 (2005): 1022-1036.

Heilman, Robert B. "Charlotte Brontë's 'New' Gothic." *From Jane Austen to Joseph Conrad.* Eds. Robert C. Rathburn and Martin Steinmann, Jr., Minneapolis: U of Minnesota P, 1958. 118-132.

Hope, Trevor. "Revisiting the Imperial Archive: *Jane Eyre, Wide Sargasso Sea,* and the Decomposition of Englishness." *College Literature* 39.1 (2012): 52-73.

Jafari, Morteza. "Freud's Uncanny: The Role of the Double in *Jane Eyre* and *Wuthering Heights.*" *Victorian Newsletter* 118 (2010): 43-53.

James, Henry. "French Writers." *Literary Criticism, Volume 2.* New York: The Library of America, 1984. 1-900.

Kaplan, Carla. "Girl Talk: *Jane Eyre* and the Romance of Women's Narration." *Novel* 30.1 (1996): 5–31.

Kapurch, Katie. "Unconditionally and Irrevocably: Theorizing the Melodramatic Impulse through the *Twilight Saga* and *Jane Eyre.*" *Children's Literature Association Quarterly* 37.2 (2012): 164-187.

Leavis, Q.D. "*Jane Eyre.*" *Collected Essays, Volume 1: The Englishness of the English Novel.* Ed. G. Singh. New York: Cambridge UP, 1985. 172-194.

Lerner, Laurence. "Bertha and the Critics." *Nineteenth-Century Literature* 44.3 (1989): 273–300. Lewes, George Henry. Rev. of *Jane Eyre*. *Fraser's Magazine*. Dec. 1847. Allott 83-87.

_____. Rev. of *Jane Eyre*. *Westminster Review*. Jan. 1848. Allott 87-88.

London, Bette. "The Pleasures of Submission: *Jane Eyre* and the Production of the Text." *ELH* 58.1 (1991): 195-213.

Moglen, Helene. *Charlotte Brontë: The Self Conceived*. Madison, WI: U of Wisconsin P, 1984.

Nelms, Ben, Beth Nelms, and Mark Vogel. "Young Adult Literature: Starting Out: Personal Odysseys of the Young." *The English Journal* 75.5 (1986): 80-83.

Oliphant, Margaret. *Blackwood's Magazine* Sept. 1867. Allott 390-391.

_____. Rev. of *Jane Eyre*. *Blackwood's Magazine,* May 1855. *The Brontës: The Critical Heritage*. Ed. Miriam Allott. Boston, MA: Routlege and Kegan Paul, 1974. 311-314.

Pell, Nancy. "Resistance, Rebellion, and Marriage: The Economics of *Jane Eyre*." *Nineteenth- Century Fiction* 31.4 (1977): 397-420.

Poovey, Mary. "The Anathematized Race: The Governess and *Jane Eyre*." *Uneven Developments: The Ideological Work of Gender in Mid-Victorian England*. Chicago: U of Chicago P, 1988. 126-163.

Rathburn, Robert C. and Martin Steinmann, Jr., eds. *From Jane Austen to Joseph Conrad*. Minneapolis: U of Minnesota P, 1958.

Renk, Kathleen Williams. "Jane Eyre as Hunger Artist." *Women's Writing* 15.1 (2008): 1-12

Rev. of *Jane Eyre*. *Atlas* 23 Oct. 1847. *The Brontës: The Critical Heritage*. Ed. Miriam Allott. Boston, MA: Routlege and Kegan Paul, 1974. 67-69.

Rev. of *Jane Eyre*. *Christian Remembrancer.* Apr. 1848. *The Brontës: The Critical Heritage*. Ed. Miriam Allott. Boston, MA: Routlege and Kegan Paul, 1974. 88-92.

Rev. of *Jane Eyre*. *Era.* 14 Nov. 1847. *The Brontës: The Critical Heritage*. Ed. Miriam Allott. Boston, MA: Routlege and Kegan Paul, 1974. 78-80.

Rev. of *Jane Eyre*. *Spectator.* 6 Nov. 1847. *The Brontës: The Critical Heritage*. Ed. Miriam Allott. Boston, MA: Routlege and Kegan Paul, 1974. 74-75.

Rich, Adrienne. "The Temptations of a Motherless Woman." *On Lies, Secrets, and Silence: Selected Prose, 1966-1978*. New York: Norton, 1986. 89-106.

Rodas, Julia Miele. "On the Spectrum": Rereading Contact and Affect in *Jane Eyre*. *Nineteenth-Century Gender Studies* 4.2 (2008): n. pag. Web. 18 Oct. 2013.

Rigby, Elizabeth. Rev. of *Jane Eyre. Quarterly Review.* Dec. 1848. *The Brontës: The Critical Heritage.* Ed. Miriam Allott. Boston, MA: Routlege and Kegan Paul, 1974. 105-112.

Thackeray, William Makepeace. "Letter to W. S. Williams." 23 Oct. 1847. *The Brontës: The Critical Heritage.* Ed. Miriam Allott. Boston, MA: Routlege and Kegan Paul, 1974. 70.

Schwartz, Nina. "The Logic of the Supplement in *Jane Eyre.*" *Jane Eyre.* Ed. Beth Newman. New York: Bedford/St. Martin's, 1996. 549-564.

Showalter, Elaine. *A Literature of Their Own: British Women Novelists from Brontë to Lessing.* Princeton: Princeton UP, 1977.

Smith, Margaret. Introduction. *Jane Eyre.* By Charlotte Brontë. New York: Oxford UP, 1975. v-xxvii.

Swinburne, Algernon Charles. *A Note on Charlotte Brontë.* London: Chatton and Windus, 1877.

Warhol, Robyn H. "Double Gender, Double Genre in *Jane Eyre* and *Villette.*" *Studies in English Literature 1500-1900* 36.4 (1996): 857-875.

Watson, Melvin R. "Form and Substance in the Brontë Novels." *From Jane Austen to Joseph Conrad.* Eds. Robert C. Rathburn and Martin Steinmann, Jr., Minneapolis: U of Minnesota P, 1958. 106-117.

Whipple, Edwin Percy. "Novels of the Season." Rev. of *Jane Eyre. North American Review.* Oct. 1848. Allott 97-99.

Woolf, Virginia. "A Room of One's Own." *The Longman Anthology of Women's Literature.* Ed. Mary K. DeShazer. New York: Longman, 2001. 16-72.

Wyatt, Jean. "A Patriarch of One's Own: *Jane Eyre* and Romantic Love. *Tulsa Studies in Women's Literature* 4.2 (1985): 199-216.

Zonana, Joyce. "The Sultan and the Slave: Feminist Orientalism and the Structure of *Jane Eyre.*" *Signs* 18.3 (1993): 592-617.

Shameful Signification: Narrative and Feeling in *Jane Eyre*

Ashly Bennett

> "For shame! for shame! . . . What shocking conduct, Miss Eyre."
> —Charlotte Brontë, *Jane Eyre* (9)

Is Jane Eyre the heroine of shame? Would such a reframing of the character famously dubbed the "heroine of fulfillment" constitute its own shamefully "shocking conduct"?[1] Widely understood as a model of engaging and empowered female voice, *Jane Eyre*'s distinctive "I" has often seemed bolstered, especially, by the emotional display and pull of that voice. Not just feeling, but specific feelings have captured critical attention, with anger and sympathy attaining pride of place in feminist assessments of Brontë's novel and of novelistic feeling in both Victorian and contemporary culture. From Sandra Gilbert and Susan Gubar's influential reading of Jane Eyre's anger as exemplary of "rebellious feminism" to more recent critiques of the normalizing "triumph of sympathy" staged by the novel's end, the fraught yet potent agency, self-assertion, and emotional invitation of Jane Eyre's autobiographical narrative, and especially her voice, have been understood to thrive on anger or sympathy.[2] Yet what are we to make of that emotion which inspires the first diegetic mention of Jane Eyre's surname and punctuates her physical imprisonment in the metaphorically rich red-room as a young girl—"For shame! for shame! . . . What shocking conduct, Miss Eyre" (9)? This cry "for shame" suggests that shame constitutes both an introduction of "Miss Eyre" to the reader and an interpellation of Jane into the contours of gendered interiority and social relations. We might imagine it as the invasive voice of society threatening to repress the more authentic self-expression of the angry Jane, or, perhaps, as an affective force imposed from outside the individual that exposes the disciplinary violence inflicted by all emotions, even those seemingly more personal and salutary feelings like sympathy. In what follows, however, I want to explore the implications of this formative call "for shame" as it weaves into the presentation of Jane Eyre's interiority and personal relations, and into the novel's structure and narrative techniques, in a form not easily accounted for as either pronounced repression or covert Foucauldian discipline. For the feminist potential of *Jane Eyre*'s voice largely emanates, I argue, from Brontë's formal enactment of a shame that mingles with and negotiates the extremes of anger's potentially antisocial alienation and sympathy's potentially oppressive socialization. The novel's initial demand "for shame" accompanies Jane's experience of being forced into the red-room and "thrust . . . upon a stool," yet it sets in motion a series of shameful spectacles that Jane, as character and narrator, embodies, witnesses, *and* stages with increasing agency, aesthetic control, and erotic investment (9). From the shamings of Jane and Helen Burns at Lowood School to the shame-charged maiming and healing of Rochester's body, Brontë employs a shame-inflected narration that intersects with physical spectacles of shame both to structure *Jane Eyre* and to fashion—in lieu of a sympathetic sameness—intimate relations of difference among the novel's characters, between present and past selves and, in a more formal sense, between experience and narration, story and discourse, and reader and text.

The specific cry "for shame!" reverberates throughout the pages of the nineteenth-century British novel, ushering many of its most famously mortified heroines—Jane Eyre, Becky Sharp, and Maggie Tulliver among them—into its narratives and onto the literary scene, and shame more broadly initiates for others—like Jane Austen's consistently humiliated protagonists—climactic shifts in social and self-awareness.[3] Tracing shame's role in *Jane Eyre* thus accentuates a historical entanglement of emotions and narrative that has wider—and continuing—resonance, amplifying a resounding yet critically neglected affective note in nineteenth-century literature and culture. In *Jane Eyre* we particularly hear this note in an empowered voice that showcases the productive, revisionary valences of novelistic engagements with shame throughout the period. Indeed, Brontë's novel offers a striking instance of shame *as voice*, in both the political and narratological senses of the term that Susan Lanser elaborates when she notes that voice, for contemporary feminism, often functions as a political concept—a "trope of identity and power"— kept distinct from the formal emphasis of narrative poetics, where "'voice' attends to the specific forms of textual practice" (3, 5). Thus the cry "for shame!" that hovers, at the start of *Jane Eyre*, around Jane's forcibly raised body encapsulates an interplay of embodied and voiced shame that develops over the course of the novel's plot and further characterizes Brontë's experimentation with narrative techniques that heighten the possibilities of novelistic shame. This interplay emblematizes how nineteenth-century novelists from Austen to Oscar Wilde significantly, if variously, enact shame in story *and* discourse—using it to motivate dramatic plot points *and* innovative narrative techniques, to stage social spectacles of shame *along with* a distinctive way of telling about them. *Jane Eyre* specifically provides a rich instance of the set of narrative techniques that I term shameful signification—techniques that disrupt and revise the sentimental signification so central to the development of the British novel. As an alternative to the sentimental signification novelists often use to support the affective aim of sympathetic identification, shameful signification enables possibilities of intimate relational difference within social relations, subjectivity, novelistic form, and literary hermeneutics.

My discussion of *Jane Eyre* and its revisionary, rather than simply repressive, forms of shame begins by considering Eve Kosofsky Sedgwick's account of shame and Adam Smith's mid-eighteenth-century theory of sympathy (which, as we will see, also advances a less explicit theorization of shame). Both Sedgwick and Smith approach shame through thought experiments that not only highlight the oddly individuated relationality that shame can accommodate, but also suggest how shame's relational potential might be a function of form, especially of the staging of a contagiously emotive spectacle that can be incorporated in varying ways into social scenarios and cultural and personal narratives. Reading *Jane Eyre* against the background of Smith and Sedgwick brings into relief the revisionary valence of the shameful spectacle as a function specifically of novelistic form, and, aligning their affect theory with narrative theory, I explore how Brontë innovates with focalization and retrospective narration to stretch shame's potential as a relational and representational alternative to the sympathetic imperative of strict identification. This potential speaks to the problematic allure of identification in our current cultural climate, and in my concluding section I return to the prominent place *Jane Eyre* holds in discussions of gender and modern individualism, considering how an attention to shame in Brontë's novel—particularly as it emerges in the "terrible spectacle" of the novel's romantic resolution (375)— can help us further to understand and shape the affective terms of ongoing feminist discussions of the possibilities and limitations of novelistic feelings.

Shame's Form

Theorists of emotion have been drawn to shame's ability to produce compelling, embodied spectacles that exert a strong relational pull without reinforcing strict identification with others, or with social norms more broadly. Certainly social norms, and a communal sense of those norms, can create punitive shameful spectacles; at the same time, however, both the shamed subject and the spectator can recognize the signified shame and even feel for others through shared proximity to that shame, without fully accepting it as their own interior emotional content or demanding it of another. The spectacle of shame can compel identificatory socialization; but it can also produce more differentiated relations around the form of shame. In her important work on shame, Eve Kosofsky Sedgwick, drawing on the affect theory of Silvan Tomkins, focuses on the theatrical performativity of shame that establishes communication despite disrupted identification. Adam Smith's influential *Theory of Moral Sentiments*—first published in 1759—suggests a similar formal feature of shame, while placing shame in relation to the popular discourse of sympathy. Reading Sedgwick's theory of shame next to Smith's discussion of sympathy thus allows us to tease out those formal aspects of shame uneasily present alongside the historically situated affective mode, discourse, and aesthetics of sympathy with which Brontë is deeply engaged.

Sedgwick investigates shame's disruptions of identification—disruptions that do not, as a result, obliterate interest, communication, or identity. Using the posture of lowered eyes and bowed head to capture shame's distinctive relationality, she focuses on the protoform "moment when the circuit of mirroring expressions between the child's face and the caregiver's recognized face . . . is broken" (36). This prototypical "disruptive moment, in a circuit of identity-constituting identificatory communication," exemplifies Sedgwick's more generalized assertion that shame can round out and fuel such a circuit—rather than just break it—by ushering in new forms of communication and new forms of identity-constitution less dependent on absolute interest or identification (36). Shame, she writes, "is itself a form of communication. Blazons of shame, the 'fallen face' with eyes down and head averted . . . are semaphores of trouble and at the same time of a desire to reconstitute the interpersonal bridge"; likewise, "in interrupting identification, shame, too, makes identity" (36). Shame simultaneously operates as a truly theatrical performance of disconnection, in the sense that it is dramatized for the other, and as a performative act, in the sense that it makes the self. Sedgwick thus describes "the double movement shame makes: toward painful individuation, toward uncontrollable relationality," as it "mantles the threshold between introversion and extroversion, between absorption and theatricality, between performativity and—performativity" (37, 38).

Sedgwick's efforts to recuperate shame depend, to a certain extent, on emphasizing its basic structural capacity for forging identity and communication in ways that do not depend on strict identification and, in fact, thrive on identification's inevitable breakdowns. Through such emphasis, she pressures understandings of shame as purely prohibitive or repressive, instead casting shame as an affective mode that can accommodate—even drive—identificatory elasticity and revision within still legible and sociable identity and group formations. This space of revision, rather than pure rupture, depends on shame's potent communicative quality. Sedgwick locates an alternative social glue in the fact that "shame is both peculiarly contagious and peculiarly individuating," and this strangely individualized contagion stems, I argue, from shame's form (36).

Though the form of shame I am underlining is not discussed by Sedgwick, it can be seen in an extended scenario with which she illustrates shame's contagious quality. She recounts that in lectures on the topic of shame,

> I used to ask listeners to join in a thought experiment, visualizing an unwashed, half-insane man who would wander into the lecture hall mumbling loudly, his speech increasingly accusatory and disjointed, and publicly urinate in front of the room, then wander out again. I pictured the excruciation of everyone else in the room: each looking down, wishing to be anywhere else yet conscious of the inexorable fate of being exactly there, inside the individual skin of which each was burningly aware; at the same time, though, unable to staunch the hemorrhage of painful identification with the misbehaving man. (37)

Here, the odd structure of "painful identification" evokes shame's capacity to bind individuals through spectacular, visualized form despite unstable content. For Sedgwick's "misbehaving man" displays little or no shame of his own; instead, what is noteworthy is his apparent lack of it. The shame the audience catches, then, comes from recognizable form without certain content, from a scenario that demands shame according to social convention, while its primary signifying subject does not have to feel it for it to be transmitted to others. The shameful scenario binds members of the audience without the affective content of shame truly belonging to them, either; what Sedgwick calls their "painful identification with the misbehaving man" is in some sense an identification with a *lack* of required shame: it evacuates each audience member's shame even as the scenario produces and spreads it. To the extent that the audience member comes into even closer proximity to shame than its apparent source—the "misbehaving man"—"identification" fails really to be established at all.

Just as the shame in this thought experiment proves hard to pin down, its results are also difficult to fix: Sedgwick "picture[s]" the audience's "painful identification," but one could imagine shame's "double movement" veering "toward painful individuation," with onlookers feeling less connection through shame than anger with or contempt for the "misbehaving man," and trying to put squarely on him the shame he maddeningly refuses. Or the movement could swerve "toward uncontrollable relationality," with the man fully succumbing to shame and closely identifying witnesses feeling similarly overcome. Sedgwick's thought experiment lingers, however, on the space between these poles, the oscillating "movement" along a spectrum of opposition and identification that constitutes shame's productive terrain. Her spectacularly shameful scenario thus lays bare the *form* of a shame that can produce relational transactions—akin but not reducible to "identification"—in which, despite "the excruciation of everyone," no one actually owns the circulating shame.

The distinction I am drawing between shame's fluid relationality and one of stricter identification depends on recognizing a number of distinctions within Sedgwick's thought experiment itself: between the scenario, the signifying body of the "misbehaving man," and each individual's interior emotional content. In fleshing out these distinctions, we can usefully turn to another thought experiment that engages the same features but puts them to the opposite use of solidifying identification: Adam Smith's oft-cited example of sympathy with "our brother upon the rack" (11). Smith introduces his theorization of sympathy—the centerpiece of his *Theory of Moral Sentiments*—with an image of sympathy at the height of its effect. The relational goal is the closest emotional equivalence possible: while Smith acknowledges that individualized sensations and senses pose barriers to actual transmission of the "immediate experience of what other men feel," representational features nonetheless can align to convey, with a certain immediacy, feelings that, "though weaker in degree," are "not altogether unlike" the feelings of others (11). The most important of these features is the scenario—the "like situation":

Though our brother is upon the rack, as long as we ourselves are at our ease, our senses will never inform us of what he suffers. They never did, and never can, carry us beyond our own person, and it is by the imagination only that we can form any conception of what are his sensations. Neither can that faculty help us to this any other way, than by representing to us what would be our own, if we were in his case. . . . By the imagination we place ourselves in his situation, we conceive ourselves enduring all the same torments, we enter as it were into his body, and become in some measure the same person with him, and thence form some idea of his sensations, and even feel something which, though weaker in degree, is not altogether unlike them. His agonies, when they are thus brought home to ourselves, when we have thus adopted and made them our own, begin at last to affect us, and we then tremble and shudder at the thought of what he feels. (11–12)

In Smith's account, sympathy works primarily through the pull of the scenario and its capacity to facilitate the spectator's imaginative insertion into it. But the sympathetic transmission of pain in this example depends not only on the dramatic, encompassing scenario of the rack, but also on the way that this particular scenario minimizes representational or responsive wiggle room, violently forcing continuity between scenario, signifying body, and interior emotional content in order to guarantee unambiguous and quick communication to the sympathetic spectator. The hyperbolically constrictive structure of the scenario pins the signifying body into a highly visible and legible place with a limited range of likely emotional responses, virtually ensuring suffering as both the victim's and the viewer's only, near-identical response. The rack captures sympathy's most seamless workings, modeling its spectacular and transparent signification and connecting such representational techniques with the relational imperative of emotional equivalence between individuals as the grounds of intimacy and sociability. The rack exemplifies, for Smith, the form of sympathy, a form whose spectacular emotional pull is similar to that of the form of shame in Sedgwick's thought experiment, but which significantly demands the neat alignment of interior emotional content as well.

Smith's *Theory* also, however, illustrates how historical accounts of sympathy themselves sought to loosen the rigidity of sympathetic imperatives, turning to shame in the process of imagining other forms of individualized relations. Shame emerges in Smith's text as a feeling that marks and fills the cracks of sympathy's fragility. Next to the rack, one could place his invocation of the pillory to figure an alternative relational model, built around shame, that the text gingerly but consistently approaches:

> A brave man is not rendered contemptible by being brought to the scaffold; he is, by being set in the pillory. His behaviour in the one situation may gain him universal esteem and admiration. No behaviour in the other can render him agreeable. The sympathy of the spectators supports him in the one case, and saves him from that shame, that consciousness that his misery is felt by himself only, which is of all sentiments the most unsupportable. There is no sympathy in the other; or, if there is any, it is not with his pain, which is a trifle, but with his consciousness of the want of sympathy with which this pain is attended. It is with his shame, not with his sorrow. Those who pity him, blush and hang down their heads for him. He droops in the same manner, and feels himself irrecoverably degraded by the punishment, though not by the crime. (71)

Smith initially notes shame as merely the affective sign of obliterated sympathy: shame is synonymous with the man in the pillory's "consciousness that his misery is felt by himself only." He immediately retreats from this extreme notion of shame, though, positioning it more specifically as an aftermath to ruptured sympathy. A connection felt by the spectator, restricted to a shared sense of the man's shame, takes the place of sympathy's more complete alignment of emotion. The assertion that "There is no sympathy in the other" is qualified: "or, if there is any, it is not with his pain, which is a trifle, but with his consciousness of the want of sympathy with which this pain is attended." The disruption of sympathy itself opens up a space of near-sympathetic connection around a shared awareness of sympathy's breakdown. In the possibility that one can still sympathize with the man in the pillory's "shame," if "not with his sorrow," a relational space unfolds that is not quite sympathy and that relies on the mutual recognition that sympathy is compromised and complete sympathetic identification is impossible. Shame's continued relationality depends on the "consciousness of the want of sympathy" that is embedded within it—an embedding of lack quite different from the mere absence of sympathy.

The physical mirroring of the sympathetic spectacle remains intact, here, but with dramatically different signification. Rather than acting as transparent signs of interior emotional content and its identical communication, the heads we see "droop[ing] in the same manner" bespeak a relational disconnection that resists equivalence but also avoids total illegibility. Incorporating aspects of the rack's sympathetic signification, Smith's pillory theatrically demands recognition and response: this form, however, encompasses a range of emotional options and interpretive possibilities that can still constitute communication and sociability, if not of sympathy's ideal kind. On the one hand, the scenario spectacularly binds the man and his observers despite varied emotional states. On the other hand, the scenario also accommodates a split within the victim's own experience of shame, as he "feels himself irrecoverably degraded by the punishment, though not by the crime." Similar to the shame-forged sympathy that is not *quite* sympathy, the victim is both shamed and not ashamed: he has a palpable relation to the form of shame, but does not entirely possess its intended content. Even more than in Sedgwick's thought experiment, the signifying body and its spectators are here linked by the irresistible contagion of a punitive form embodying social convention, while none are fully conscripted into its universalizing mandates.

In *Jane Eyre,* Brontë exhibits and extends the sorts of relational and representational permutations of sympathy that theoretical valorizations of sympathy, like Smith's *Theory,* were themselves pursuing. *Jane Eyre* employs formal shifts in novelistic representation that could be considered shameful signification, as opposed to—but also deeply entwined with—sentimental signification. A rich body of critical work has delineated how formal strategies support the affective aim of sympathetic identification in the eighteenth- and nineteenth-century development of the British novel: drawing on such work, I characterize sentimental signification as a set of narrative techniques defined by, and pursuing, an ideal of sympathetic continuity between interior emotional content and the signifying body, and between feeling subjects (including characters and readers) linked through emotional identification, physical mirroring, and identically shared feelings.[4] An alternative representational mode of shameful signification emerges in tandem and in tension with sentimental signification in the eighteenth century, and becomes increasingly important in shaping formal features of the nineteenth-century novel. As deployed and developed by Brontë, shameful signification engages the representational techniques that sentimental novelists used for sympathetic mimesis, and it adapts these techniques to accommodate greater emotional disjunctions among characters, between text and reader, and among readers. Brontë's exploration of the ideological and formal potential of shame in *Jane Eyre* draws on the compelling, spectacular form of shame that we find in both Smith and Sedgwick, a form that can relationally bind individuals through shameful scenario and signifying body, while loosening the rigid continuity of interior emotional content. Throughout the novel, Brontë develops formal strategies of shameful signification in which she seeks shame's distinctive relational pull not only through the staging of physical spectacles in the novel's plot, but also through effects of focalization and retrospective narration that mimic and stretch these spectacles' accommodation of individualized difference.

Reading Shame

In the sequence at Lowood School, and especially in Jane's relationship with Helen Burns, Brontë most directly connects the relational possibilities of shame to a literary hermeneutics and to the formal permutations of sentimental signification that I have described as shameful signification. *Jane Eyre* positions shame as a relational, representational, and reading mode in the depiction of Jane's childhood encounters with Helen at Lowood. We see the problem of individualized subjectivity and social relation that haunts Jane's first days at Lowood in her fuzzy perception of her new surroundings, and especially the other girls, as an indistinguishable mass. She can only register the "hum of many voices" and their seemingly "countless" number, and the difficulty of differentiation spreads from Jane's surroundings to her thoughts, even impinging on narration: "My reflections were too undefined and fragmentary to merit record: I hardly yet knew where I was" (37, 42). Only two "marked event[s]" cut through the perceptual and descriptive haze of Jane's first day: Helen reading and Helen being publicly shamed (44). In each instance, Jane recognizes another individual and interrogates possible forms of intimate interaction with her. The narration similarly finds in Helen an individual character around which to organize Jane's past perceptions and present memories: Helen, and Jane's reactions to her, "merit record." Through the same dynamic of shame that she uses to negotiate relations with others in the story, the narrating Jane resists both sympathetic submission to her past self and self-estrangement. *Jane Eyre* enacts this dynamic of shame in terms of not only relationality, but also interiority and narrative form—a dynamic that, as we will see, provides a significant model of readerly engagement as well.

When Helen first comes into Jane's view, she conjures the prospect of sympathetic identification:

> I saw a girl sitting on a stone bench near; she was bent over a book, on the perusal of which she seemed intent: from where I stood I could see the title—it was "Rasselas;" a name that struck me as strange, and consequently attractive. In turning a leaf she happened to look up, and I said to her directly; —"Is your book interesting?" I had already formed the intention of asking her to lend it to me some day. . . . I hardly know where I found the hardihood thus to open a conversation with a stranger; the step was contrary to my nature and habits: but I think her occupation touched a chord of sympathy somewhere; for I too liked reading, though of a frivolous and childish kind; I could not digest or comprehend the serious or substantial. (42–43)

Jane initially attempts to assimilate the "stranger" to her investment in sympathetic likeness, and, by staging this potentially sympathetic scene specifically as a scene of reading, Brontë extends the subsequent disruption of Jane's limited sympathetic idealization to literary investments. For the "chord of sympathy" is plucked only to be loosened: a sympathetic paradigm of close identification with novelistic content, as well as other readers' responses, is frustrated when Jane actually looks inside the coveted book, "a brief examination" of which "convinced me that the contents were less taking than the title: 'Rasselas' looked dull to my trifling taste; I saw nothing about fairies, nothing about genii; no bright variety seemed to spread over the closely printed pages" (43). Jane's interest in Helen persists in spite of their discordant reading practices, however. The "chord of sympathy" that can be touched through reading—as a generalized activity—is made to accommodate differences in understanding and affective engagement. Like shame—and sharing its paradigmatic bent posture, here "bent over a book"—the scene of reading provides a form that can bind those drawn to reading both despite and through pointed divergences of reading practice and response. To distinguish Brontë's conceptualization of reading from more fixed sympathetic hermeneutics and sentimental signification, it is useful to recall the constitutive aspects—scenario, signifying body, and interior emotion—of Smith's classic sympathetic scene, as well as Smith's and Sedgwick's shameful reconfigurations of it. Reading, broadly defined, acts as a compelling scenario with a strong relational pull: Jane is initially intrigued simply because "I too liked reading." The signifying body, here, entails both a physical body—Helen's bent posture—and a textual one—the book cover bearing the "strange, and consequently attractive" title of *Rasselas*. Unlike the rigid sympathetic continuity of signifying form and interior emotional content, however, there is here room for variance. The actual "contents" of *Rasselas* diverge between "dull" and absorbing, depending on the distinct responses of readers whose own interior emotional content—while evoked by the shared posture and scenario of reading—can diverge as well without breaking the bond of reading.

Following this initial upset of a strict sympathetic connection, Jane continues to attend to the "stranger," and an intense bond between Jane and Helen develops that is especially forged through shameful reading. While remaining an explicit figure of reading, Helen also morphs increasingly into the text Jane most longs to read—one that can be most intimately and closely read through shame. In the second "marked event" of Jane's initial day at Lowood, Helen's shameful "disgrace," like her reading, draws Jane into a compelling spectacle that pulls the novel's relational alternative to sympathy into sharper focus (44). Before turning to this spectacle, however, we should first consider another, later exhibition of Helen's shame that threatens to push Jane past relational disconnection and into angry, antisocial alienation. The representational features of this scene of humiliating exposure illuminate those aspects of sentimental signification that Brontë seeks to revise in other scenes of more conditional shameful exhibition. The scene also occurs during Jane's stay at Lowood, and in it Helen is literally transformed into a text of shame:

> Miss Scatcherd wrote in conspicuous characters on a piece of pasteboard the word "Slattern," and bound it like a phylactery round Helen's large, mild, intelligent, and benign-looking forehead. She wore it till evening, patient, unresentful, regarding it as a deserved punishment. The moment Miss Scatcherd withdrew after afternoon-school, I ran to Helen, tore it off, and thrust it into the fire: the fury of which she was incapable had been burning in my soul all day, and tears, hot and large, had continually been scalding my cheek; for the spectacle of her sad resignation gave me an intolerable pain at the heart. (64)

Though Helen is shamed, here, her shame has much of the representational rigidity of Smith's sympathetic rack, rather than his shameful pillory. The shaming scenario, imprinted onto the signifying body with a horrifyingly fixed materiality and explicitness of signification, secures, in turn, the interior content of that body: Helen regards the sign of "Slattern" "as a deserved punishment." An excruciating continuity and transparency of sentimental signification traps Jane, as spectator, between the extremes of hyper-socialized submission—akin to Helen's response here—or antisocial revolt. Jane's responding anger not only severs connection with clearly oppressive forces, represented by Miss Scatcherd, but also imperils any affective continuity between herself and Helen: Jane feels "the fury of which [Helen] was incapable." Jane's response here approaches—as it does in an earlier scene in which Helen's shame is branded directly onto her body through a beating—"a sentiment of unavailing and impotent anger" (46).

Yet the first shaming of Helen that Jane witnesses—to return to the second "marked event" of her first day at Lowood (44) — strikingly contrasts with the inflexible signification represented by the material label of "Slattern." Similar to Smith's pillory and Sedgwick's thought experiment, a scenario demanding shame here circulates a palpably communicative feeling that still fails to define entirely any individual's interior content or to produce strict identification between individuals:

> The only marked event of the afternoon was, that I saw the girl with whom I had conversed in the verandah, dismissed in disgrace, by Miss Scatcherd, from a history class, and sent to stand in the middle of the large schoolroom. The punishment seemed to me in a high degree ignominious, especially for so great a girl—she looked thirteen or upwards. I expected she would show signs of great distress and shame; but to my surprise she neither wept nor blushed: composed, though grave, she stood, the central mark of all eyes. "How can she bear it so quietly—so firmly?" I asked of myself. "Were I in her place, it seems to me I should wish the earth to open and swallow me up. She looks as if she were thinking of something beyond her punishment— beyond her situation: of something not round her nor before her. I have heard of day-dreams—is she in a day-dream now? Her eyes are fixed on the floor, but I am sure they do not see it—her sight seems turned in, gone down into her heart: she is looking at what she can remember, I believe; not at what is really present. I wonder what sort of a girl she is—whether good or naughty?" (44–45)

As in the previous scene of reading, Jane is frustrated in any easy application of a sympathetic hermeneutics to Helen's compelling spectacle. She fails to trace the expected continuity of shaming scenario and concrete physical signs—"signs of great distress and shame"—as Helen "neither wept nor blushed," and appears "composed, though grave." Instead, the bowed head—"her eyes fixed on the floor"—again allows for diverse interior content, bringing Helen and Jane into a shameful scenario whose form nonetheless accommodates other feelings and affectively binds Jane to Helen despite her sense of their divergent emotions and thoughts.

Narrating Shame

The spectacle of Helen's extreme, visual exposure as "she stood, the central mark of all eyes" further is alleviated of an all-consuming shame by layered acts of thinking—Jane thinking that Helen "looks as if she were thinking of something beyond her punishment—beyond her situation." Through this "thinking," Helen attains some distance from the explicit affective demand of her shaming "punishment." The precise structure of this thought is provocative: Jane imagines that Helen finds relief from a highly visible shame, even as that spectacle draws others toward her, because "she is looking at what she can remember, I believe; not at what is really present." Helen's remembering doubles Jane's own narratorial stance of establishing proximity to shame through retrospection. That Helen's remembering is accessible only through Jane's telling about it highlights the way in which it figures Jane's narrative act, emphasizing how certain forms of both perceiving and telling about shame can enhance the possibilities of a conditional relation to its punitive spectacle.

Jane's own remembered perceptions of Helen's acts of remembering capture the individuated intimacy enabled by shame that Brontë further accentuates through effects of focalization. When Jane thinks, "Were I in her place, it seems to me I should wish the earth to open and swallow me up," she focalizes an overwhelming perception of shame both on behalf of herself and Helen and, in a sense, for no one. Through what remains a merely hypothetical focalization of self-eviscerating shame, Brontë enacts an intimate contact between the two girls' still distinct thoughts and feelings, as well as a friction between each girl's interior emotional content and the form of shame's spectacle.[5] For Jane is not "in her place" and recognizes as much in her thoughts, which emphasize her own distance from the shame she only hypothetically perceives. Neither does the perception of intense shame appear to apply to the stoic Helen's actual feelings in that shaming "place." This hypothetical focalization of shame captures shame's potential to combine fragile yet marked distinctions with a tangible sense of closeness, as Jane and Helen are drawn near both the "punishment" of shame and each other's interiority, yet escape undifferentiated merging. In its absolute exposure of the experiencing Jane's thoughts, the hypothetical focalization of shame provides a formal, interior equivalent of the scene of shame's ability to create a spectacularly visualized body that can bind individuals in relational difference. Further, Jane here—in her keen engagement that is not reducible to identification—offers a figure for the reader's own relation to such novelistic spectacles of shame.

While the formulation "Were I in her place" gives Jane and Helen some distance from the threat of overwhelming shame, when Jane actually *is* put "in [Helen's] place," such distance is still preserved through layers of retrospection that come together within Jane's interiority. Soon after Helen's public shaming, Jane finds herself hoisted on a stool in the schoolroom for Mr. Brocklehurst's public condemnation of her, and the perception of shame that Jane had experienced in relation to Helen's exposure enables a meeting with her own past self as well as with Helen:

There was I, then, mounted aloft: I, who had said I could not bear the shame of standing on my natural feet in the middle of the room, was now exposed to general view on a pedestal of infamy. What my sensations were, no language can describe: but just as they all rose, stifling my breath and constricting my throat, a girl came up and passed me: in passing, she lifted up her eyes. What a strange light inspired them! What an extraordinary sensation that ray sent through me! How the new feeling bore me up! It was as if a martyr, a hero, had passed a slave or victim, and imparted strength in transit. I mastered the rising hysteria, lifted up my head, and took a firm stand on the stool. Helen Burns asked some slight question about her work of Miss Smith, was chidden for the triviality of the inquiry, returned to her place, and smiled at me as she again went by. What a smile! I remember it now, and I know that it was the effluence of fine intellect, of true courage; it lit up her marked lineaments, her thin face, her sunken grey eye, like a reflection from the aspect of an angel. (58–59)

The narrator here brings her present-tense "I" into retrospective contact with two past "I"s: the "I, then, mounted aloft" and the "I, who had said I could not bear the shame." The experiencing Jane, "mounted aloft," engages in the same act of remembering a past proximity to shame as the narrating "I," offering a model for the narrator's ability, through shameful retrospection, to bring together yet differentiate between moments making up the self. The complex interaction of closely connected yet distinct "I"s enabled by Jane's "expos[ure] to general view on a pedestal of infamy" encapsulates not just shame's relational possibilities, but the affectively charged narrative structure of *Jane Eyre*'s retrospective autobiographical form and its shamedelineated space of intimate relational difference between story and narrating.

In considering this retrospective narrative structure, we might usefully turn to Gérard Genette's discussion of voice in *Narrative Discourse*, in which he provocatively alludes to the differentiating work that shame might perform. Observing the especially fragile temporal distinctions of interpolated narrating, or narrating "between the moments of action," common in epistolary novels, Genette writes, "the extreme closeness of story to narrating produces . . . most often, a very subtle effect of friction (if I may call it that) between the slight temporal displacement of the narrative of events ('Here is what happened to me today') and the complete simultaneousness in the report of thoughts and feelings ('Here is what I think about it this evening')" (217–18). This "friction" often entails a barely perceptible difference between story and narrating, hero and narrator: "Here, the narrator is at one and the same time still the hero and already someone else: the events of the day are already in the past, and the 'point of view' may have been modified since then; the feelings of the evening or the next day are fully of the present, and here focalization through the narrator is at the same time focalization through the hero" (218). In Genette's example, from Choderlos de Laclos's *Les Liaisons Dangereuses,* one feeling particularly embodies the "friction" of past experience and present feelings:

> Cécile Volanges writes to Mme. de Merteuil to tell her how she was seduced, last night, by Valmont, and to confide in her her remorse; the seduction scene is past, and with it the confusion that Cécile no longer feels, and can no longer even imagine; what remains is the shame, and a sort of stupor which is both incomprehension and discovery of oneself . . . The Cécile of yesterday, very near and already far off, is seen and spoken of by the Cécile of today. We have here two successive heroines, (only) the second of whom is (also) the narrator and gives her point of view, the point of view—displaced just enough to create dissonance—of the immediate *post-event* future. (218)

In general, Genette's example portrays the "friction" inherent in interpolated narrating, a friction any number of emotions could join with the form to display. Yet in specifically bringing shame together with the "friction" produced by the epistolary mode, Genette's illustration also suggests how this formal effect and shame amplify each other: shame, here, appears especially potent affective material for marking subtle distinctions of focalization and voice when temporal proximity threatens to elide them. A point of view tinged with shame—and its performance of disrupted identification—will be "displaced just enough to create dissonance" but not enough to break close contact with past perspectives. Through shame, the interpolated narration even more tangibly rubs up against an immediately preceding yet distinct affective experience, keeping the past self who is perceived as a compelling spectacle of shame "very near and already far off." Shame fortifies an autobiographical characterization containing "two successive heroines, (only) the second of whom is (also) the narrator," and these "successive heroines" accumulate into a coherent identity—an autobiographical "I"—that changes and encompasses affective deviations over the temporal progression of the novel.

If we consider interpolated narrating not only as a broad narrative category but also in the specific context of the sentimental novel that often adopts this form, then the changing heroine represented through shame becomes especially significant. While Genette focuses primarily on the temporal "closeness of story to narrating" that can blur the experiencing and narrating heroine, the sentimental novel puts this temporal closeness within a larger relational and representational logic of sympathetic equivalence. In such a context, it is not just the affective differences between individuals that can fade, but also those within an individual character. In novels such as Samuel Richardson's *Pamela* and *Clarissa*, for example, the mimetic structure of one character sympathetically reproducing another's feelings extends to a mimetic structure of interiority, in which past and present selves replicate relatively unvarying emotional responses. By extension, the epistolary or journaling narrator tends to replicate and reinforce her earlier affective experience during a sympathetic revisiting. In a sentimental interpolated narrative, the "dissonance" and "friction" between experience and narrating that Genette particularly evokes through shame thus could not only instate fragile yet distinct differences in voice and focalization, but also, in so doing, disrupt the larger mimetic logic of the narrative.

Jane Eyre does not, of course, include interpolated narrating, falling firmly into the category of subsequent narrating, "the classical position of the past-tense narrative" (Genette 217). Nonetheless, shame's differentiating potential in interpolated narrating helps to isolate a similar effect in Brontë's novel. *Jane Eyre* incorporates shame's "friction" into a much wider temporal gap between story and narrating, reinforcing a "dissonance" between a past and present "I" that also disrupts sympathetic idealization and sentimental signification. In adapting shame's "friction" from interpolated narrating, *Jane Eyre* not only creates dissonance but also preserves an intimate closeness between a past and present self—a closeness which is not, as in interpolated narrating, enacted through temporal nearness. Harnessing shame's capacity to stage "successive heroines" who are both "very near and already far off" from one another, the novel creates, through shameful retrospection, a sense of affective contact in the place of literal temporal proximity (Genette 218). By stretching the temporal interval between experience and memory, Brontë pushes the limits of relational difference between the experiencing and narrating Jane, while using shame to preserve intimacy and prevent an alienating break within the autobiographical "I." Similar to the eighteenth-century novels Genette invokes, *Jane Eyre* "exploit[s] that narrative situation propitious to the most subtle and the most 'irritating' counterpoints: the situation of the tiniest temporal interval" (Genette 218). Brontë, however, innovatively furthers this exploitation by replacing the irritation of the "tiniest temporal interval" with the purely affective substitute of shame's differentiated closeness.[6] *Jane Eyre* thus explores the possibilities of an intimate dynamic of shame in terms of social relations, interiority, and narrative form.

Jane's schoolroom exposure culminates in a moment that conveys the intimate friction such spectacles of shame can produce. The narrating *and* experiencing Janes' memories of differentiated past selves are linked to another significant memory related to Jane's shaming—Helen's smile. The affectionate observation "What a smile!"—like the memory of shame—briefly bridges the voice and focalization of the experiencing and narrating Jane, while the subsequent interjection, "I remember it now," reinstates the difference of time.[7] The smile brings Jane's differentiated "I"'s together with Helen in a moment of acute connection that—unlike the sympathetic paradigm—depends on distinctions within the self and between the self and others. The affective intensity of the smile derives in part from the sequence of shifting postures that precedes it and wavers between relationality and disconnection: Helen "lifted up her eyes" to make contact with Jane's bowed head; and Jane in turn "lifted up [her] head," as Helen "passed." These postures— variously mismatched and corresponding, rather than stagnantly mirroring—culminate in the momentary, intimate contact of the smile—a moment the narrator lingers over still.

The affective intensity of Helen's smile further derives from the ways in which it makes manifest much of the agency and intimacy embedded in the previous scene of Jane watching Helen's "disgrace." In the earlier spectacle Helen stood still with "her eyes . . . fixed on the floor": but now Helen moves, lifts her gaze, and smiles, actively responding to and physically advancing the reach that Jane had before extended toward her in thought only. Helen's smile and Jane's response enact the intimate differentiation of Jane's formulation "Were I in her place" as a now tangible point of connection, as Helen directly acknowledges Jane's shameful scenario while also prompting her to move beyond its limiting, oppressive contours. And Jane's own layered memories at this moment, producing palpable contact between past and present selves around the spectacle of shame, further draw out the processes implicit in Helen's earlier "look[ing] as if she were thinking of something beyond her punishment" because she seemed to be "looking at what she can remember." The convergence of these two scenes' spectacles of shame particularly illustrates how the autobiographical subject's recognition and staging of differences within a coherent self can inform an increased attention to— even seeking of—compelling difference in others. To recognize, here, how *Jane Eyre*'s autobiographical narrative of development reinforces the novel's investment in relational difference is to begin to challenge the common critique of Jane Eyre's interiority and voice, especially from her concluding position as a bourgeois domestic woman, as effecting a normalizing and exclusionary idealization of sympathetic identification.

Shame's "terrible spectacle"

Any unsettling of *Jane Eyre* as a narrative idealizing sympathetic union must account for Jane's final romantic reunion with Rochester and particularly for the two spectacles that seem to position this reunion as a highly sympathetic one: Rochester's inexplicable call, which leaves Jane's "flesh quiver[ing] on my bones," and his disfigurement, which renders Jane, through his devotion to and physical dependence on her, "absolutely bone of his bone and flesh of his flesh" (369, 397). To be sure, each of these spectacles touches a palpable "chord of sympathy," but they also function beyond the immediacy of their purely sympathetic displays. Indeed, it is through subsequent narrations of these seemingly sympathetic spectacles, by Jane and by other characters, that Brontë establishes an erotics of shame—an erotics that constitutes the novel's affective closure in a form that also, I suggest, helps to keep *Jane Eyre* open to readers' diverse engagements and critical concerns.

Rochester's call to Jane might at first appear the antithesis of, even the antidote for, the cry "for shame!" that forces the young, alienated Jane—"a thing that could not sympathize with one amongst" the Reeds—into the red-room (12). When Jane, despite their gaping geographic separation, experiences a heightened sense of Rochester's feelings, her histrionic body responds to Rochester's emotion with classic sympathetic susceptibility: "My heart beat fast and thick," then "stood still to an inexpressible feeling that thrilled it through, and passed at once to my head and extremities," she explains (369). Along with her sympathetic, bodily response, however, Jane also registers a voice: "I saw nothing: but I heard a voice somewhere cry—'Jane! Jane! Jane!' nothing more" (369). While an "inexpressible feeling" threatens to merge completely with Jane's responsive body, the compelling, individuated voice remains distinct, for "it was the voice of a human being—a known, loved, well-remembered voice—that of Edward Fairfax Rochester" (369). This deviation from the sympathetic paradigm continues, veering closer to the cry for shame, as the following narration explains Rochester's "cry" by linking it to his desperate "call" to his wife, Bertha Mason. When Jane investigates the meaning of her uncanny experience by returning to Thornfield Hall, an innkeeper provides background on the "terrible spectacle" of its burning and Rochester's doomed attempt to remove his wife (375):

He . . . went back to get his mad wife out of her cell. And then they called out to him that she was on the roof; where she was standing, waving her arms, above the battlements, and shouting out till they could hear her a mile off; I saw and heard her with my own eyes. She was a big woman, and had long black hair: we could see it streaming against the flames as she stood. I witnessed, and several more witnessed Mr. Rochester ascend through the skylight on to the roof: we heard him call "Bertha!" We saw him approach her; and then, ma'am, she yelled, and gave a spring, and the next minute she lay smashed on the pavement. (377)

Rochester's thoroughgoing public exposure and reverberating call to Bertha provide his intimate cry—"Jane! Jane! Jane!"—with a dramatically humiliating source. The spectacle on the rooftop, widely witnessed and heard "a mile off," literalizes a scenario that Rochester only imagines early in his relationship with Jane, in his coy hint that he has hidden "defects," "a past existence, a series of deeds, a colour of life to contemplate within my own breast, which might well call my sneers and censures from my neighbours to myself" (118–19). Rochester gestures at self-exposure in this early statement but firmly limits this possibility to private "contemplat[ion] within my own breast." The actual revelation of his "defects" and "past existence" to the surrounding neighborhood thus dramatically inverts a tactic of not just privacy but extreme secrecy and disavowal, which Rochester has taken toward the shame that Bertha represents for him. Rochester's call on the rooftop places him in spectacular relation to the shame he has so persistently hidden and rejected— now given concrete form in the figure of Bertha and in the witnessing crowds who hear and see him.

"Shame," writes Michael Warner, "is an experience of exposure, in which I become suddenly an object through the eyes of another; it thus resonates powerfully in situations of erotic objectification, visuality, and display" (290). Indeed, at the point of Rochester's dramatic display on the rooftop, such shameful exposure has accumulated an intense erotic allure in Brontë's narrative, having provided Jane with a space of intimacy with others and even her own memories. From the beginning, Jane's relationship with Rochester is driven by an erotics of shameful exposure: in this sense, the "terrible spectacle" of his long-hidden shame finally delivers on the eroticized, potential surfacing of error and degradation that has enticed Jane. Like Helen, Rochester is a text whose vulnerable physical surface fascinates Jane, especially as it suggests depths that Jane desires to read through shame. Early in their relationship, when Rochester intently gazes at Thornfield Hall, Jane just as intently scrutinizes the mysterious glint in his eyes, puzzling over the "pain, shame, ire" she perceives wrestling in the "quivering conflict in the large pupil dilating under his ebon eyebrow" (125). Critics often have turned to the roles of rebellious anger (or "ire") and sympathy (often thriving on "pain") in reading Jane's conflicted romance with Rochester and the ideological and aesthetic implications of its resolution. Yet Jane's ruminations on the happiness in store for Blanche Ingram, as Rochester's intended bride, suggest that shame, particularly, constitutes the desired depth of Rochester's impenetrable eye and that its materialization would offer for her something akin to erotic climax and marital closure. Jane worries about her increasing tendency toward "forgetting all his faults, for which I had once kept a sharp look-out" and reinstates the watch (165):

> And as for the vague something—was it a sinister or a sorrowful, a designing or a desponding expression?—that opened upon a careful observer, now and then, in his eye and closed again before one could fathom the strange depth partially disclosed; that something which used to make me fear and shrink, as if I had been wandering amongst volcanic-looking hills, and had suddenly felt the ground quiver, and seen it gape; that something I at intervals beheld still, and with throbbing heart, but not with palsied nerves. Instead of wishing to shun, I longed only to dare—to divine it; and I thought Miss Ingram happy, because one day she might look into the abyss at her leisure, explore its secrets, and analyse their nature. (165)

Jane's imagining of the fleeting revelation of Rochester's secret as a sudden "gap[ing]" of the "ground" she traverses echoes the imagery of her conditional relation to Helen's shameful exposure: "Were I in her place, it seems to me I should wish the earth to open and swallow me up." The spectacular surfacing of Rochester's shameful, "vague something" on the burning rooftop—and Jane's own mediated contact with this spectacle through the inn-keeper's later narration of it—allows her once again to approach the "open[ing] and swallow[ing]" earth that figures the *frisson* of partial contact with another's shameful exposure. For as with Helen's display, Rochester's spectacle of shame produces a compelling form with uncertain content, a form that preserves his interior emotions as "a strange depth" still only "partially disclosed." Reading Rochester's call to Jane in relation to his call to Bertha, and especially the shame that it signifies, illuminates the full erotic significance of the oft-cited romantic call and response and allows it a greater textual function than the consolidation of a normalizing sympathetic bond between the lovers. The fervent call and response between Rochester and Jane presents a moment of precarious intimate connection, the erotics of which depends, like the smile Jane shares with Helen, on proximity to a shameful spectacle that both exposes another and enticingly obscures the full transparency of that other's distinct interiority.

While the spectacle of Rochester's shame forwards the novel's erotic resolution, it is also significant that Bertha Mason has been incorporated into the scenario. As we have seen in Jane's shame-fueled relations with both Helen and her own past selves, the scene of shame in *Jane Eyre* is also, often, a scene of productive individuation and intimate relation through difference. Yet Bertha, as many critics have contended, is the character who most pressures the novel's capacity to tolerate difference.[8] From this perspective, Bertha's integration into a relational spectacle of potential individuation—with Rochester, her most virulent critic and oppressor, no less—suggests Brontë's attempt to push the limit of difference that the novel's dynamic of shame can accommodate. The violent death of Bertha, as she "lay smashed on the pavement," undeniably marks this limit and shame's potential for damaging effects and normalizing demarcations (377). Bertha's frantic, ultimately self-destructive gestures and unintelligible response to Rochester's call seem designed to keep her on the cusp of relationality: the legibility of Jane's answer ("I am coming") to Rochester's cry of "Jane! Jane! Jane!" is withheld from Bertha, whom onlookers have seen "waving her arms" and "shouting out" before she "yelled, and gave a spring" in response to Rochester's "call" of "Bertha!" (369, 377). But Rochester's call to Bertha, in its partial parallels to his romantic cry to Jane, also offers a fleeting extension of individualized identity and relationality to the one character to whom they have been consistently denied—both by Rochester and by the text more generally. We can more fully understand the complex, and often contradictory, aesthetic and cultural impact of Victorian shame (and Victorian emotions more broadly) by recognizing that here, the novel allows Bertha the most legibility and recognition she receives from other characters, not in spite of shame's exclusionary effects, but through shame's relational dynamic.

Brontë's novel further counters the embodiments of shame's indisputable violence with the striking revision of shame's form in subsequent narrations of Rochester's injuries. When Jane reunites with Rochester, he relates the "terrible spectacle" of Thornfield's burning, Bertha's end, and his own misfortunes in more indirect fashion than the inn-keeper, interpreting the events, and especially his maimed body, as a just and long-overdue shaming punishment for "my stiffnecked rebellion" (393):

> "Divine justice pursued its course; disasters came thick on me. . . . *His* chastisements are mighty; and one smote me which has humbled me for ever. You know I was proud of my strength; but what is it now, when I must give it over to foreign guidance, as a child does its weakness" (393).

As his narration continues, Rochester's cry to Jane is positioned as the direct outgrowth of his humbling—particularly his physical humiliation. Rochester's renarrating of his earlier cry places him in a relational dynamic with Jane organized around his humiliated body, a dynamic that echoes the emotional proximity established between Helen and Jane around their physical exposures in the schoolroom. Jane further renarrates this moment for the reader in a way that remakes her bond with Helen, bringing both Rochester and the reader into the scene. In Jane's previous perception, Helen had alleviated the shame of her spectacular punishment through a physical posture suggesting memory: "Her eyes are fixed on the floor, but I am sure they do not see it—her sight seems turned in, gone down into her heart: she is looking at what she can remember, I believe; not at what is really present" (45). Now Rochester stands, like Helen before him, "bending his sightless eyes to the earth . . . in mute devotion," while Jane repeats Helen's reflective turn "into her heart": "Reader . . . I listened to Mr. Rochester's narrative; but made no disclosure in return. . . . I kept these things then, and pondered them in my heart" (394). The narrator explicitly invokes the "Reader" as a witnessing participant, invited into the erotic structure of shame and positioned much like the young Jane in her prior scene of intimacy with Helen, which this scene reenacts—a reenactment that constitutes romantic reunion with Rochester.

When Jane recollects Rochester's physical dependence on her due to his blindness, she lingers on his seemingly shameful body, which encompasses not just "Divine justice" but also bitter-sweet love: "there was a pleasure in my services, most full, most exquisite, even though sad—because he claimed these services without painful shame or damping humiliation" (397). Jane's description emphasizes the form of shame—present in Rochester's physical condition and its expected "painful shame or damping humiliation"—while embedding this form in acts of narration that mitigate shame's hold. Jane alleviates Rochester's sense of shame by "putting into words" the world he can no longer see, thus disrupting the rigid alignment of shameful scenario, signifying body, and interior emotional content that his lost "strength" initially inflicted on him (397). Revising the indelible signification of absolute shame into more conditional shame, Jane also claims the happiness she had earlier imagined for Blanche Ingram: Jane now "might look into the abyss" of her husband's shameful eye "at her leisure," but she also relieves the shame caused by that blinded eye by looking and narrating on its behalf (165). The possibility of revising the shamefully signifying body further materializes when Rochester's blindness begins to heal, but not completely, and not before it "drew us so very near" (397). When Jane first discerns the "quivering conflict" of "pain, shame, ire" in Rochester's eye, he rejects it as posing "obstacles to happiness" (125); but her concluding narration of and for this eye brings shame into close and productive contact with other feelings—with a "sad[ness]" and pain inextricable from "pleasure" (397)—such that "Edward and I, then, are happy" and "those we most love are happy likewise" (398). Shame—as much as "pain" and "ire"—facilitates happiness: in both preserving and reworking the form of "painful shame or damping humiliation," Brontë's novel reimagines felicitous selfhood and relationality.

Feminism and Novelistic Feeling

Yet however comfortably happy Jane Eyre seems by the novel's end, Brontë's heroine also raises numerous, often uncomfortable questions about the costs of such happiness for the self and for others. For contemporary feminist criticism, for which *Jane Eyre* remains a touchstone text, such questions often revolve around the costs of emotional identification, cast specifically in terms of anger and sympathy. Observing the "highly charged contentious response" *Jane Eyre* continues to elicit, Cora Kaplan postulates that Brontë's novel "condenses unresolved questions in and for feminism today," questions concerning how "the status of female feelings in feminism" relates to "the status of female individualism" (25). In her characterization of the "emotive history" of this criticism (25), Kaplan foregrounds the specific feelings of anger and sympathy and links them to the issue of "identification": a history of "angry or sympathetic identification with the text" of *Jane Eyre* "and its heroine" has, she suggests, also "produced a second order set of feelings about the critical debates, for which, nevertheless, *Jane Eyre* remains a referent" (31). The most influential exemplar of "angry . . . identification" would, of course, be Gilbert and Gubar's *The Madwoman in the Attic*, with its centerpiece reading of anger in *Jane Eyre*. In mapping a feminist poetics centered on anger, this landmark study entails problematic demands for emotional identifications that define the "female" and the "feminist." While the madwoman figures an attractive "rebellious feminism" for Gilbert and Gubar (338), the subversive energy of anger must be distinguished from potentially antisocial or illegible madness, and the challenges of maintaining this distinction appear to motivate the claim that the angry double in nineteenth-century literature serves to "act out the subversive impulses *every woman inevitably feels* when she contemplates the 'deep-rooted' evils of patriarchy" (77; emphasis mine). The madwoman is kept legible and relational as "every woman," but at the risk of universalizing female emotional makeup—what "every woman inevitably feels"—through a hermeneutics of identification involving the shared anger of literary characters, authors, and readers. Thus in their reading of *Jane Eyre*,

Gilbert and Gubar's emphasis on a "constitutional *ire*"—in various stages of repression—that emotionally defines not only Jane Eyre and her double, Bertha Mason, but all of the other major female characters, begins to function less as an uncovering of personal emotion and more as a pervasive mandate for truly feminist—or even female—feeling (349). In order for the angry double to qualify as a subversive rather than a monitory literary figure, the author also must manifest traceable identification with her rage, and, for the feminist potential of this identification to take full effect, the reader must acknowledge—and even better, share—this anger as well.

In highlighting the problems of such universalizing of gendered emotion, revisionist feminist criticism of *Jane Eyre* has often focused on sympathy in order to pose the risk of a coercive idealization of emotional identification. In her recent study *How Novels Think*, for example, Nancy Armstrong positions *Jane Eyre*'s romantic resolution as representative of the Victorian novel's "project of universalizing the individual subject" through the "fantasy of domestic plentitude or wholeness of being within the household" (10, 25). Armstrong does not discuss sympathy explicitly in her reading of *Jane Eyre,* but she situates the novel's idealization of naturalized domesticity—which, she claims, reproduces emotional connections within and between "almost indistinguishable" happy homes as novelistic closure (144)—as exemplary of a restrictive phase of a paradoxically self-regulating individualism that she links, in her introduction, to the "logic of sympathy" (15). Amit Rai and Lorri Nandrea also critique sympathy in *Jane Eyre* as a predominantly normalizing mode of emotional identification that can solidify individual and group identities, but at the expense of excluded others. Rai traces "the narrative of Jane's assumption of a sympathetic police-agency" (99); and Nandrea describes as the "triumph of sympathy" the oft-noted "manner in which the end of the novel emphasizes Jane's success in eliminating all possible threats to her newly attained subject position" through "a systematic negation of others and otherness" (119). Yet while Rai and Nandrea critique a dominant narrative of the "triumph of sympathy" in *Jane Eyre*, Rai also maintains that "the trajectory of Jane's assumption of power gives off a certain haunting," a faint, mainly disavowed "signal [of] the possibility of another relationship between subjectivity, sympathy and spirituality" (103–104). Nandrea more thoroughly engages with an affective "undercurrent to the major narrative trajectory of the text," one that, she argues, revels in the "disempowering pleasures of sensibility" (119). Both usefully seek to uncover additional affective facets of *Jane Eyre*, suggesting that a critique of sympathy's problematic imperative of identification need not entail a critical rejection of all emotional connections within (or, to a certain extent, with) the novel.

If we heed Brontë's call "for shame," acknowledging it as a central affective strand of *Jane Eyre*—one that insistently appears in the form of compelling spectacles of relational difference—we can recognize the novel as less a triumphant march toward normalizing identification than an exploration of shame as an alternative for shaping individuated, intimate social relations. Insofar as shame encompasses, for Brontë, a mode of readerly engagement, its insistent presence in *Jane Eyre* asks us to think again about the ideological implications of the relationship between emotion and form in the development of the nineteenth-century novel. Indeed, shame's role in *Jane Eyre* as an affective mediator between coercive overidentification and potentially alienating emotional ruptures perhaps accounts for the rapt scrutiny the novel continues to inspire in readers looking to Victorian literature to find points of affinity with—as well as instructive differences from—current investments in issues of affect, gender, identification, and novel form. "Pain, shame, ire": as critics responsive to, while also thinking and telling about, the affective impact of novels, we might find ourselves suggestively, because imperfectly, reflected in Jane's hope, and Brontë's seeming confidence, that the registering and narrating of such conflicting feelings could forward productive forms of individual and relational happiness.

From NARRATIVE, Vol. 18, No. 3 (October 2010) *by Ashly Bennett.* © *2010 by The Ohio State University Press.All rights reserved. Reprinted with permission.*

Notes

I would like to thank Ellis Hanson, Laura Brown, Harry E. Shaw, and James Phelan for their comments and advice on drafts of this essay.

1. Elaine Showalter reads Jane Eyre as the "heroine of fulfillment" in *A Literature of Their Own: British Women Novelists from Brontë to Lessing* (112).

2. Carla Kaplan provides a useful overview of feminist criticism's longstanding investment in reading Jane Eyre's personal fulfillment and ownership in relation to her authentic and empowered voice: noting that Jane "does move from silence to speech, thus providing a model of feminist resistance and liberation," Kaplan finds it "hardly . . . surprising that feminist criticism would borrow much of its romance with women's narration, its metaphorics of voice, and its own self-understanding as an enterprise from this novel" (6). For Gilbert and Gubar, Jane Eyre's anger is central to her "rebellious feminism" (338). Those critics who have more recently shifted the focus to sympathy in *Jane Eyre* include Armstrong, Kees, Rai, and Sharpe, and I borrow the phrase "triumph of sympathy" from Lorri Nandrea (119).

3. In William Makepeace Thackeray's *Vanity Fair*, Amelia Sedley cries, "Oh Rebecca, Rebecca, for shame . . . how dare you have such wicked, revengeful thoughts?" as she and Becky Sharp depart from Miss Pinkerton's academy to enter "the world . . . before the two young ladies" (10), while in the opening pages of George Eliot's *The Mill on the Floss*, Maggie Tulliver is scolded "—do, for shame; an' come an' go on with your patch-work, like a little lady" (13). Particularly memorable humiliations of Austen's heroines occur in *Northanger Abbey, Pride and Prejudice*, and *Emma.*

4. See, for example, Ablow, Armstrong, Barker-Benfield, Benedict, Frank, Jaffe, Johnson, Marshall, Mullan, Nandrea, Pinch, Rai, and Todd.

5. I draw the term "hypothetical focalization" from David Herman's work on "the use of hypotheses, framed by the narrator or a character, about what might be or might have been seen or perceived—if only there were someone who could have adopted the requisite perspective on the situations and events at issue" (*Story Logic* 303). Herman also develops the concept in his article "Hypothetical Focalization."

6. Susan Lanser suggestively reads Brontë's engagement with epistolary form as part of "the narrative practices that create Jane Eyre's singular voice," a "narrative voice, which has been perceived as almost tyrannical in its power to impose a stance" and historically "has no precedent in the authority it claims for a female personal voice" (182, 176–77). For Lanser a new "kind of public epistolarity becomes the narrative sign, then, of Jane's quest for . . . a blend of intimacy and autonomy"; but Lanser implies that this blend is a

reaction against (rather than, as I argue, an extension of) Jane's experiences of shame, when she asks, "Who can blame her (to paraphrase Jane) if, abandoned by family and publicly shamed, Jane might anxiously seek the approval of a larger audience?" (186).

7. James Phelan's concept of "dual focalization" in character narration—"a narrative situation . . .[that] involves a narrator perceiving his former self's perceptions"—helps to describe this moment and to explain its effect of intimate differentiation (215). As Phelan suggests in a discussion of Vladimir Nabokov's *Lolita*, "story and discourse overlap" in moments of dual focalization, but important distinctions are preserved insofar as "the narrator's focalization does not drop away. Instead, the narrator's focalization contains the character's" (118–19).

8. In his analysis of Bertha Mason's central role in readings of *Jane Eyre* as well as studies of the Victorian novel, Laurence Lerner usefully outlines three common critical approaches to Bertha: "Bertha as representing Jane's repressed sexual desire, Bertha as representing Jane's suppressed anger, and . . . Bertha-Antoinette as representing the colonial subject" (279). Across each broadly defined approach, Bertha tends to be read as the figure of excessive or foreign elements—whether elements of desire, emotion, or racial and national identity—that the novel represses or violently marginalizes. For a detailed discussion of representative criticism, see Lerner.

Works Cited

Ablow, Rachel. *The Marriage of Minds: Reading Sympathy in the Victorian Marriage Plot*. Stanford: Stanford Univ. Press, 2007.

Armstrong, Nancy. *How Novels Think: The Limits of British Individualism from 1719–1900*. New York: Columbia Univ. Press, 2005.

Austen, Jane. *Emma*. Edited by Stephen M. Parrish. 3rd ed. New York: Norton, 2000.

———. *Northanger Abbey*. Edited by Susan Fraiman. New York: Norton, 2004.

———. *Pride and Prejudice*. Edited by Donald Gray. 3rd ed. New York: Norton, 2001.

Barker-Benfield, G. J. *The Culture of Sensibility: Sex and Society in Eighteenth-Century Britain*. Chicago: Univ. of Chicago Press, 1992.

Benedict, Barbara M. *Framing Feeling: Sentiment and Style in English Prose Fiction, 1745–1800*. New York: AMS Press, 1994.

Brontë, Charlotte. *Jane Eyre*. Edited by Richard J. Dunn. 2nd ed. New York: Norton, 1987.

Eliot, George. *The Mill on the Floss*. Edited by Gordon S. Haight. Boston: Houghton Mifflin, 1961.

Frank, Judith. *Common Ground: Eighteenth-Century English Satiric Fiction and the Poor*. Stanford: Stanford Univ. Press, 1997.

Genette, Gérard. *Narrative Discourse: An Essay in Method*. Translated by Jane E. Lewin. Ithaca: Cornell Univ. Press, 1980.

Gilbert, Sandra M. and Susan Gubar. *The Madwoman in the Attic: The Woman Writer and the Nineteenth-Century Literary Imagination*. New Haven: Yale Univ. Press, 1984.

Herman, David. "Hypothetical Focalization." *Narrative* 2.3 (1994): 230–53.

————. *Story Logic: Problems and Possibilities of Narrative*. Lincoln: Univ. of Nebraska Press, 2002.

Jaffe, Audrey. *Scenes of Sympathy: Identity and Representation in Victorian Fiction*. Ithaca: Cornell Univ. Press, 2000.

Johnson, Claudia L. *Equivocal Beings: Politics, Gender, and Sentimentality in the 1790s: Wollstonecraft, Radcliffe, Burney, Austen*. Chicago: Univ. of Chicago Press, 1995.

Kaplan, Carla. "Girl Talk: *Jane Eyre* and the Romance of Women's Narration." *Novel* 30.1 (1996): 5–31.

Kaplan, Cora. *Victoriana: Histories, Fictions, Criticism*. New York: Columbia Univ. Press, 2007.

Kees, Lara Freeburg. "'Sympathy' in *Jane Eyre*." *Studies in English Literature, 1500–1900* 45.4 (2005): 873–97.

Lanser, Susan Sniader. *Fictions of Authority: Women Writers and Narrative Voice*. Ithaca: Cornell Univ. Press, 1992.

Lerner, Laurence. "Bertha and the Critics." *Nineteenth-Century Literature* 44.3 (1989): 273–300.

Marshall, David. *The Figure of Theater: Shaftesbury, Defoe, Adam Smith, and George Eliot*. New York: Columbia Univ. Press, 1986.

Mullan, John. *Sentiment and Sociability: The Language of Feeling in the Eighteenth Century*. Oxford: Clarendon Press, 1988.

Nandrea, Lorri G. "Desiring Difference: Sympathy and Sensibility in *Jane Eyre*." *Novel* 37.1–2 (2003): 112–34.

Phelan, James. *Living to Tell about It: A Rhetoric and Ethics of Character Narration*.Ithaca: Cornell Univ. Press, 2005.

Pinch, Adela. *Strange Fits of Passion: Epistemologies of Emotion, Hume to Austen*. Stanford: Stanford Univ. Press, 1996.

Rai, Amit S. *Rule of Sympathy: Sentiment, Race and Power, 1750–1850*. New York: Palgrave, 2002.

Sedgwick, Eve Kosofsky. *Touching Feeling: Affect, Pedagogy, Performativity*. Durham: Duke Univ. Press, 2003.

Sharpe, Jenny. *Allegories of Empire: The Figure of Woman in the Colonial Text.* Minneapolis: Univ. of Minnesota Press, 1993.

Showalter, Elaine. *A Literature of Their Own: British Women Novelists from Brontë to Lessing.* Rev. ed. Princeton: Princeton Univ. Press, 1999.

Smith, Adam. *The Theory of Moral Sentiments.* Edited by Knud Haakonssen Cambridge: Cambridge Univ. Press, 2002.

Thackeray, William Makepeace. *Vanity Fair.* Edited by Peter L. Shillingsburg. New York: Norton, 1994.

Todd, Janet M. *Sensibility: An Introduction.* New York: Methuen, 1986.

Warner, Michael. "Pleasures and Dangers of Shame." In *Gay Shame*, edited by David M. Halperin and Valerie Traub, 283–96. Chicago: Univ. of Chicago Press, 2009.

Passion and Economics in *Jane Eyre* and *North and South*

Thomas Recchio

Charlotte Brontë and Elizabeth Gaskell first met in the summer of 1850, and they remained friends until Brontë's death in 1855. They exchanged visits to Brontë's village home in Haworth and Gaskell's city home in Manchester, they read each other's novels, and they corresponded about their lives and work as women novelists over those five years. Gaskell helped smooth the way for Brontë's marriage in 1854, and after Brontë's death, she wrote a two-volume biography that is generally considered the finest literary biography of the nineteenth-century. (That same biography is also credited with creating the myth of Brontë as one of a group of reclusive sisters, isolated in a dark parsonage on the moors, oppressed by an unpredictable and cranky father, who poured all their frustrated longing for a full and sensual life into writing stories in an eccentric, coarse style.)

Despite their relatively close friendship, there was an "enormous gulf between Gaskell's and Charlotte's attitudes toward art, femininity, and sexuality" (51), according to Lucasta Miller, who bases that observation on the contrast between the passivity and lack of passion of the main character in Gaskell's second novel (*Ruth*) and the imaginative energy and passion of the main character in Brontë's fourth novel (*Villette*). A careful analysis of the main characters in Brontë's second novel, *Jane Eyre*, and Gaskell's fourth novel, *North and South*, however, complicates the stark contrast drawn by Miller. Both novels feature economically compromised heroines who struggle to understand, contain, and ultimately express their passion for a powerful male figure. The narrative movement toward final union in both cases is hampered by economic inequalities that, once resolved through the women achieving economic independence, enables them to act upon rather than misunderstand and thus repress their legitimate desires. Gaskell and Brontë, through the art of the novel, explore issues of femininity and sexuality in a social context where economic factors impinge on a woman's options to act on her own self-understanding. An analysis of the intersections of economic inequality and passionate motives for self-expression and autonomous action for Jane, the heroine of *Jane Eyre*, and Margaret Hale, the heroine of *North and South* will show that Gaskell and Brontë understand that intersection in similar ways. The narrative resolution of each novel, however, suggests that Brontë's conclusions about the scope of female action in the world, once economic and psychological inequalities have been mitigated, is less expansive than Gaskell's conclusions.

The intensity of the collision between economic inequality and passion is rendered with great power in the opening chapter of *Jane Eyre*. Jane, an orphan under the reluctant care of her widowed aunt and her three children, sits in isolation in a window seat, heavy curtains drawn, reading the section of Bewick's *History of British Birds* that "treat[s] of the haunts of sea-fowl" in "the vast sweep of the Arctic Zone." Those "death-white realms" (40) serve as metaphors for Jane's domestic alienation as she sits reading and hidden while her cousins "clustered around their mamma in the drawing-room . . . by the fireside," looking "perfectly happy" (39). That apparent happiness masks a potential for brutality that quickly erupts when Jane's cousin John comes looking for her. He finds her and "all at once, without speaking, he struck [Jane] suddenly and strongly" (42). Jane, "accustomed to John Reed's abuse" prepares "to endure the blow which would certainly follow" (42). Rather than a blow, John reprimands her for daring to read one of the family's books: "You have no business to take our books," he says, threateningly: "you are a dependent, mamma says; you have no money; your father left you none; you ought to beg, and not live here with gentlemen's children like us, and eat the same meals we do, and wear clothes at our mamma's expense" (42). He then prepares to "hurl" (42) the book she was reading at her; the book hits her, causing her to fall against the door, cutting her head. John then, "ran headlong at [her]: [Jane] felt him grasp [her] hair and [her] shoulder" (43). Jane defends herself, receiving "him in a frantic sort" (43). Her aunt and two servants intervene, and, in the process of the adults separating them, Jane hears these words directed at her: "Did ever anybody see such a picture of passion!" (43). Jane is then carried off to the "red-room . . . upstairs" (43). Jane's dependency, it seems, justifies John's abuse, and her lack of financial resources renders her powerless.

That scene, which strikes the keynote for the novel, introduces a series of images and associations that help structure the narrative: the isolation behind the curtains in the window seat and subsequent confinement to the red-room; Jane's inner life rendered in landscapes, such as the "death-white realms" of the "Arctic Zone;" passion as both desire and the potential for violence; and lack of financial resources as justification for physical privation. These themes all revurberate throughout the novel. As Sandra M. Gilbert and Susan Gubar argue, the opening scene of the novel "is in itself a paradigm of the larger drama that occupies the entire book: Jane's anomalous, orphaned position in society, her enclosure in stultifying roles and houses, and her attempts to escape through flight, starvation and . . . madness" (341). Jane's narrative, they suggest, "consists of a series of experiences which are . . . variations on the central red-room motif of enclosure and escape" (341). Figuring the movement of the novel as a pilgrimage through five allegorical locations—beginning at Gateshead; moving to the "Institution" of Lowood (a boarding school with a convent-like architecture); then Thornfield (where Bertha Rochester, the madwoman, is concealed); then through a literal cold, barren landscape to Marsh End (the home of another set of cousins); and finally to Ferndean (where she re-unites with Rochester)—Gilbert and Gubar argue that Jane's is a pilgrimage to family and "selfhood" (364), ending with a "marriage of true minds at Ferndean" (371), an asocial, "natural paradise" (370). While such an allegorical structure certainly functions as described, there is an economic dynamic that serves as the fuel for the repeated pattern of frustrated passion, subsequent enclosure, and escape. So rather than *Jane Eyre* being, in Sally Shuttleworth's words, "a drama of the psyche" alone, the novel explores "the ways in which ideological pressures of class, gender, and economics are played out in the domain of subjectivity" (105), or, in other words, the individual mind.

Even in one of the most heightened and purely inter-personal scenes in the novel—when Rochester first proposes marriage to Jane—the economic disparity between the two puts pressure on Jane's thinking in her dialogue with Rochester. Anticipating that Rochester is about to announce his imminent marriage to Miss Ingram, Jane resolves to leave. Rochester plays along with Jane's misapprehension, vowing to "look out for employment and an asylum" (279) for her in Ireland. Since Jane has already revealed to the reader her love for Rochester, we readily understand why the prospect of her going to Ireland would strike her heart cold, first because of the sea that would separate them, and second for the "coldest remembrance of the wider ocean—wealth, caste, and custom" that, she reflects, has "intervened between me and what I naturally and inevitably loved" (280). In those words, Jane places love against systems of economics, social class, and accepted behaviors, and she seems to accept the dominance of social form over natural passion. As a result, when Rochester insists she stay despite the fact of his impending marriage, Jane replies, "'I tell you I must go!' . . . roused to something like passion" (281). She then asserts, in one of the novel's most famous speeches, the fundamental equality between her small, young, plain, female self and Rochester's large, striking, powerful, male self, in words that reject the dominance of human-made systems over the heart and soul of the individual:

> "Do you think I can stay to become nothing to you? Do you think I am an automaton? – a machine without feelings? And can bear to have my morsel of bread snatched from my lips, and my drop of living water dashed from my cup? Do you think, because I am poor, obscure, plain, and little, I am soulless and heartless? You think wrong! – I have as much soul as you – and full as much heart! And if God had gifted me with some beauty and much wealth, I should have made it as hard for you to leave me, as it is now for me to leave you. I am not talking to you now through the medium of custom, conventionalities, nor ever mortal flesh: it is my spirit that addresses your spirit; just as if both had passed through the grave, and stood at God's feet, equal – as we are!" (281)

Despite the speech's emphatic affirmation of the fundamental equality of Jane and Rochester as human beings, there is a clear recognition that such equality can only be imagined outside the context of economic and social inequalities. As Jane's cousin John's treatment of her has shown, because she is poor, she need not be treated with any recognition of her humanity; and as Jane's reference to "much wealth" suggests, wealth would have changed the terms of relation between her and Rochester in this world. It is only through imagining having passed through death that equality in terms of spirit can be conceivable, for in the world Jane inhabits, she has learned the determining power of money. Even though Rochester, soon after Jane's speech, tells her "it is you only I intend to marry" (282), the marriage cannot legally be, since Rochester is already married—through nuptials arranged because, as the younger son, Rochester had to "be provided for by a wealthy marriage" (332). Cash, custom, and conventionalities—not spirit—remain the dominant determinants.

So although Jane is, as she says, a "free human being with an independent will" (282), her scope of action is highly constrained by her lack of money when she leaves Rochester. That point is rendered powerfully as Jane wanders across the countryside in search of some form of work through which she can earn money and thus provide herself with both sustenance and dignity. When she comes to a village toward the end of her wanderings, she observes, "I could hardly tell how men and women in extremities of destitution proceeded" (352). She enters a shop, inquires about work—sewing, service, factory labor—and finds none. Then she asks a question that applies not only to her but to most women in her culture: "What do the women do?" (353). This question raises an issue that haunts *Jane Eyre* as a whole (and that haunts *North and South* as well): the issue of a woman's vocation. That is, if a woman is not financially independent (perhaps even if she is) and she is not married, what work can she do that has both social and personal meaning? Jane leaves the village with no clear answer to her question; the question remains open even after she finds refuge with St. John Rivers and his three sisters, who turn out to be Jane's cousins.

When Jane faints from hunger and exposure to the elements outside their door, they take her in, and when she is able, Jane describes the help she needs as follows: "getting work which I can do, and the remuneration for which will keep me" (373). Rivers eventually provides that work when he asks Jane to serve as the first school mistress for poor girls in the village of Morton. Jane accepts, with "all my heart" (381). But Rivers has doubts. "'You will not stay at Morton long: no, no!'" he says. "'Why?'" Jane responds. "'I read it in your eyes; it [the position] is not of that description which promises the maintenance of an even tenor in life,'" Rivers answers. Jane points out that she is not "ambitious," and Rivers responds by noting he was not going to say that. Rather "'I was going to say, impassioned . . . [by which] I mean that human affections and sympathies have a most powerful hold on you'" (382). Rivers' response changes the question from one of vocation to one of passion, from economic to emotional necessities, which Brontë works to reconcile through the rest of the novel. Jane's economic difficulties disappear when she receives an inheritance from her uncle in Madeira. And her impassioned desire for affection and sympathy is satisfied in what follows when she and Rochester meet "in spirit"—as he cried out for her in the night, and Jane's "soul," as Rochester puts it, had "wandered from its cell to comfort mine" (472): he avows "his dependence" (464), and they marry. With financial independence, Jane can embrace her male counterpart in full equality, but not before Rochester is emotionally and physically diminished. (He was blinded and partially maimed in the Thornfield fire that killed his first wife). The upshot seems to be that only in isolation, away from the workings of the larger world, can equality be possible in the world of *Jane Eyre*. Faced with a similar problem of narrative resolution in *North and South*, Elizabeth Gaskell suggests a wider possibility.

Despite the fact that Margaret Hale, the heroine of *North and South*, values modesty so highly—she is never subject to the passionate outbursts associated with the young Jane Eyre—Gaskell communicates her passionate nature deftly, if indirectly, by associating Margaret's beauty and vitality with the energies of nature and by the depth of passion she inspires in others, most notably, the industrialist John Thornton. After spending much of her childhood in London, living with her Aunt Shaw and cousin Edith early in the novel, Margaret returns to her parents' village home of Helstone, where, the narrator notes, "The forest trees were all one dark, full, dusky green; the fern below them caught all the slanting sunbeams; the weather was sultry and broodingly still. Margaret used to tramp along by her father's side, crushing down the fern with cruel glee, as she felt it yield under her foot, and send up the fragrance peculiar to it" (48). Unlike the outburst of Jane towards her cousin John, this characterization of Margaret's fundamental passion is subtle, suggested in the quality of the weather ("sultry and brooding") and in the gentle violence of Margaret's foot releasing the fern's fragrance by crushing it, her happiness a "cruel glee." This strategy, to suggest passion as it is filtered through external objects (the weather, the fern) and as it is manifest in the way others look at and respond to Margaret's body and speech, characterizes the novel as a whole.

For example, when Margaret first meets John Thornton upon her family's removal from their home village to the industrial city of Milton-Northern, Thornton directly perceives the tension between Margaret's personal modesty and passionate nature. Narrating through Thornton's point of view, the narrator says: "Margaret could not help her looks; but the short curled upper lip, the round, massive up-turned chin, the manner of carrying her head, her movements, full of soft feminine defiance, always gave strangers the impression of haughtiness" (100). Margaret's physical presence is imposing, her "soft" femininity so defiant that, in the case of Thornton, it evokes a physical response as he becomes aware of his own body, which "felt more awkward and self-conscious in every limb than [it] had ever done in all his life before" (101). Margaret is, in this scene, as Terrence Wright puts it, "all woman" (103).

The narrative extends the hint of sexual tension in their first meeting when describing Thornton's perception of Margaret as she makes tea during Thornton's first formal visit to the Hales' home as tutor to Margaret's father. Once again, the narrative is filtered through Thornton's point of view, and we are told that, while serving tea, Margaret:

> looked as if she was not attending to the conversation, but solely busy with the teacups, among which her round ivory hands moved with pretty, noiseless daintiness. She had a bracelet on one taper arm, which would fall down over her round wrist. Mr. Thornton watched the replacing of this troublesome ornament with far more attention than he listened to her father. It seemed as if it fascinated him to see her push it up impatiently, until it tightened her soft flesh; and then to mark the loosening—the fall. He could almost have exclaimed— "There it goes again" (120)

The physical detail of Thornton's perceptions—the "ivory hands," "taper arm," "round wrist," and "soft flesh," along with the repetitive rise and fall of the "troublesome bracelet"—marks his attraction to her as sexual, born of his recognition of her capacity for passion that expresses itself through her body more than her words. Sexual passion in the novel is thus evoked through image, through bodily expression, and internal, unspoken impression rather than explicit description and articulation. Passion is in this way dispersed; it is apprehended more than comprehended through most of the novel. And while sexual passion would seem to be bounded by intimate, interpersonal relations, language associated with sexual passion permeates the scene of most intense political conflict: the labor strike and confrontation at Thornton's mill.

The passionate atmosphere that encompasses the strike scene becomes discernible as Margaret walks toward Thornton's mill to borrow a waterbed for her ill mother's comfort. The narrator tell us:

> She was struck with an unusual heaving among the mass of the people in the crowded road . . . there was a restless, oppressive sense of irritation abroad among the people; a thunderous atmosphere, morally as well as physically, around her . . . she looked round and heard the first long far-off roll of the tempest; saw the first slow-surging wave of the dark crowd come, with its threatening crest, tumble over, and retreat . . . (226)

The crowd, like an ocean wave, heaves, rolls, surges, crests, and retreats, its energies akin to the motion of the sea, natural, unstoppable. Later, when Thornton confronts the strikers, "Margaret felt intuitively, that in an instant, all would be uproar . . . —that in another instant the stormy passions would have passed their bounds, and swept away all barriers of reason, or apprehension, or consequence" (233). She fears for Thornton's life, shielding his body with her own just as the "reckless passion" of the strikers "carried them too far to stop," and she is struck by a "sharp pebble" that grazed her "forehead and cheek," drawing blood and, for the moment, "blinding" her. Sobered by the sight of "the thread of dark-red blood" (235) that marked Margaret's face, and challenged by Thornton's defiant rage, the strikers retreat, and Thornton takes the opportunity provided by the ensuing lull to declare his love to an unconscious Margaret! "'Oh, my Margaret—my Margaret! No one can tell what you are to me! Dead—cold as you lie there, you are the only woman I ever loved! Oh, Margaret—Margaret!'" (236). The passionate energies generated by the economic deprivation of the mill workers and the sexual passion of John Thornton, the mill owner, merge in unsettling ways in the scene; the impassioned struggle for economic equity between employer and workers bleeds into the inchoate romantic passions between a man and a woman.

That conflation of passions suggests that one task Gaskell has set for herself in *North and South* is to show how difficult it is to keep economic inequities separate from a woman's desire to feel genuinely and fully equal with her possible marriage partner, a point solidified by Thornton's mother's assumption that Margaret, like other unnamed women in the novel, wants to marry Thornton for his wealth and position. Just as Brontë had done in *Jane Eyre*, Gaskell offers a prelude to the possibility of equality between the sexes by having Margaret address her need to find a way to work productively in the world before it becomes possible to achieve what we might call an equality of passion. For Brontë and for Gaskell, the prerequisite for that seems to be the establishment of a woman's economic independence.

After a series of personal traumas—the death of Margaret's mother, the final exile of her brother Frederick, and the sudden death of her father—Margaret inherits the estate of her father's closest friend, an estate that includes the property on which John Thornton's mill is built. Estranged from Thornton at this point in the narrative, Margaret returns to her aunt's family in London, and she resolves to take "her life into her own hands" (508). One of the things "she had learnt," the narrator notes, is "that she herself must . . . answer for her own life, and what she had done with it; and she tried to settle the most difficult problem for women, how much was to be utterly merged in obedience to authority, and how much might be set apart for freedom in working" (508). Margaret thus defines her challenge as a woman as the need to reconcile the cultural expectations that a woman be subordinate to male authority with her sense of her own capacity to do productive work in the world. Later in the chapter, she articulates a conservative version of that challenge when she says to her cousin Edith: "Only as I have neither husband nor child to give me natural duties, I must make myself some" (509), acceding thereby to her culture's conventional thinking.

But when the time comes for Margaret and Thornton finally to acknowledge their passion and love for each other, the possibility of their relationship conforming to the social conventions of a woman's "natural" obedience and duty to male authority is powerfully qualified. First of all, as Thornton puts it, when Margaret inherited the estate, she became his "landlord" (514). Second, after Thornton's mill had failed and after he thought he had lost Margaret forever, he reflected on what he had learned through his experience as a mill owner in connection to what his previous history with Margaret had taught him about human relations. In a conversation with a Member of Parliament, Thornton explains one of the conclusions he had come to: "My only wish is to have the opportunity of cultivating some intercourse with the hands [i.e. workers] beyond the mere 'cash nexus' [the exchange of money for labor]" (525). That statement, coupled with the nature of Thornton's ideas for mill reform, which center on food and communication, suggest that Thornton has recognized that certain values associated with women and the home (such as food and intimate communication) need to animate the workplace, breaking down the false separation between the values associated with work and the values associated with home. Third, Thornton is able to act on his new thinking when Margaret offers to lend him the money to set up a new mill operation. Consequently, while their projected marriage may look like it means Margaret surrenders responsibility for her own life to the authority of her husband, her financial strength and his new set of values redefine what the convention of marriage means for them as individuals.

In the closing scene of the novel, Gaskell draws together the economic and the passionate threads of the narrative by echoing two earlier scenes: the riot and the "gentle violence" of Margaret's village walks as a young woman. When he embraces Margaret after she agrees to marry him, Thornton "laid her arms as they had once before been placed to protect him from the rioters." Moments later, Margaret tries to take some dried Helstone roses from Thornton's hand "with gentle violence" (530). Those quiet echoes evoke the inchoate passion of the young Margaret, wedding it to the economic struggles of industry and labor that takes up most of the novel. Just as Charlotte Brontë had closed *Jane Eyre* by redressing the economic and interpersonal power imbalance between Rochester and Jane, Gaskell closes *North and South* by redressing those same imbalances. The geographic isolation and the physical disfigurement of Rochester make Brontë's ending more idiosyncratic, something limited to two peculiar characters. The fusion of industrial labor and romance in Gaskell's novel, in contrast, makes the ending of *North and South* more resonant; it suggests larger possibilities than just the reconciliation of two individuals.

Works Cited

Brontë, Charlotte. *Jane Eyre*. Harmondsworth: Penguin, 1982.

Gaskell, Elizabeth. *North and South*. Harmondsworth: Penguin, 1977.

Gilbert, Sandra M. and Susan Gubar. *The Madwoman in the Attic: The Woman Writer and the Nineteenth-Century Literary Imagination*. New Haven: Yale UP, 2000.

Miller, Lucasta. *The Brontë Myth*. New York: Alfred A. Knopf, 2003.

Shuttleworth, Sally. "*Jane Eyre*: Lurid Hieroglyphics." *Charlotte Brontë's* Jane Eyre*: A Casebook*. New York: Oxford UP, 2006.

Wright, Terence. *Elizabeth Gaskell "We are not angels": Realism, Gender, Values*. New York: St. Martin's Press, 1995.

CRITICAL READINGS

Women's Place: Home, Sanctuary, and the Big House in *Jane Eyre*

Katherine Montwieler

In their classic study, *The Shell and the Kernel*, practicing psychoanalysts Nicolas Abraham and Maria Torok argue that children carry with them the scars of their parents' neuroses. Though not necessarily afflicted by the trauma that originally affected their parents, children still bear the symptoms of their progenitors—doomed to repeat them, in part, because they are unaware of the underlying cause that precipitated the neuroses. Within this essay is an exploration of how the houses within *Jane Eyre* function as metaphors for the social bodies of mid-Victorian England. In other words, just as individuals carry with them scars of traumas (that they may or may not have been exposed to, as Abraham and Torok tell us), so the massive mansions of *Jane Eyre* display—to the sensitive eye—the marks of the social traumas that were partially responsible for the ostensibly civilized achievements of Victorian England. More specifically, it is argued here that the novel's great houses—particularly Gateshead Hall and Thornfield Hall, which, on the surface, appear to be facades of strength, power, and control—also reveal the wounds and violence that enabled their existence. The homes of *Jane Eyre* embody not only the private, personal suffering of the people who originally inhabited them, but also the wounds of the bodies on which the Victorian Empire was built: namely, the working poor and the slaves of the Caribbean sugar plantations.[1] At the same time, great houses also offer *some* of their inhabitants a kind of sanctuary, a sort of oasis of domestic tranquility. This is embodied particularly in female servants, who do the work of building a feminine community for the novel's heroine. If such work would later be idealized by Coventry Patmore and satirized by Virginia Woolf as the tasks of the "angel of the house," Charlotte Brontë presciently critiques the ideology by portraying feminine mentoring not as an instinctive, "natural" process, but as paid labor performed by working-class women, even if it's not the mentoring that they're being paid for. Thus, great houses paradoxically function both as sites of trauma and sites of refuge.

Until the climactic burning down of Thornfield Hall—an event that neither the reader nor Jane Eyre herself actually witnesses—the houses stand as visual testaments to patriarchy and imperialism, but concurrently those houses and their inhabitants also bear witness to the traumas that created these institutions and the houses themselves. Houses, by their very nature, serve multiple, sometimes conflicting functions. If they publicly display, they also privately conceal. A great house may stand for centuries, but fall it eventually will, and so its very existence speaks to both impermanence and the desire to endure, just as it does its public and private functions. Much of the labor of working-class women is unseen, but its effects shine in the glistening banisters, polished floors, and formal gardens of the family manse. Publicly, however, as Anne Williams tells us, the great house is "a cultural artifact linked with the name of a particular family" (44). Houses serve to promote particular families' reputations, and they also conceal family secrets. Brontë's mansions function as many do in gothic fiction. Williams continues, "a house makes secrets in merely being itself, for its function is to enclose spaces. And the larger, older, and more complex the structure becomes, the more likely it is to have secret or forgotten rooms" (44). In fact, within *Jane Eyre,* Brontë shows her readers that the very sociocultural institutions of Victorian England—embodied within the house—are based on violence, but a violence they necessarily hide. Closeted secrets haunt the heart of gothic fiction, gothic castles, and gothic families. Brontë's novel is no exception. As Jane comes to learn, Thornfield Hall, like Edward Rochester, its master, carries within it "the concealed shame of [the family]" (Abraham and Torok 188). Bertha Mason's eruptions of laughter, violence, and arson are ascribed variously to ghosts or drunken servants that haunt Thornfield Hall. To Jane, they seem "strange and incongruous … acts" (Abraham and Torok 188), but as she, Rochester, and the reader come to learn, it is not just Bertha or even her abusive husband who is responsible for all of the suffering and the cicatrizes of Thornfield; rather, it is the nation of England that bears responsibility for the sins of imperialism, patriarchy, primogeniture, and violence against women and children (to name a few).

The first big house to appear in *Jane Eyre* is Gateshead Hall, where our protagonist feels an interloper within the home and within the Reed family: "I was like nobody there; I had nothing in common with Mrs. Reed or her children, or her chosen vassalage.... an uncongenial alien permanently intruded on [the] family group" (12-13). If Gateshead appears "such a fine place to live" (19), the home also houses and hides sites of abuse. As Jane explains to the reader, if to no one else, her cousin John Reed "bullied and punished me; not two or three times in the week, nor once or twice every day, but continually: every nerve I had feared him, and every morsel of flesh on my bones shrank when he came near" (8). When she complains, she is punished for speaking out and is locked in the Red-Room where she becomes hysterical. The traumatic events are both physical—the abuse by John Reed—and emotional—the indifference of Mrs. Reed to her niece's suffering. Jane's punishment is to be hidden away in an act that, of course, presages Bertha's later confinement. Gateshead hides and houses the neglect and abuse of the child.[2] Again, following Williams, the house:

> has a private and a public aspect; its walls, towers, and ramparts suggest external identity, the 'corridors of power,' consciousness; whereas its dungeons, attics, secret rooms, and dark hidden passages connote the culturally female, the sexual, the maternal, the unconscious. It is a public identity enfolding (and organizing) the private, the law enclosing, controlling, dark 'female' otherness. (44)

What Williams reads in psychoanalytic terms, I'd like to extend culturally. That is, just as the little body of Jane Eyre, which is beaten and ignored and which cries out for freedom, represents the bodies of the workers whose labor and profits built Gateshead, so the Red-Room, in its showy display, alludes to not only the profits, but also the sins of colonialism.[3]

The Red Room becomes a site of punishment, fear, violence, and an attempt to contain the female child. When Jane is in the room, she thinks she sees the ghost of her uncle. I think this vision is crucial; rather than perceiving the ghost as a benevolent, avuncular spirit who would protect her, Jane sees the ghost as frightening. Family does not comfort the child—but paid workers do. Neither family nor ghosts soothe the grieving girl; Bessie, the family's nursemaid does. Jane thinks she is to blame for her punishment in the Red-Room, and her later banishment to Lowood. What she doesn't realize—but can intuit—is, following Abraham and Torok, "what haunts are not the dead, but the gaps left within us by the secret of others" (171). That unvoiced secret may be the hostility Mrs. Reed feels for tending to Jane, a hostility that the mature Jane can accept and forgive in later years, but as a child, Jane hysterically projects onto the vision of a ghost.

Young Jane is terrified of being locked in the Red-Room, for "it was in this chamber [Mr. Reed] breathed his last; here he lay in state; hence his coffin was borne by the undertaker's men" (11). Jane does not yet realize that what is terrifying is not the ghost of Mr. Reed—as she surmises—but the cruelty and indifference of her guardian. The Red-Room houses both, and Jane's imprisonment within the room, as Sandra Gilbert tells us, "is in itself a paradigm of the larger drama that occupies the entire book: Jane's anomalous, orphaned position in society, her enclosure in stultifying roles and houses, and her attempts to escape through flight, starvation, and… madness" (341). Escape—of a kind—she finds, though again her temporary home is marked less by its warmth and more by its lack of it.

It is only when the servants fear for Jane's health that she is released to see the apothecary, who initiates Jane's later removal to Lowood. To the gentle doctor who asks Jane how she likes living in "beautiful" Gateshead, she replies, "'it is not my house, sir; and Abbot says I have less right to be here than a servant'" (19). Her discomfort is important; Jane's alienation at home mirrors her outsider status within the family. Brontë and Jane draw our attention to class distinctions here. Two paid employees of the Reeds—the apothecary and the servant Bessie—show kindness to Jane; perhaps they do so out of some instinctive generosity of spirit, or perhaps because they recognize in Jane another victim of class privilege, or perhaps because the Reeds pay them to care for others, sentimental work that would later become coded less as labor and more as feeling as the century progressed.

Lowood School is another site of feminine control and containment, run by the theoretically beneficent and generous Reverend Brocklehurst. Unfortunately, as Jane soon finds out, Brocklehurst is a Christian in name only and regularly shames, starves, and physically punishes the students of Lowood. The school, like its headmaster, is unforgiving. Nominally, girls are sent there to grow and to develop into young, educated, marketable women, but the locale sickens and kills them instead of nurturing them. A typhoid outbreak hits the school: "semi-starvation and neglected colds had predisposed most of the pupils to receive infection.... Many, already smitten, went home to die: some died at the school, and were burned quietly and quickly, the nature of the malady forbidding delay" (65). If, on the surface, the school appears to house girls with no friends, family, or future, it also kills them, sapping their spirit and the very life within them. Again, Jane finds some small comfort in a paid employee: here it is Miss Temple who soothes, nurtures, and feeds the lonely child. Brontë draws the reader's attention to the nourishing qualities of female friendship, but rather than sacralizing the relationship (as the name Temple suggests), Brontë carefully characterizes the relationship as teacher-student. Caring for Jane is work for Miss Temple. Jane does form a sentimental friendship with Helen Burns, yet since Helen dies, Brontë again underscores the transience rather than the immutability or perfection of such bonds. Marriage takes Miss Temple from Jane. If Helen is too good to survive in the world, Miss Temple, Bessie, and, later, Mrs. Fairfax all offer Jane a realistic portrayal of the labor women do to keep others happy, safe, and as healthy as possible.

Jane meets Mrs. Fairfax when she travels to Thornfield Hall to work. As M. Jeanne Peterson explains, as a governess, Jane is in a liminal position. A woman with an education and a job, she uneasily negotiates the servants' hall and the public rooms, finding herself uncomfortable, and in some ways, a stranger in both environs. Like her alter ego, Bertha Mason, Jane does not belong, and she is keenly aware of her inability to acclimate to life at Thornfield Hall. Just as she did as a child, Jane lingers in doorways, on windowsills, transitional spaces that bespeak her twin desires to move out and to stay still. But, if Bertha screams, tears Jane's wedding dress, attacks her jailers, and sets rooms on fire, Jane is more reserved in her outbursts. She explores the house, contemplates her situation, and criticizes the wealthy—silently—but she does not commit any active violence. She's learned self-control and submissive behavior at Lowood; yet deep within the breast of this small young woman lingers a raging child disgusted by the injustices of the world, particularly those that affect her personally.

As Jane walks on the roof of Thornfield, she considers,

> Nobody knows how many rebellions besides political rebellions ferment in the masses of life which people earth. Women are supposed to be very calm generally: but women feel just as men feel; they need exercise for their faculties and a field for their efforts as much as their brothers do. (93)

Neither, as Jane hints and Sandra Gilbert points out more explicitly, is Jane the only liminal figure at Thornfield. Adèle Varens, Blanche Ingram, Grace Poole, and of course Bertha Mason, do not belong either—the house is full of inconvenient women who trouble the idea of *la femme couverte*. Jane finds freedom outside the walls of the house, when she stands on the balcony looking out over the countryside. This moment shows her autonomy and her strength. Her now famous reverie is disrupted by Bertha Mason's equally famous laugh, indicating the women's similarity and perhaps the irony of Jane's quest for freedom and the poignancy of her complaint.

Thornfield Hall appears grand, but behind its walls hides a canker; its sore is not just primogeniture, aristocracy, sugar plantations, or patriarchy, but a combination of all of these institutions built on the back of slaves, women, second or third or fourth sons,

---

and the working poor. The façade would not exist without the people whose sweat and blood made it possible. Bertha Mason's body and madness make those sins visible. Her body and her jail in the attic of Thornfield bear the traces of those institutions that cement the great house's foundation. It's ironic that she is housed in the attic, when it is the very structure of the house that is rotten.

Jane comes across Bertha Mason a few times in the course of her stay at Thornfield. Most of these encounters are not actual interactions, but, like the laugh whose echo lingers in the air, moments where Jane recognizes only the uncanny traces of Bertha's presence: Rochester's burning room, Mason's injured arm, Jane's own torn veil. Bertha and Jane finally come face to face when Mason interrupts the wedding of Rochester and Jane. Rochester presents his first wife to the assembled parties: "What it was, whether beast or human, one could not, at first sight, tell: it groveled, seemingly, on all fours; it snatched and growled like some strange wild animal: but it was covered with clothing; and a quantity of dark grizzled hair, wild as a mane, hid its head and face….The maniac bellowed; she parted her shaggy locks from her visage, and gazed wildly at her visitors" (250). Jane is dismayed by Bertha, whom she cannot identify as a fellow human being. Maria Tatar takes the heroine to task for her blindness, claiming she is:

> determined to preserve at least one delusion…a kind of moral blind spot. Just as she was unwilling to press her husband for knowledge about the forbidden chamber in the attic, so too she fails to interrogate and contest Rochester's treatment of Bertha Mason…. Jane's happiness rests on a willingness to shut out the deeper knowledge of the ways in which her own social identity is built on the domination, suppression, and elimination of Rochester's first wife. (74)

While I appreciate the sensitivity Tatar shows Bertha, and agree that Jane does not show compassion to the woman before her, I think Tatar does not sympathize with Jane's hopeless predicament enough. Jane herself, at this point, is a character in crisis, facing a moment of trauma—not just caused by seeing Bertha and realizing the man she thought she would marry is not what she imagined and that she is on the verge of an extra-legal union, but also because seeing Bertha recalls for Jane her own displacement in the world and her impossible position. Seeing Bertha causes Jane to look inward, and such a gesture is understandable, self-protective, and deeply human, particularly when we recall how children react to trauma. If Bertha sees herself when she looks at Jane, it is conceivable that Jane sees herself when she looks at Bertha, and this causes a crisis in her ego, recalling, as Gilbert points out, her earlier experience with hysteria in the Red-Room. The madwoman is not just Bertha, but could also be Jane herself.

Rochester offers to make Jane his mistress, but she refuses. She will not be a concubine (neither, of course, will Bertha). Instead, Jane decides to leave Thornfield. The patriarchal manse will not keep her, and so, in act of spectacular individuation and agency, she decides to set off, alone, into the wilderness. At the same time, and this is crucial to an understanding of Jane as a character damaged by traumatic events—even those which she has not experienced firsthand—at this moment of crisis, she *hears her mother's voice* that "spoke to my spirit: immeasurably distant was the tone, yet so near, it whispered in my heart—'My daughter, flee temptation!'" (272). Jane listens and obeys, devastated by Bertha's appearance and Rochester's confession, and she attempts to rectify the situation by leaving. Why, we might ask, is she so upset?

Jane's decision to leave Thornfield, a grand house whose wealth comes from colonialism, duplicity, and physical and emotional violence is not just one of self-control, but is also figured as a retreat into a kind of childish fantasy. Jane fears becoming Rochester's sexual partner. If she is comfortable doing some women's work (teaching and caring for the young Adèle Varens), sexual labor is not one of the tasks she's willing to take on. Seeing Bertha and listening to Rochester's proposal of a paid sexual relationship unconsciously reminds Jane of her own mother and the tragedy that befell her after she married and became sexually active. In hearing her mother's voice, Jane hears the siren sound of a lullaby she never heard when she was a child. She hopes to return to a prelapsarian, infantile state, away from the house of patriarchy, although she does not realize how elusive and impossible such a wish is.

Abraham and Torok offer another angle on Jane's excessive reaction to her predicament:

> A symbolic allusion to another object of fear must be involved, an object that is the more unknown for not being derived from the child's own desires or drives but from another place: the father's or the mother's unconscious, in which are inscribed the parents' unspoken fears, their apprehensions, the reasons for their enslavement, their hidden faults. (180)

In other words, Jane's devastation speaks not just to her current situation, but to her mother's abandonment as well. Jane's mother ran off, eloped, and was never forgiven by her family. Unconsciously, Jane has internalized her mother's shame, and she is driven by a desire to abandon this home because she feels she doesn't deserve one; she has assumed the punishment and condemnation bestowed on her parents, without engaging in the activity that precipitated it. Jane's very wandering and isolation may be the result of having "no way of directly evoking the contents of [her] crypt…. The only resolution available to [Jane] is to *use [her] own body in a quasi-hysterical fashion, thereby avoiding the fantasy of endocryptic identification*" (163; italics theirs).

Jane exhibits trauma but cannot articulate it because she does not consciously understand her mother's desire, disobedience, and disgrace. Like her mother, she runs away—not with a partner, but as a single woman alone in a cold, cruel, and indifferent world. Jane nearly dies of hypothermia, starvation, and dehydration, dissolving into hysterical fantasies, as she traverses the moors, looking for a home that does not yet exist. Jane idealizes her comfort on the moor by feminizing the landscape, claiming she finds the mother she lacks:

> Nature seemed to me benign and good; I thought she loved me, outcast as I was; and I, who from man could anticipate only mistrust, rejection, insult, clung to her with filial fondness. Tonight, at least, I

---

would be her guest—as I was her child; my mother would lodge me without money and without price. (276)

But tonight, Mother Nature disappoints and Jane finds only temporary succor. As her earlier experiences have made painfully clear, she needs real working women to protect her.[4]

Jane's lonely existence is an elegy then to her father, her mother, and also to her very childhood. Just as Jane retreats, so does Rochester, both looking for the woman he has most recently lost (as opposed to his first wife and mother) and also isolating himself. Both characters follow Abraham and Torok's diagnosis of depression:

> The ego begins the public displace of an interminable process of mourning. The subject heralds the love-object's sadness, his gaping wound, his universal guilt—without ever revealing, of course, the unspeakable secret, well worth the entire universe. The only means left by which the subject can covertly revive the secret paradise taken from him is to stage the grief attributed to the object who lost him…. The more suffering and degradation the object undergoes (meaning: the more he pines for the subject he lost), the prouder the subject can be: "he endures all this because of me." Being a melancholic, I stage and let everyone else see the full extent of my love object's grief over having lost me….If there is any aggression at all, it is shared between the love object and the melancholic subject in being directed at the external world at large in the form of withdrawal and retreat from libidinal investments. (Abraham and Torok 136-7)

While Jane waxes melancholic, she claims Rochester causes all of her sadness. She cannot admit the more painful memory of her initial abandonment by both parents. In a similar vein, Rochester, too, claims his worry is all over Jane. Unconsciously, however, his sense of guilt and anxiety is caused by his treatment of his first wife, itself an action that compensates for his own abuse at the hands of his father and brother. But that filial abuse is too painful for him to accept. Instead, he projects his own abandonment onto his most recent love object.

Following her leave-taking from Thornfield, Jane spends three nights outside. She's frail, not strong enough to care for herself. If disappointing to contemporary readers who long for a heroine who can thrive in the wilderness, Brontë instead gives us a weak figure who submits to her situation, divorced from the feminine communities that have protected and housed her all her life. Once again, she is starving, cold, and alone—very much the girl-child of Lowood, but now there is no Bessie or Helen Burns or Miss Temple or Mrs. Fairfax for Jane. As Gilbert points out, Jane's "terrible journey across the moors suggests the essential homelessness—the nameless, placeless, and contingent status—of women in a patriarchal society" (364). For all of its problems, the house of patriarchy also offers some small protection to Jane in the hands of the women who support it. Outside of that structure, apart from those women, she cannot survive.

Miraculously, at her moment of greatest need, Jane finds a home and a family. Nearly fainting from hunger and cold, standing again in the liminal space of a doorway, Jane is rescued by her cousin, St. John Rivers. Yet it is his sisters and their skeptical servant, Hannah, who do the work of nursing Jane back to health. The comfortable cottage of Moor House is the closest Jane comes to domestic tranquility until the novel's very end.[5] In this house, too, Jane is an interloper, a welcomed guest, but a guest nonetheless. Once she recovers, Jane realizes, "Happy at Moor House I was and hard I worked; and so did Hannah: she was charmed to see how jovial I could be amidst the bustle of a house turned topsy-turvy—how I could brush, and dust, and clean, and cook" (33).

If the home offers sanctuary to Jane, it too, bears the traces of imperialism and patriarchy, particularly in the form of St. John as he prepares to travel to India as a missionary. He wants to take Jane with him as his wife, and she rebuffs him. In that act of rhetorical refusal, Jane commands her own autonomy and agency, allowing she will travel as his sister but not his wife, an arrangement St. John cannot tolerate, perhaps because if she travels as his sister, Jane will have a freedom and autonomy that repulses her would-be fiancé.

Once again, Jane is unhappily stuck, ill at ease at a home that has no place for her.

Fortunately, in another mystical trance, Jane hears Rochester calling, and so she begins her search for a kind of transcendent reunion that can't occur in the big house, but only in a space—that if still haunted by the uneasy relation to the profits that made its existence possible, is more naturalized, akin to the English landscape rather than the English empire. As Gilbert points out:

> the house itself, set deep in a dark forest, is old and decaying: Rochester had not even thought it suitable for the loathsome Bertha....Ferndean is notably stripped and asocial, so that the physical isolation of the lovers suggests their spiritual isolation in a world where such egalitarian marriages as theirs are rare, if not impossible. True minds, Charlotte Brontë seems to be saying, must withdraw into a remote forest, a wilderness even, in order to circumvent the strictures of a hierarchical society. (369)

If Ferndean is a remote sanctuary, the lovers, however, cannot hide from each other. The scars and sins, the marks of their individual journeys, are out in the open. Jane and Rochester have recovered, not meeting each other as blind young lovers in the public drawing room, but as older, wiser, disappointed beings in the quiet of a private house. Jane has physical and financial power at the novel's end. And in that independence, she can mother herself, Rochester, and the son she will soon bear, albeit complemented by the work of at least two servants, Mary and John.

The houses, thus, are vexed sites, for while they bear the scars of patriarchy and imperialism, they also house within them kind women who tend to Jane's emotional and physical needs, though they cannot assuage the sins of the family manse. The big house offers a sanctuary, and it is also a jail, a prison. On one level,

> Jane's evolution is articulated through a clearly defined progression of houses with the female protagonist moving from orphaned social outcast to security as wife and mother [showing...] a direct connection between the changing architectural domestic spaces—

houses galleries, bed-chambers, passages, windows, doors and hiding places—and the heroine's self-development. (Tommaso 84)

Yet, this evolution is not a simple path, and its destination is muddied. Look what Brontë demands of her readers: the family manse displays wealth, grace, power, and privilege, but beyond the doors are the women who keep the house running, the slaves whose bodies provided the wealth for bricks and mortar. If Bertha Mason burns the big house down, Charlotte Brontë does not go quite so far. She allows Rochester to live after all, wounded, blinded, crippled, a shadow of his former self who needs to bring his helpmeet out of the shadows in order to survive. The end of the novel then puts Jane back into light, gives her narrative control and a very real physical power—she has money and sight at the book's end, she is the leader of the house.

As mistress, mother, and wife, Jane embodies the tangible and intangible work that goes into housekeeping and homemaking. Rochester's body, too, becomes like Thornfield. Although at first, it is a display of wealth, arrogance, masculinity, patriarchal and imperial power, he becomes broken and blinded. The novel's satisfaction lies in this tying up, this acknowledgment of the sins of the father—those sins are borne out in the destruction of Thornfield and the destruction of Rochester's body. Brontë forces her readers to see the scars, not to shy away from the ugliness of the past. In so doing, she offers her readers a model for coping with trauma: to see and to recognize that visibly damaged bodies and houses (preferably employing women whose labor keeps the operation running smoothly) make for happy homes.[6]

Notes

1. Thornfield Hall and Gateshead Hall are not alone in this vexed literary representation. After all, as Karen Chase and Michael Levenson relate, in Victorian fiction more generally, great houses are also always already "shadowed by contradictions, resistance, refusal and bewilderment" (Chase and Levenson 5).

2. Perhaps, in returning to Gateshead as an adult, Jane shows the maturity of an individual who has recognized and can move beyond her childhood trauma.

3. Certainly, all of Jane's allusions to slavery and tyranny bear out this reading. Jane sees herself as a "slave" revolting against the murderous "slave-driver" John Reed (8).

4. Jane herself seems to unconsciously intuit this realization, as she asks, when going from door to door, "what do the women do" (278).

5. Perhaps the most unsatisfying part of the novel is Jane's brief stint as a teacher at the village school of Morton. As the schoolmistress, Jane "became a favourite in the neighbourhood," and yet, each night she "rushes" into "dreams many-coloured, agitated, full of the ideal, the stirring, the stormy— dreams where, amidst unusual scenes, charged with adventure, with agitating risk and romantic chance, I still again and again met Mr. Rochester" (312). While Jane is good at the work she does and is beloved by her students and their families, she is also happy to leave it when she finds herself an heiress who has the chance to live in her own home rather than work as a paid employee. She chooses financial independence, to return to Moor House, to her family, rather than to work as a teacher to a number of working-class girls. This decision privileges domestic, private labor over the public good. But such a position of course is only possible if one has wealth from other means.

6. This is true at least for Jane, Rochester, and, presumably, their son. Jane's sending Adèle off to boarding school is not critiqued within the novel, but an astute reader might notice that Jane's compassion has limitations, and that a "happy home" is happy for only some of its family members.

Works Cited

Abraham, Nicolas and Maria Torok. *The Shell and the Kernel: Renewals of Psychoanalysis*. Ed. and Trans. Nicholas T. Rand. Chicago: U Chicago P, 1994.

Brontë, Charlotte. *Jane Eyre*. Ed. Richard J. Dunn. New York: Norton, 2001.

Chase, Karen and Michael Levenson. *The Spectacle of Intimacy: A Public Life for the Victorian Family*. Princeton: Princeton UP, 2000.

Gilbert, Sandra M. "A Dialogue of Self and Soul: Plain Jane's Progress." *The Madwoman in the Attic: The Woman Writer and the Nineteenth-Century Literary Imagination*. Eds. Sandra M. Gilbert and Susan Gubar. New Haven: Yale UP, 1979, 336-371.

Peterson, M. Jeanne. "The Victorian Governess: Status Incongruence in Family and Society." *Victorian Studies* 14.1 (1970): 7-26.

Tatar, Maria. *Secrets Beyond the Door: The Story of Bluebeard and His Wives*. Princeton: Princeton UP, 2004.

Tommaso, Laura. "Space, Evolution and the Function of the House in *Jane Eyre*." *The House of Fiction as the House of Life*. Eds. Francesca Saggini and Anna Enrichetta Soccio. Newcastle Upon Tyne: Cambridge Scholars Publishing, 2012. 83-89.

Williams, Anne. *Art of Darkness: A Poetics of Gothic*. Chicago: U Chicago P, 1995.

Sins of the Mother: Adèle's Genetic and National Burden in *Jane Eyre* _____

Mara Reisman

For contemporary readers, the story Edward Rochester tells the governess Jane Eyre about the background of her pupil, Adèle Varens, is one of the shocking aspects of Charlotte Brontë's *Jane Eyre* because it necessarily includes details about his French mistress. Equally shocking was Jane's complacency at Rochester's recitation. As Elizabeth Rigby notes of this scene in her 1848 article for the *Quarterly Review*:

> He pours into her ears disgraceful tales of his past life, connected with the birth of little Adèle, which any man with common respect for a woman, and that a mere girl of eighteen, would have spared her; but which eighteen in this case listens to as if it were nothing new, and certainly nothing distasteful. (Eastlake 60)

Rigby was not alone in her concerns about the impropriety of Rochester's tale. James Lorimer also finds this scene disturbing. In his 1849 piece for the *North British Review*, he notes that "the matter-of-course way in which she, a girl of nineteen, who had seen nothing of the world, receives his revelations of his former life, is both revolting and improbable" (qtd. in Allott 114). Both reviews reflect contemporary conservative attitudes about sexuality and emphasize the expectation that a young, unmarried woman should be ignorant of this kind of sexual knowledge. This sexual ignorance would have been even more important for a governess. Mary Poovey argues that Victorians were anxious about governesses being unable to "regulate . . . their sexuality," thereby introducing a sexual threat to the household (131). As a result, they linked governesses to the socially disruptive figures of the lunatic and the fallen woman (129), which are represented in *Jane Eyre* by Bertha and Céline.

Rochester's confession also invokes the issue of national morality because the past life he describes to Jane is one of dissipation and sexual adventures with foreign mistresses in foreign countries. His three mistresses of note are the French Céline Varens (Adèle's mother), the Italian Giacinta, and the German Clara. Rochester's relationship with Céline connects Adèle with his time abroad. As a result, although only a child, Adèle comes to represent the world of experience rather than the innocence of childhood. Rochester's descriptions of Adèle as the "'illegitimate offspring of a French-opera girl'" (170) and "'a French dancer's bastard'" (348) further emphasize the sexual and national taints associated with Adèle. This essay focuses on the ways in which Adèle is central to Jane Eyre's ideological messages about nationality, sexuality, and education, and it argues that, according to Brontë, Adèle may become more civilized and more moral through an English education. However, this education cannot make Adèle English.

Jane's first impressions of Adèle are benign and leave out her nationality, but they have important implications in terms of Adèle's character and the book's politics. When Jane first sees Adèle, she notices her stature and her hair, observing that "[s]he was quite a child—perhaps seven or eight years old—slightly built, with a pale, small-featured face, and a redundancy of hair falling in curls to her waist" (119). The "redundancy" of "curls" may seem simply descriptive, but it has meaning in relation to Jane's experience at Lowood. Curls there carry a class message and are characterized as frivolous and unbefitting to the school's lower-class pupils. The school's philosophy is one of austerity, and Mr. Brocklehurst, the headmaster, extends this philosophy to the girls' appearance. Although the hair of pupil Julia Severn is natural, Mr. Brocklehurst objects to her "'[r]ed hair . . . curled all over'" (75), because it is "'in defiance of every precept and principle of this house'" (76). This "'abundance'" of hair represents "'vanity'" and "'the lusts of the flesh'" (76) rather than class-appropriate plainness, modesty, and grace.

That Mr. Brocklehurt's objection is class-related becomes even more apparent when Mrs. and the Misses Brocklehurst enter the schoolroom, and their curled hair and splendid dress are not a matter of concern for Mr. Brocklehurst. The Misses Brocklehurst have "a profusion of light tresses, elaborately curled" while their mother wears "a false front of French curls" (77). In this context, curls indicate for Jane luxury, indulgence, vanity, and worldliness. She may not consciously associate these qualities with Adèle when she meets her, but later, the text confirms that Jane sees these as attributes of Adèle's character. In addition, the French curls symbolically link artificiality, vanity, and foreignness, associations that are reproduced on a larger scale in terms of Brontë's representation of national character, particularly that of non-English character.

Even more than her curls, what really defines Adèle is that she is not English. As Mrs. Fairfax explains to Jane:

> "The nurse [Sophie] is a foreigner, Adela was born on the Continent; and, I believe, never left it till within six months ago. When she first came here she could speak no English; now she can make shift to talk it a little. I don't understand her, she mixes it so with French; but you will make out her meaning very well, I daresay." (119-20)

There is a lot at stake in this description in terms of national identification. From Mrs. Fairfax's perspective, Adèle and Sophie's foreignness is problematic because she cannot understand their words. The further implication is that their behavior is similarly incomprehensible to Mrs. Fairfax, whom Adèle rightly describes as "'all English'" (120). When she differentiates Adèle's being born "'on the Continent'"—someplace at least familiar to the English—from Sophie being "'a foreigner,'" Mrs. Fairfax suggests that there are degrees of foreignness. That Adèle is not quite as foreign as Sophie is important because, although Adèle may never quite be English (although she is potentially half English if she is Rochester's child), she is not so foreign, like Sophie or Bertha, that she is excluded from the possibility of moral and social redemption represented by England and Englishness.

Mrs. Fairfax's comment about Adèle's language also speaks to the issue of Victorian education. As Mrs. Fairfax correctly expects, Jane can understand Adèle, because her education at Lowood included instruction in French. The curriculum at the Clergy

Daughters' School, the model for Lowood that Charlotte Brontë and her sisters attended, taught reading, writing, math, sewing, grammar, geography, history, and the accomplishments of French, music, and drawing (Barker 128). Students' training was partly dictated by vocation, so not all students received an equal education in the accomplishments. However, those who were "to be educated for a governess . . . received lessons in French and drawing" (Barker 129). As instruction in French demonstrates, French could be a respectable part of one's language education. However, as the depictions of Adèle and Céline show, French is not respectable as an identity. Similarly in Elizabeth Barrett Browning's *Aurora Leigh*, a text contemporary to *Jane Eyre*, French is an important part of Aurora's education, but it is equally important that she learn "classic French / (Kept pure of Balzac and neologism)" (16), which suggests that there is a hint of immorality associated with France and with French authors, like Balzac, who write about vice.

Adèle's early education has been focused on accomplishments rather than academics. Her mother trained her to sing, dance, recite, and perform for their guests, and when Adèle meets Jane, she insists on showing off these skills. Adèle's fondness for performance indicates a streak of vanity. For Jane and her contemporaries, performance also would have indicated vulgarity. Actresses were linked to prostitution, and their public displays were regarded as distasteful. Along these lines, there are moral and sexual implications to Adèle's performance. Adèle's performance is skilled, but the subject of "love and jealousy" is not appropriate to her age (121). Jane not only takes note of the subject matter but also of Adèle's staging: "she came and placed herself on my knee; then, folding her little hands demurely before her, shaking back her curls, and lifting her eyes to the ceiling, she commenced singing a song from some opera. It was the strain of a forsaken lady" (121). Like Adèle's careful preparation to sing, her poetic recitation indicates that she has been "carefully trained" to act and, in particular, to act like a little woman: "Assuming an attitude, she began 'La Ligue des Rats; fable de La Fontaine.' She then declaimed the little piece with an attention to punctuation and emphasis, a flexibility of voice, and an appropriateness of gesture, very unusual indeed at her age" (121-22). Adèle is accomplished in these arts, yet from Jane's English perspective, something is not quite right. What is not quite right is Adèle's Frenchness and the related problem that she has too much knowledge of the world and sexuality, even if it is only mimickry rather than empirical knowledge. There is also something artificial about Adèle's character that is implied in her ability to act so convincingly.

Although proficient in these accomplishments, Adèle is less adept in academic subjects. Jane observes, "I found my pupil sufficiently docile, though disinclined to apply" (122). Despite the criticism implied in Jane's words about Adèle's lack of motivation, Adèle's docility and her recitation skills are a benefit because they suggest that she can be trained. This malleability is significant because, if Adèle can be educated in a proper English manner, she potentially can be saved from her corrupt background.

The association of France with corruption and England with purity is evident in both Rochester's description of how Adèle came to live with him after Céline "abandoned" her and in his project for Adèle's improvement. He explains:

> "I acknowledged no natural claim on Adèle's part to be supported by me, nor do I now acknowledge any, for I am not her father; but hearing that she was quite destitute, I e'en took the poor thing out of the slime and mud of Paris, and transplanted it here, to grow up clean in the wholesome soil of an English country garden. Mrs. Fairfax found you to train it." (170)

Rochester's words imply that Adèle's national and maternal background negatively affects her character, but that a "wholesome" English influence might correct these defects.

Rochester then proposes that Adèle's dubious background might make Jane like her less, but Jane defends Adèle, arguing that she "'is not answerable for either her mother's faults or yours'" (170). Despite this vocal protestation, Jane's thoughts betray a similar opinion to Rochester's about the origin of Adèle's flaws.

In the same scene, she observes that Adèle's superficial character is "inherited probably from her mother" and is "hardly congenial to an English mind" (170). Jane's words are one example of how Brontë sets up England and the English as the normative and desired nationality in the text.[1] Jane makes similar national judgments when she recognizes that the alternative to her dull life at the Morton school would be a life of dissipation in France.[2] She couches her emotional dilemma in sexual and national terms that reaffirm the goodness of England when she asks herself: "Whether it is better . . . to be a slave in a fool's paradise in Marseilles—fevered with delusive bliss one hour—suffocating with the bitterest tears of remorse and shame the next—or to be a village school-mistress, free and honest, in a breezy mountain nook in the healthy heart of England?" (414).

Jina Politi argues that this contrast is at the root of the text's ideological message:

> the nationalist code articulated in Charlotte Brontë's *Jane Eyre* (1848), structured on the cultural opposition French/English, in turn subsumes antithetical representations of "natural" and "un-natural" political and gender identities. In the text, revolution, insanity and sexuality are threats reaching England from "abroad." (98)

The depiction of England as a healthy, wholesome space in contrast to unhealthy, immoral France is part of a larger discourse in the text about "contamination from abroad" (Meyer 84). "[W]hat is clean," Susan Meyer argues, "is represented as intrinsically English" (84). This portrayal applies to the characters from these countries as well. Along these lines, Jane becomes the quintessential English woman in contrast to the West Indian Bertha or the French Céline.[3]

Rochester's love for Céline, his *"grande passion"* (165), initially mitigates his moral judgments about her character and nationality, but even at the start, he situates their relationship in terms of national identity. Rochester tells Jane that he was so "'flattered by this preference of the Gallic sylph for her British gnome, that I installed her in an hotel; gave her a complete establishment of servants, a carriage, cashmeres, diamonds, dentelles, etc.'" (165). He also positions the economic component of their relationship in national terms when he notes that Céline "'charmed my English gold out of my British breeches'" (163). The relationship ends when Rochester discovers that Céline has another admirer. This revelation understandably provokes a change in his feelings for Céline, whom he subsequently associates with faithlessness. He also blames her for his "'ruin,'" "'shame,'" and "'destruction'" (165). Significantly, Rochester's opinions about Céline are not just personal. They come to describe a national character in which Céline represents France, sexual immorality, and economic greed.

Rochester links all of Céline's faults to Adèle when he describes her as a "'miniature Céline Varens'" (163). Adèle's new "dress of rose-coloured satin" and "silk stockings and small white satin sandals" (163) visually transform Adèle into a little Céline. The resemblance, however, does not end there. Rochester also compares Adèle's character to Céline's. He uses Adèle's delight in the dress as proof that, like Céline, "'coquetry runs in her [Adèle's] blood, blends with her brains, and seasons the marrow of her bones'" (163). Rochester's words further imply that loose morals and manipulative sexuality are an integral part of Adèle's character.

This connection between mother and daughter is confirmed even more when Adèle bounds into the room, dances for Rochester, and then

> drop[s] on one knee at his feet, exclaiming—
> "Monsieur, je vous remercie mille fois de votre bonté;" then rising she added, "C'est comme cela que maman faisait, n'est-ce pas, monsieur?"
> "Pre-cise-ly!" was the answer; "and, 'comme cela,' she charmed my English gold out of my British breeches' pocket." (163)

Adèle is pleased by herself as a spectacle and hopes that her display emulates her mother because she loves her mother and wants to be like her and because she saw men admire her mother, and Adèle likes admiration. In this passage, Rochester equates Céline's

French identity with mercenariness. Rochester's description of the economic component of his relationship with Céline also emphasizes that he now has economic responsibility for Adèle, which, it can be argued, is dependent on her charm. Despite his protests about Céline and Adèle's behavior, Rochester chooses to take Adèle in, care for her, and spoil her. Along these lines, he selects and buys the dress for Adèle that turns her into a miniature Céline, knowing that it will delight her and that it will remind him of Céline. These actions suggest that France and Céline, represented by the "'French floweret'" Adèle (163), still hold some allure for Rochester.

Paternity might be another explanation for Rochester's actions, except he denies being Adèle's father. Rochester's denials may be wishful rather than proof that he is not her father; readers are never given a definitive answer. There are, however, consquences to Rochester denying paternity or, as Angela Carter puts it, leaving the question "interestingly moot" (166). Without this issue resolved, Adèle's social status is compromised. Rather than being the daughter of an English gentleman and a French mother, she is described alternately as a ward, an orphan, and a bastard, none of which give her good English social standing. Moreover, because Adèle's paternity is not clear, her identification with Céline, a promiscuous French woman, wholly defines her. As a result of this undiluted genetic association, Céline passes onto her daughter the sins of nationality and sexuality.

Adèle's symbolic relationship with Bertha also has important implications for Adèle's fate. Like Céline, Bertha represents the sins of nationality and sexuality. When Rochester first meets Bertha, he is enticed by her sexual allure: "'She flattered me, and lavishly displayed for my pleasure her charms and accomplishments'" (352). In this passage, Rochester could easily be describing his relationship with Céline, who flatters him by her attention and displays herself on the stage and in private. In addition, as I discuss above, these charming qualities are part of Adèle's character as well, which suggests that although Adèle is a child, Rochester associates her with the manipulative sexuality of his wife and his former mistress.

Like Céline, Bertha also falls in Rochester's esteem, and he feels degraded by association when he learns more about her character and background, which is interesting considering that he is the mercenary, marrying her for her money. Bertha's faults, according to Rochester, include rampant sexuality, foreignness, and madness, and Rochester traces all of these flaws back to Bertha's mother, noting:

> "Bertha Mason is mad; and she came of a mad family; idiots and maniacs through three generations! Her mother, the Creole, was both a madwoman and a drunkard! . . . Bertha, like a dutiful child, copied her parent in both points. . . . Bertha Mason, the true daughter of an infamous mother, dragged me through all the hideous and degrading agonies which must attend a man bound to a wife at once intemperate and unchaste." (337, 353)

Bertha's behavioral problems are linked to race and to maternal dissolution. Elaine Showalter argues that Brontë's depiction of Bertha's madness as related to her mother "echoes the beliefs of Victorian psychiatry about the transmission of madness: since the reproductive system was the source of mental illness in women, women were the prime carriers of madness, twice as likely to transmit it as were fathers" (67). Showalter also offers a Victorian context for the sexual component of Bertha's madness, noting that "Bertha suffers from the 'moral insanity' associated with women's sexual desires" (67).

Rochester's description of Bertha's mother as the root of Bertha's problems mirrors the genetic burden that Adèle carries. Adèle's problems, like Bertha's, are due to being the daughter of a non-English mother. Emphasizing the connection between Adèle and Bertha, Rochester describes Bertha as "'the true daughter of an infamous mother'" (353), which is reminiscent of the language he uses to describe Adèle, the "'genuine daughter of Paris.'" Also like Bertha, whom Rochester describes as a "'dutiful child'" in "'cop[ying]'" her mother, Adèle likes to imitate her mother's behavior and dress. The potential implications for Adèle are troubling. Like Bertha, Adèle shares the taint of an infamous mother and a foreign birthplace. Moreover, Adèle's mother is linked to immorality by being French, being on the stage, having multiple suitors, and engaging in sex outside of marriage. With this kind of dubious cultural and maternal backgound, Bertha's fate—madness and death—is Adèle's possible future.

What saves Adèle, at least in part, is her connection to Jane. Jane serves as Adèle's educational guide, "'petite maman Anglaise'" (284), and civilizing influence. Their relationship is established formally through Jane's position as governess and informally through the connections Jane makes between Adèle and herself. For example, Jane as a governess and Adèle as a ward share an ambiguous status in the household. The governess, as Poovey points out, represented a position between the middle-class mother and the working-class woman. Similarly, Adèle is neither daughter nor guest.[4] As a result, both Jane and Adèle are simultaneously an integral part of the family, yet separate from it. Their roles also imply economic dependence on the head of the family. Consequently, both must act appropriately in order to keep their place. Although the position of a ward may seem more secure in this regard, Jane's expulsion from the Reed family shows the precarious position of wards. Cousin John Reed clarifies Jane's unstable position and economic dependency when he tells her: "'You have no business to take our books; you are a dependent, mamma says; you have no money; your father left you none; you ought to beg, and not to live here with gentlemen's children like us, and eat the same meals we do, and wear clothes at our mamma's expense'" (13). Adèle might not encounter such harsh treatment as John metes out, but she can still be sent away whenever Rochester desires.

That both are orphans—or in Adèle's case, at least symbolically so—is another bond between Jane and Adèle. This connection allows Jane to see herself in Adèle and, therefore, to empathize with her. As Jane explains to Rochester, "'now that I know she is, in a sense, parentless—forsaken by her mother and disowned by you, sir—I shall cling closer to her than before. How could I possibly prefer the spoilt pet of a wealthy family, who would hate her governess as a nuisance, to a lonely little orphan, who leans towards her as a friend?'" (170). In a novel where likeness is crucial to personal relationships, social interactions, and national politics, this relationship between Jane and Adèle is essential to Adèle's development. It ensures that Jane will be invested in Adèle's training and future, which allows Adèle the opportunity to change her moral character and become more like Jane, more English.

Although Rochester "'transplants'" Adèle from France, he is less interested than Jane in Adèle because he sees in her no likeness to himself. Jane recognizes this reason for his detachment when she observes: "I sought in her [Adèle's] countenance and features a likeness to Mr. Rochester, but found none: no trait, no turn of expression announced relationship. It was a pity: if she could but have been proved to resemble him, he would have thought more of her" (170). Jane comes to this conclusion, because as a child she experiences the same distancing by Mrs. Reed and her children; they find the character of young Jane alien to their own. Jane comments retrospectively:

> I was a discord in Gateshead Hall; I was like nobody there; I had nothing in harmony with Mrs. Reed or her children, or her chosen vassalage. . . . They were not bound to regard with affection a thing that could not sympathise with one amongst them; a heterogeneous thing, opposed to them in temperament, in capacity, in propensities. (19)

The other connection between Jane and Adèle and the reason that neither fits fully into the household is due to their mothers' fraught relationships with the heads of household. Sins of the mother, therefore, connect the two, despite their difference in nationality. In Jane's case, Mrs. Reed explains that her dislike of Jane has to do with her dislike of Jane's mother, "'for she was my husband's only sister, and a great favourite with him: he opposed the family's disowning her when she made her low marriage; and when news came of her death, he wept like a simpleton'" (267). Like Céline's indecent behavior, Jane's mother's misstep has an economic component. Yet Jane's mother's choice is bad in terms of marrying down rather than bad in terms of being a kept mistress, a position that also has immoral sexual connotations. Nevertheless, both mothers' relationship decisions result in their children's morality being questioned. Rochester thinks Adèle is a coquette; Mrs. Reed thinks that Jane is a liar. For both girls, attempts are made to educate them out of their "bad" behavior.

At Lowood, Jane is educated and socialized into more proper English behavior, which means quelling some of her rebelliousness. Along these lines, Sue Zlotnick argues that "[a]t Lowood, Jane simultaneously becomes a governess and one who can govern herself, so that by the end of her years there, she emerges as a model young woman, one who has learned to (self) govern all the passionate indignation that marred her girlhood" (33). Learning to govern herself is crucial to Jane fitting better into proper English society, and through Miss Temple's influence, Jane becomes the ideal of English domesticity. Zlotnick contends that "by transferring Jane's allegiances from rebellion to 'duty and order' (116), she [Miss Temple] enables Jane's conversion from heathen child to Englishwoman" (37).

Jane's allegiance to this model for her own teaching can be seen in her attempts to convert Adèle from a French heathen child to a proper Englishwoman. Jane engages in this same civilizing work at the school in Morton. In both cases, behavioral civilizing, missionary work, nationalism, and education are interconnected. Education helps to correct class and national defects and, as such, serves a moral and social mission.[5] Adèle may not be openly rebellious, but she is associated with the potentially rebellious, disorderly, dangerous France. France, at the time, was inextricably linked to the upheaval of the French Revolution and with fears about revolution in England. Accordingly, in *Jane Eyre*, the "anxiety about revolution" is "coded as French and immoral" (Meyer 73).

Jane's English influence helps to save Adèle from her two biggest problems: her associations with France and her mother's immorality. Jane is able to enact this change in Adèle's behavior because, although Adèle is easily distracted, she is tractable. She also is living in England and has no contact with her mother. Jane emphasizes the significance of these factors when she observes: "My pupil was a lively child, who had been spoilt and indulged, and therefore was sometimes wayward; but as she was committed entirely to my care, and no injudicious interference from any quarter ever thwarted my plans for her improvement, she soon forgot her little freaks, and became obedient and teachable" (128). Without outside interference, Jane's English authority, her missionary work on the homefront, can prevail.

Adèle's English education and socialization, which Jane sees as positive, raises complicated political issues. Politi rightly argues that both are part of a larger national agenda, whereby Adèle's voice is stifled in order to curb rebellion at home:

What Elizabeth Rigby failed to see was that the other tone of mind and thought which strengthened authority, preserved by wile and force every code human and divine and brutally suppressed Chartism and rebellion at home, was also insidiously writing itself into Jane Eyre, effectively silencing the other. Jane Eyre, when she assumes the status of governess, conspires with Mr. Rochester to stifle little Adèle's speech. (81)

This suppression of speech is part of what Zlotnick sees as a colonization project, which imposes the English language and English values on those who are not English. What makes Adèle "available for colonization" is her foreignness, illegitimacy, and youth (Zlotnick 37). Zlotnick argues that "[t]hroughout *Jane Eyre*, Brontë distinguishes between who should and should not be converted" (Zlotnick 37). Adèle is one who should be and can be converted because she is neither too foreign nor too defiant and is a child.

This conversion relies as much on Adèle's social education as on her academic education, and Jane is instrumental in this as well. Early in the text, when Adèle wants a flower to complement her dress, Jane chastises her for her attention to dress—a lesson about proper English behavior—but also indulges her, giving her a lesson in kindness.

"You think too much of your 'toilette,' Adèle," Jane chides, "but you may have a flower." And I took a rose from a vase and fastened it in her sash. She sighed a sigh of ineffable satisfaction, as if her cup of happiness were now full. I turned my face away to conceal a smile I could not suppress: there was something ludicrous as well as painful in the little Parisienne's earnestness and innate devotion to matters of dress. (198)

By the end of the text, Adèle has learned both lessons and is more devoted to Jane than to her dress. Through her influence, therefore, Jane does manage to change Adèle's character for the better.

Even after Jane has stopped being Adèle's governess, she continues to influence her education. When Jane returns to Rochester, she visits Adèle at her boarding school. There, she finds a forlorn Adèle: "She looked pale and thin: she said she was not happy. I found the rules of the establishment were too strict, its course of study too severe, for a child of her age" (518). This discontent at school provides another connection to Jane; it is a situation with which Jane can empathize because of her unhappy time at Lowood. Jane intends to take Adèle home and "become her governess once more" (518), but, as she explains, it was "impracticable; my time and cares were now required by another—my husband needed them all" (518). Jane's solution is to find a school better suited to Adèle. In the new, more lenient school that Jane chooses, Adèle "[makes] fair progress in her studies" (519). Even though Adèle only realizes "fair progress" rather than great strides in her academic work, this schooling helps to further socialize her. As Jane notes, "a sound English education corrected in a great measure her French defects; and when she left school, I found in her a pleasing and obliging companion—docile, good tempered, and well-principled" (519). Adèle's education may make her much better, but it does not make her entirely English. Moreover, Jane's words imply that the education Adèle receives corrects her chracter in "great measure," yet it does not makes up entirely for her French defects, defects that Jane continues to connect with Adèle's nationality.

The end suggests that Adèle has become more English, or at least can behave as such, but her identity is still that of a foreigner, albeit an English-educated one. As a result, she cannot entirely be assimilated into English domestic life. Furthermore, although Adèle is saved from Bertha's fate—Meyer argues that Bertha is killed off at the end in order to quell anxieities about foreign influence, inappropriate sexuality, and madness (66-67)—it could be argued that Adèle is also eliminated, albeit in a different way. She is invoked by Jane only to be dismissed again. In the end, Adèle does not have a place in the reestablished English family—the symbol of English purity, wholesomeness, honesty, health, and morality—which consists of Rochester, Jane, and their son, the legitimate heir.

Notes

1. Brontë's distinctions between Englishness and otherness/Continentalness also appear regularly in *Villette*.

2. Her other alternative would be a loveless marriage in India, which Jane acknowledges would be a "monstrous . . . martyrdom" (467). Moreover, the non-English climate would not be conducive to Jane's health; to go to India would be to "go to premature death" (466).

3. In *Adèle: Jane Eyre's Hidden Story* (2002), Emma Tennant challenges these national axioms in a number of ways. Most crucially, it is the "all English" Mrs. Fairfax who poses the danger to the household—a danger from within—rather than the French influence of Adèle or the West Indian influence of Bertha. Mrs. Fairfax surreptitiously murders Bertha (paving the way for Rochester to remarry) and later Grace, whom she dresses in Bertha's clothes so it appears that Bertha has commited suicide by jumping from the roof. She then tries to frame Jane for the murder. Earlier, Mrs. Fairfax has cast suspicion on Adèle for a fire at Thornfield. Her goal is to get both Adèle and Jane out of the way so that Blanche can take her rightful place in the household. Mrs. Fairfax sees this marriage as a more appropriate social and class alliance than Rochester's relationship with Jane. Mrs. Fairfax's actions challenge the inherent goodness of England. In other ways, too, Tennant reverses the ideological message in Brontë's text that equates Englishness with goodness and foreignness with badness and a threat to civility and civilization. Tennant's version makes the relationship between Rochester and Céline more complex. In *Adèle*, Rochester is genuinely in love with Céline and continues to be. "Céline," he thinks to himself, "your spirit walks this house as my wife, my true wife. I cannot live without you" (35).

Rochester also admits that Céline is not the mercenary he made her out to be (125). In fact, rather than trying to charm the gold out of Rochester's English pockets, Céline feels oppressed by the gifts he gives her (22). In another reversal, whereas in *Jane Eyre*, Adèle's flaws and deceptiveness are linked to her French mother, in *Adèle*, they are linked to Adèle's English father, Rochester. In addition, Adèle impugns Rochester's sexuality rather than her mother's. Tennant also presents a more sympathetic and human portrayal of Bertha, whom Adèle befriends because they share a common language and an outsider status. Tennant suggests that Bertha's illness may have hereditary causes, but that it is exacerbated by Bertha being in "wholesome" England.

4. In *Adèle*, Tennant emphasizes that because Rochester does not openly claim Adèle as his daughter, she experiences the "uncertainty of her status" (45) as "neither gentry nor servant class" (44). Adèle feels this acutely, and when Blanche objects to Adèle's presence in a room, she wonders "Was I not the daughter of the house?" (46). What being Rochester's daughter also means is that Adèle and Mrs. Fairfax are related, something that Mrs. Fairfax would be loathe to acknowledge. Adèle, though, makes the connection when she admits: "Sometimes . . . I misbehave simply to gain the attention of this cousin of Papa (so is she my cousin also? I hardly think she desires me as kin)" (44).

5. St. John is also involved in this ideological project through his establishment of the schools in Morton and through his missionary work in India.

Works Cited

Allott, Miriam, ed. *The Brontës: The Critical Heritage*: Boston: Routledge, 1974.

Barker, Juliet R. V. *The Brontës*. New York: St. Martin's P, 1994.

Brontë, Charlotte. *Jane Eyre*. 1847. New York: Penguin, 2006.

Browning, Elizabeth Barrett. *Aurora Leigh*. 1857. New York: Oxford UP, 2008.

Carter, Angela. "Charlotte Brontë: *Jane Eyre*." *Expletives Deleted*. London: Vintage, 1993. 161-72.

Eastlake, Elizabeth Rigby. "Review of *Vanity Fair* and *Jane Eyre*." *A Serious Occupation: Literary Criticism by Victorian Women Writers*. Ed. Solveig C. Robinson. Peterborough, ON: Broadview Press, 2003. 46-73.

Meyer, Susan. "'Indian Ink': Colonialism and the Figurative Strategy of *Jane Eyre*." *Imperialism at Home: Race and Victorian Women's Fiction*. Ithaca: Cornell UP, 1996. 60-95.

Politi, Jina. "*Jane Eyre* Class-ified." Jane Eyre: *Contemporary Critical Essays*. Ed. Heather Glen. New York: St. Martin's Press, 1997. 78-91.

Poovey, Mary. "The Anathematized Race: The Governess and *Jane Eyre*." *Uneven Developments: The Ideological Work of Gender in Mid-Victorian England*. Chicago: U of Chicago P, 1988. 126-63.

Showalter, Elaine. *The Female Malady: Women, Madness and English Culture, 1830-1980*. New York: Penguin, 1987.

Tennant, Emma. *Adèle:* Jane Eyre*'s Hidden Story*. New York: Harper, 2002.

Zlotnick, Susan. "Jane Eyre, Anna Leonowens, and the White Woman's Burden: Governesses, Missionaries, and Maternal Imperialists in Mid-Victorian Britain." *Victorians Institute Journal* 24 (1996): 27-56.

"That Better Part Which Cannot Be Taken From You": Varieties of Christian Experience in *Jane Eyre* _____

Jennie-Rebecca Falcetta

When readers name their reasons for loving and rereading *Jane Eyre,* they often cite the compelling attraction between Jane and Edward Fairfax Rochester, the intriguing gothic element of the mad first Mrs. Rochester, or the surprising self-possession and self-worth belonging to a heroine without beauty, name, or fortune to recommend her. With all these narrative delights in store for Brontë's readers, it might be easy to overlook the penetrating religious currents and themes of the novel. But Charlotte Brontë, herself the daughter of a Church of England minister, infuses the story with critiques and models of Christianity alike. Despite Jane's hard lot and mistreatment at the hands of many people, she possesses a deep, sincere, and animating Christian faith, one that evolves over the course of the novel. Considering *Jane Eyre* as a *Bildungsroman* (a novel of education), one can trace the forces that shape and define Jane's religious belief, most notably her school friend Helen Burns and her clergyman-cousin St. John Rivers—who occupies a good third of the book, and to whom Charlotte Brontë gives the novel's last words.[1] An examination of the religious themes of *Jane Eyre*, as figured forth in the spiritual practices of and distinctive rhetoric of significant characters, reveals a variety of Christianities. However, the novel clearly advocates for a Christian belief, in which human and Divine love are not mutually exclusive, but companionable, as embodied in Jane's eventual union to a newly penitent Mr. Rochester.

As a genre, the nineteenth-century English novel *teems* with clergymen, who are, more often than not, targets of criticism. The Church of England's central role in the sociocultural lives of nineteenth-century English citizens meant that everyone had a local clergyman, and some parish priests and curates were better than others. If novelists did not paint an outright negative picture of these men of the cloth (the unfeeling pedant Reverend Casaubon of *Middlemarch* comes to mind), they might at least gently satirize them (e.g. *Pride and Prejudice*'s obsequious Mr. Collins). *Jane Eyre* has its share of clerical portraits, beginning with Jane's late father, a poor clergyman of whom she has no memory. More present to her consciousness is the hypocritical Mr. Brocklehurst (with his appropriately prickly name), director of Lowood Institution. Brontë uses him to illustrate both an Evangelical extremism and a gross class prejudice that often characterized attitudes to the poor.[2] Early in Jane's narrative, this man excoriates the "vanity" of a Lowood student whose curly hair refuses to lie straight. He rages at the supreme cheek of these girls who "in defiance of every precept and principle of this house, ... conform to the world so openly—here in an *evangelical*, charitable establishment" (126, my italics).[3]

Although the word "evangelical" might suggest to twenty-first century readers a certain flavor of American Christianity marked by political conservatism, Biblical literalism, and low church worship (all overgeneralizations, of course), the Evangelicalism of eighteenth and nineteenth century England was of a slightly different cast. Born of a desire to reform the Church of England (not, like dissenters such as the Quakers, to leave it), Evangelicals were influenced by the preaching of John and Charles Wesley, the founders of Methodism, and, less directly, by the teaching of John Calvin. Calvinist (or Reform) doctrine emphasizes, among other teachings, the sinful depravity of all, and the election and redemption of only those chosen (or predestined) by God. These chosen few could never lose their salvation. While on the one hand, they concerned themselves with outward works of mercy and conversion of fellow men and women to Christ, Evangelicals can be held "responsible for many of the attitudes today thought of as 'Victorian,'" writes George Landow (par. 1). Their zeal for reform was often accompanied by strict, legalistic attitudes governing behavior, pleasure, gender roles, and social interactions.

Given an emphasis on human sinfulness, self-denial and the mortification of the flesh took on a greater importance in the Evangelical wing than in the more mainstream Church of England. This explains Mr. Brocklehurst's severity toward the Lowood students and his self-identified quest "to mortify in these girls the lusts of the flesh; to teach them to clothe themselves with sobriety, not with braided hair and costly apparel" (Brontë 127). While we might disagree with his extremism, we *might* also concede that his plan of female modesty has some merit to it. We might, that is, until Brocklehurst's own daughters enter the schoolroom and parade around in their feathered hats and silk pelisses like popinjays while his wife wears an alliterative "false front of French curls," which is nothing more than a hair extension. The stark visual contrast between the drab schoolroom attire of the Lowood girls and the Brocklehurst ladies' lavish dress needs only Jane's innocent reportage to critique it. Brocklehurst's not-so-subtle message, of course, is that fashion and vanity are not appropriate for poor girls. Certainly, for charity students to become habituated to a luxury that their subsequent lives would likely not support would be cruel. However, for Mr. Brocklehurst, the "lusts of the flesh" apparently include simple, wholesome food, heated rooms, and naturally curly hair.

Yet, if Brocklehurst is fearsome and detestable, he is hardly as powerful an influence on Jane as the long-suffering and spiritually wise Helen Burns. Ill with tuberculosis and frequently called out for her slovenliness by the schoolmistresses Helen nonetheless displays patience and a touching belief in her own need for reform and grace. Her beatified death prefigures the predicted martyrdom of St. John Rivers, and both contribute to Jane's own spiritual development. On one level, Helen is a type, a young, virginal, too-good-for-this-world martyr—like Beth March from *Little Women* or Eva in *Uncle Tom's Cabin*. These characters' narrative function is to die, thus saving others and equipping them with virtues for the living of life. Despite the typology, however, Brontë constructs Helen with a believable dimension and depth, giving her some of the loveliest speeches in the book.

One of Jane's few friends at Lowood, Helen impresses the younger, more rebellious girl with her perfect submission to the punishments and privations of her life. While Jane wonders at Helen's "doctrine of endurance [and] the forbearance she expressed for her chastiser" she somehow understands "that Helen Burns considered things by a light invisible to my eyes" (117). While Jane struggles with her natural, inborn inclinations to love only where she is loved, resist against perceived injustice, and "strike back again very hard" when struck, Helen gently encourages her toward a pure Christianity, unmuddied by doctrinal debates and sectarianism: "Read the New Testament, and observe what Christ says, and how he acts—make his word your rule and his conduct your example" (119-120). Although a cough—a symptom of the tuberculosis that soon fells her—is the first Jane hears from her, Helen's speech is gorgeously metaphysical, her eyes fixed on eternity. She can bear wrongs and hardship because she sees beyond them:

> Life appears to me too short to be spent in nursing animosity or registering wrongs. We are, and must be, one and all, burdened with faults in this world: but the time will soon come when, I trust, we shall put them off in putting off our corruptible bodies; when debasement and sin will fall from us with this cumbrous frame of flesh, and only the spark of the spirit will remain,--the impalpable principle of light and thought, pure as when it left the Creator to inspire the creature: whence it came it will return; perhaps again to be communicated to some being higher than man--perhaps to pass through gradations of glory, from the pale human soul to brighten to the seraph! Surely it will never, on the contrary, be suffered to degenerate from man to fiend? No; I cannot believe that: I hold another creed: which no one ever taught me, and which I seldom mention; but in which I delight, and to which I cling; for it makes Eternity a rest—a mighty home, not a terror and an abyss. (120-121)

I quote at length to showcase the soaring flight of Helen's rhetoric, unusually transcendent and articulate in a girl so young, but fitting for her discourse on eternal glory. Contrast her beautiful language with the crabbed and dire tone of Brocklehurst's dicta. Helen's expression of belief is alliterative (e.g. "spark of the spirit"), vividly descriptive ("cumbrous frame of flesh"), and theologically complex, as she compares the ineffable soul to various forms of light. Her reference to the creed "which no one ever taught me" suggests the doctrine of universal salvation, the belief that *all* of creation—not only those who call themselves Christians—will eventually be redeemed and reconciled to God. All will enjoy eternal life in His presence, without "a terror [or] an abyss." Although this theory has had its adherents from the beginning of Christianity, it is not a generally accepted mainstream teaching, and certainly not a tenet of Evangelicalism. Helen's compassionate belief in a more comprehensive program of redemption would be rejected by the likes of Brocklehurst.[4]

In Helen's character, we see the confluence of several currents of Christian thought; while she believes in her own imperfection and need for repentance and grace, she is nonetheless deeply compassionate to others. And, while she can love the things of this earth (like *Rasselas* or her native Northumberland countryside), she sees past them to a bright eternity that will not pass away. Helen's spiritual practice holds in tension the opposites of sinfulness and redemption, submission and active love, temporal and eternal. She simultaneously loves Jane as she is and encourages her toward the firmer spiritual ground of forgiveness and a simple belief in "My Maker and yours, who will never destroy what he created" (147). From their brief but intense friendship and the example of Helen's tranquil passing to "her long home," Jane inherits Helen's belief in a loving God and a deep trust in His care. The genuine faith Jane cultivates is the root of both her self-worth (she is God's greatly loved child) and the source of her principled integrity.

If Helen shows Jane the way of righteousness, St. John Rivers nearly tempts her to a path of holy falseness. As clergy go, Mr. Brocklehurst is obviously full of error and easily dismissed, but St. John Rivers is a compelling and far more dimensional figure. He and his complex brand of Christianity occupy a central position in the novel and in Jane's own self-realization. Even his harmonious name—St. John Rivers—is suggestive. Whether his namesake is John the Baptist, who foretold the coming of Christ, or John the Apostle who wrote both the Gospel bearing his name and the extraordinary visions of the Book of Revelation, St. John's given name practically predestines him for a life of Christian service. "Rivers" has its own connotations—of baptism, of fluidity, of movement—for a man who aspires to leave behind the waterways he knows for the faraway shores of the Ganges. While it has been a critical commonplace to view St. John as a symbol of a rigid religious patriarchy that Jane must oppose and reject, he is worth a nuanced examination.[5] On the one hand charismatic, compelling, and nearly irresistible to Jane, he is also a "cold cumbrous column," against which she sharpens and defines her own lived Christianity (491). Understanding him assists the reader in understanding Jane's spirituality, the context of her return to Rochester, and the last words of the novel.

After her discovery that Mr. Rochester "has a wife now living," Jane flees Thornfield, misplaces her purse, and wanders for three days. Reduced to begging, she seeks shelter at Moor-House, the Rivers family home. The servant who answers the door denies her entrance, and Jane despairs aloud, "I can but die . . . and I believe in God. Let me try to wait His will in silence." Such an articulation of faithfulness makes a strong first impression on St. John, who replies, "All men must die . . . but all are not condemned to meet a lingering and premature doom, such as yours would be if you perished here of want" (428). It is a prophetic first dialogue. Jane professes her belief despite her suffering; St. John administers charity with reason and curiosity rather than tenderness, his interest piqued by Jane's being a "peculiar case" that he must "examine into" (429). This first exchange sets the tone for all their dealings to come, and the novel, via Jane's perspective, simultaneously admires and critiques St. John. In contrast to the immediate bosom friendship Jane forms with Diana and Mary Rivers, her understanding of St. John's character is hard-won, the accumulation of several episodes that Jane details for the reader. He is a complicated welter of contradictions: the cure to Brocklehurst's naked hypocrisy; a good, learned, deeply faithful man; and the object of Jane's eventual veneration. Yet, in some ways, St. John is the very embodiment of the negative example offered in I Corinthians 13:

> Though I speak with the tongues of men and of angels, and have not charity, I am become as sounding brass, or a tinkling cymbal. And though I have the gift of prophecy, and understand all mysteries, and

all knowledge; and though I have all faith, so that I could remove mountains, and have not charity, I am nothing. And though I bestow all my goods to feed the poor, and though I give my body to be burned, and have not charity, it profiteth me nothing. (I Corinthians 13: 1-3)

As she comes to know his nature, Jane testifies to St. John's eloquence ("speaking with the tongues of angels"), learning ("all knowledge"), missionary vocation ("giving my body to be burned"), and lack of doubt about his calling ("all faith"). And yet, he seems incapable of feeling a motivating love for any of his fellow humans—not even his sisters, so beloved by Jane. He is good, but not empathetic. Early in their acquaintance, she attempts to describe one of his sermons, but concludes, "it is past my power." Still, she ventures a sketch, all concentrated on the effect of his words and delivery:

> The heart was thrilled, the mind astonished, by the power of the preacher: neither were softened. Throughout there was a strange bitterness; an absence of consolatory gentleness; stern allusions to Calvinistic doctrines—election, predestination, reprobation— were frequent; and each reference to these points sounded like a sentence pronounced for doom. When he had done, instead of feeling better, calmer, more enlightened by his discourse, I experienced an inexpressible sadness. (446-447)

St. John's homily presents a system of belief that Jane must successfully negotiate in order to sustain her own Christianity. St. John's keen intellect (indeed, he does not seem to *feel* his religion at all) has embraced Calvin's teachings that God elects some to His service and thus to eternal salvation—but not others, who are passively left to their own damnation. His Calvinist leanings (not mainline Church of England teaching) and inability to console his listeners place him in opposition to the unschooled Helen Burns, with her burning compassion and radical universalism.[6] St. John's Christianity is joyless. Jane senses he "had not yet found that peace of God that passeth all understanding" (447). Jane's clear-eyed assessment of his preaching anticipates her later far less disinterested response to St. John's proposal of marriage. She is "thrilled" but not "softened," receiving the call to join him as his wife "like a sentence pronounced for doom." The occasion of Jane's inheritance and her plans to refurbish Moor-House for Christmas afford her further insight into St. John's makeup. As she joyfully shares her plans, he responds with a proprietary caution, allowing but "two months' grace . . . for pleasing yourself with this late-found charm of relationship" and urging her, "Don't cling so tenaciously to ties of the flesh; save your constancy and ardour for an adequate cause: forbear to waste them on trite transient objects" (489). Paradoxically, as J. Jeffrey Franklin points out, "it is Jane's capacity for sympathy that St. John is most critical of, *and . . .* that most strongly attracts him to her" (Franklin 467). If his manner of dismissing simple human joys and comforts calls Brocklehurst to mind, it must be pointed out that St. John hardly insists on a Lowood-like self-deprivation and poverty. Nor is he a hypocrite. He is no more severe upon those around him than he is on himself. Still, Jane's rebelliousness rears its head, claiming for herself the long-sought joy of natural affections: "I feel I have adequate cause to be happy, and I *will* be happy!" (489, Brontë's emphasis).

Jane experiences a series of epiphanies occasioned by this episode: that "the humanities and amenities of life had no attraction for him," that "he lived only to aspire," and most importantly, "that he would hardly make a good husband" (491). St. John's *intractable* ambition for the crown of righteousness is another manifestation of an Evangelical sensibility. Hardship, opposition, or persecution for the sake of the Gospel was both a mark and a means of holiness. Indeed, he says as much when he offers Jane the Morton school: "I hold that the more arid and unreclaimed the soil where the Christian labourer's task of tillage is appointed him . . . the higher the honour" (449). Earthly comforts and sensual delights only interfere with the attainment of holiness.

Yet for all his noble celestial goals, St. John is keenly aware of physical beauty. Even as Jane lay in her sickbed upon first arriving at Moor-House, he noted, "The grace and harmony of beauty are quite wanting in those features" (433). He never makes Jane to feel that she is attractive as a woman, only as a worker. Meanwhile, the single thorn in his flesh is his sensual attraction to the "exquisitely beautiful, graceful, and fascinating" Rosamund Oliver (463). In Jane's presence, he indulges in an imaginative fantasy of being Rosamund's husband and lover for a closely timed quarter-hour, as he "breathed fast and low" (470). But because Rosamund would make no good missionary's wife, even his lust for her is sacrificed at the altar of his "insatiable" need "to rise higher, to do more than others" (472). His Protestant Evangelical ethos dichotomizes *eros* and *agape*: he is incapable of imagining that sexual satisfaction and commitment to Christian mission might be supplied by one and the same woman. To make St. John an even more complicated being, Brontë endows him with a physical perfection of his own—a beauty to which Jane is not insensible and which contributes to a number of plot dynamics.[7] His perfectly chiseled and harmonious features only underscore his marble-coldness and lack of emotion. The difference between his beauty and Rochester's shaggy, dark looks externalizes the contrast between the man who claims Jane for his ambition and the one who claims her for his heart. Upon their reunion, Jane teases Mr. Rochester with descriptions of St. John's Grecian profile, causing Mr. Rochester to exclaim under his breath, "Damn him!" When Jane nearly yields to St. John's proposal of marriage, I believe his beauty is part of the reason. She is aware of his physicality throughout his strange courtship of her, as her many references to his features and bodily presence attest.

With tension and intensity, the novel lays the groundwork for St. John's proposal of marriage to Jane. She notes his "experiment kiss," his blue eyes in frequent observation of her, and her own "servitude" of "daily wish[ing] more to please him" (497). When the proposal finally comes, its expression is dramatic, leaving Jane open to being "struck and thrilled" when St. John asks, "And what does *your* heart say?" (501). The language might sound romantic, but in this context, his question refers to Christian vocation, and not to carnal love. She is so close to catching his view that, she recounts, "It was as if I had heard a summons from Heaven—as if a visionary messenger, like him of Macedonia, had enounced, 'Come over and help us'!" (501). Citing the Book of Acts and the vision that led the Apostle Paul to preach in Macedonia, Jane reveals her own biblical grounding and the attraction of a holy calling. St. John's plan is problematic on at least two counts, however. First is his troubling conviction that he has discerned God's will *for Jane*—a dynamic of mediation that Maria LaMonaca links to the secondhand Divine access granted Milton's Eve: "For contemplation he and valour form'd. . . He for GOD only/She for GOD in him" (247). Equally offensive is St. John's denial of Jane's full personhood:

> God and nature intended you for a missionary's wife. It is not personal, but mental endowments they have given you: *you are formed for labor, not for love.* A missionary's wife you must—shall be. You shall be mine. I claim you—not for my pleasure, but for my Sovereign's service! (501, Brontë's emphasis)

Typical of St. John, the language is passionate but not erotic. Contrast his rhetorical treatment of Jane with Mr. Rochester's playfully fond names for her—"faerie," "elf," "sprite"—and his assessment of her as "good, gifted,"—and most importantly— "lovely" (406). St. John does not *cherish* Jane; he only sees that she will be useful for his work. Most fatal to his own purpose, he suggests that she does not deserve love, that she was not created for it, because she lacks beauty, grace, or form.

The final time Jane and St. John discuss marriage, she nearly yields; but even as she knows "his look was not, indeed, that of a lover beholding his mistress; but it was that of a pastor recalling his wandering sheep," when he touches her, laying his hand on her head, Jane is nearly overpowered by feelings of "veneration" (518). While the language of this scene never turns away from its religious tone, it is striking that his *touch*, his nearly enfolding Jane in his arms, has as much effect on her as his words. At the very moment Jane is certain she does not love St. John, his persuasive presentation of "God's will," her need for his approval, and his rare beauty accompanied by physical touch *almost* combine into a draught too potent for her to resist.[8]

How to explain the fact that our independently minded heroine, able to quit the home of the man she loves in order to preserve her principles and honor, falls under the spell of this cold, remote taskmaster? Jane's Christianity, deep and sincere, experiences nature, human fellowship, and, we can assume, sexual union, as occasions of God's love and grace. A friendless orphan most of her life, she treasures affectionate ties with others. St. John's undue influence swings her natural affections out of balance and nearly convinces her to sacrifice human love to the Divine. In the renewal of his marriage proposal, he angles for Jane's capitulation to *his* sense of God's will with Jesus's own words from the Gospel of Luke. He half prays, half urges, "God give you strength to choose that better part which shall not be taken from you," drawing an analogy between Jane and Mary, the sister of Lazarus (518). When Mary sits at the feet of Christ, rapt and listening, instead of helping in the kitchen, her sister Martha complains to Jesus, who answers, "But one thing is needful: and Mary hath chosen that good part, which shall not be taken away from her" (Luke 10:42). After this last pronouncement of St. John's, coupled with his physical touch and "gentleness," Jane nearly mistakes his physical perfection, magnetism, and spiritual conviction for a simulacrum of passion—though never love (519).

If the true danger presented by St. John and Jane's near-acceptance of his hand doesn't come across clearly enough, perhaps a contemporary analogue to *Jane Eyre* will cast some further light. Mary Gordon's 1978 novel, *Final Payments*, reimagines Jane as Isabel Moore, a woman who emerges into delayed adulthood at age 30, after eleven confining years of nursing her ailing father. Isabel falls in love with a married man, but when his wife confronts her publically, Isabel becomes convinced of the "danger of pleasure" (Gordon 241) and retreats to a life of penance. She seeks out her father's former housekeeper, Margaret Casey—an unbeautiful, uneducated, humourless, sour, niggardly, poormouth old maid— and moves in with her. Isabel clings to the idea that to love Margaret would absolve her from her sins of carnality with someone else's husband: "I would devote myself to the person I was least capable of loving. I would absorb myself in the suffering of someone I found unattractive. It would be a pure act, like a martyr's death" (Gordon 240).

Isabel struggles, and, like Jane, nearly submerges her own will into another's. Eventually fed up with Margaret's continual self-pitying references to her own poverty (and her active dislike of *Jane Eyre*), Isabel angrily and somewhat reflexively flings at her, "The poor you have always with you!" Unexpectedly, the context of this phrase unfolds itself into a healing and redemptive understanding of Christ's words. In this passage from the Gospel of John, Mary (the same woman who earlier shirked her household duties) anoints Jesus' feet, wiping them with her hair. Judas, Christ's betrayer, complains that the money spent on this lavish gesture could have been given to the poor instead. The truth of Christ's answer, "The poor you have always with you; but me, not always" breaks like light upon Isabel's comprehension. She realizes, "What Christ was saying, what he meant, was that the pleasures of that hair, that ointment, must be taken. Because the accidents of death would deprive us soon enough. We must not deprive ourselves, our loved ones, of the luxury of our extravagant affections. We must not try to second-guess death by refusing to love the ones we loved in favor of the anonymous poor" (289). *Agape* and sensuality need not be enemies, Isabel understands. After this revelation, she is able exercise true charity toward Margaret by disbursing the "final payment" of the title. Realizing that Margaret's life would be easier if she didn't have to worry about money, Isabel gives her the proceeds from the sale of her father's house, phones her friends, and flees the poverty of her penitential existence, ready to "open the jar of ointment" (289).

Isabel Moore is rescued by a biblical epiphany, but what saves Jane Eyre is supernatural, unable to be explained in logical terms. As Jane struggles with whether it be "God's will" to marry St. John, she hears the voice of Mr. Rochester, far away, on the wind, thrice calling her name. "Where are you?" she replies. Although the sudden appearance of the supernatural element may smack of *deus ex machina,* it is logical within the terms of this novel to view it as a legitimate divine intervention. When Jane and Rochester ultimately reunite, this scene's legitimizing power is reinforced on two levels.

Firstly, Rochester admits to calling her name "two nights ago last" and hearing her response; his description only confirms her own experience. But perhaps even more importantly, Rochester's plea signals a return to prayer and a more religious life. He confesses he has begun to "experience remorse, repentance" and "the wish for reconcilement to my Maker"; these have found voice in "very brief" but "very sincere" prayers (549). In the moral terms of the novel, Rochester's restored belief softens the blow of Jane's rejection of mission work. She has not refused a missionary for an unbelieving adulterer, but for a redeemed sinner.

Of the many versions of Christian practice depicted in *Jane Eyre*, the integrated belief of the heroine is what persists. Despite her dear Helen's admonishment, "You think too much of the love of human beings" (a warning echoed by St. John), Jane holds tightly to those she loves, experiencing God in her friendships and in her marriage (133). St. John's repudiation of human ties for the sake of God's Kingdom is not for her and, in fact, would be a denial of her selfhood in God, as she understands it. Her own spiritual progress requires that she practice a Christian faith true to the integrity of her nature and her being—a nature that takes delight in human sympathies, in Nature, in artmaking, in books, and, eventually, in marriage and motherhood. Her religious devotion reveals itself in acts like the four-way division of her inheritance with the Riverses; her kindly cultivation of young minds at the Morton village school; and forgiveness offered freely to her dying Aunt Reed. Able to find some measure of contentment at Lowood, Thornfield, Moor-House, and the Morton school alike, Jane is even willing to embrace self-denial and self-sacrifice by going to India to spread the Gospel. Yet, she draws the line at self-delusion and self-immolation by false marriage. Jane knows what "better part" is true for her, and she chooses it.

With Rochester's return to belief, Charlotte Brontë presents a decided viewpoint regarding the relationship between human love and divine love. One can lead to the other; if marriage is a model of Christ's love for his Bride, the Church (that is, the body of believers), then human participation in this relationship is a sacred act. For our principled heroine, a loveless marriage entered into for the express purpose of furthering God's work is far less honorable and desirable than a partnership of true equals who love and value one another in light of their status as God's children. Jane is able to pull back from the precipice in time, realizing that the two loves are not exclusive— that indeed the first, nearer love can mirror and mediate the greater, more cosmic Love of God.

Be that as it may, the novel ends with St. John, the mouthpiece of an austere, ascetic, and unyielding—although unswerving and genuine—religious sensibility. Some critics have read this ending as problematic, but consider another angle.[9] If Jane tells her own story (writes it, even, to the frequently addressed "Reader"), her decision to conclude with sympathetic praise of St. John' imminent martyrdom reveals much about her. Although she declines to be his wife, Jane tells him she *would* have gone to India: "With you, I would have ventured much; because I admire, confide in, and, as a sister, I love you" (513). Jane Eyre says nothing she does not believe. While she returns and finds Rochester and chooses *her* better part of marriage, she never ceases admiring St. John. As a sincere Christian, Jane is bound to revere such a "firm, faithful, and devoted" follower of her Lord (555). As a further spiritual insight, she acknowledges the dualism of a presently earthbound, but ultimately eternal humanity, when she confides, "The last letter I received from [St. John] drew from my eyes human tears, and yet filled my heart with Divine joy" (556). Happy and fulfilled herself, Jane elects not to deny another his expression and experience of the greatest good. In the novel's closing words, Jane (as penned by Charlotte Brontë) quotes St. John quoting The Book of Revelation: "Amen; even so come, Lord Jesus!" Thus, the book ends intertextually, looking toward the *eschaton*, the Second Coming of Christ, the prayer of John the Revelator ringing its last note.

Notes

1. Early feminist readings of Jane Eyre, such as Gilbert and Gubar's seminal, collaborative *The Madwoman in the Attic*, generally adopted a position of skepticism toward the perceived patriarchy of religion. The tide turned in the

1990s, however, with considerations that integrated feminist concerns with the treatment of Christianity as a credible system of belief. For instance, by designating Jane Eyre a "Christian feminist bildungsroman" Susan VanZanten Gallagher opened up new interpretive avenues for the novel. See "Jane Eyre and Christianity" in *Approaches to Teaching Brontë's Jane Eyre*, edited by Diane Long Hoeveler and Beth Lau.

2. The real-life basis for Lowood was the Clergy Daughters' School at Cowan Bridge in Lancashire, which the Brontë sisters attended and where Maria Brontë, the inspiration for Helen, became infected with the tuberculosis that ended her young life.

3. See: DeVere, Laura Suzanne. "Evangelicalism at Lowood." *Victorian Web.* May 1994. Web. 27 Nov. 2013. < http://www.victorianweb.org/authors/ bronte/cbronte/jane6.html>

4. For a lucid and accessible recent discussion of universal salvation, see Rob Bell's *Love Wins: A Book About Heaven, Hell, and the Fate of Every Person Who Ever Lived* (Harper Collins, 2012).

5. In Gilbert and Gubar's (fairly representative) assessment, St. John does possess "integrity of principle," but when all is said and done he is merely "a pillar of patriarchy" (366)—not wholly inaccurate, but not attending to St. John's complexity.

6. J. Jeffrey Franklin locates in Helen the sympathetic centre of the novel, arguing that "she simultaneously brings into play issues of human sympathy and woman's identity that supersede Christian spirituality" (465).

7. Of the dozens of Jane Eyre film versions, only a select few cast St. John Rivers according to the novel's description. Handsome Andrew Bicknell in the 1983 made-for-TV version (starring Timothy Dalton as Rochester) possesses the fair coloring and noble profile Jane attributes to him. Rupert Penry-Jones, in a 1997 adaptation starring Samantha Morton as Jane, is also aptly cast. Several St. Johns, however, have been brunets and not more aesthetically pleasing than their Rochesters, which dulls the intended contrast between Apollo and Vulcan.

8. If, as I suggest, St. John fascinates Jane beyond the merely intellectual or sympathetic, J. Jeffrey Franklin holds that the reverse is also true. He ascribes to St. John darker "motives and passions" to which he is "blind," as "he has been cloaking them all along in sanctimonious rhetoric" (469).

9. Among these is Maria LaMonaca, for whom "the vexed discourses of gender, domesticity, and faith surrounding Jane Eyre's production [make] an easy reading of the book . . . neither possible nor desirable" (260).

Works Cited

Bell, Rob. *Love Wins: A Book About Heaven, Hell, and the Fate of Every Person Who Ever Lived*. New York: HarperCollins, 2012.

Brontë, Charlotte. *Jane Eyre*. Edited by Richard Nemesvari. Ontario: Broadview, 1999.

Franklin, J. Jeffrey. "The Merging of Spiritualities: Jane Eyre as Missionary of Love." *Nineteenth Century Literature* 49.4 (1995): 456-482.

Gallagher, Susan VanZanten. "*Jane Eyre* and Christianity." *Approaches to Teaching Brontë's* Jane Eyre. Eds. Diane Long Hoeveler and Beth Lau. New York: Modern Language Association, 1993.

Gilbert, Susan M. and Susan Gubar. *The Madwoman in the Attic: The Woman Writer and the Nineteenth-Century Literary Imagination*. 2nd ed. New Haven: Yale Nota Bene, 2000.

. *Final Payments*. New York: Anchor Books, 2006.

Jane Eyre. Dir. Julian Amyes. Perf. Zelah Clarke, Timothy Dalton, Jean Harvey, Andrew Bicknell. BBC, 1983. Film.

Jane Eyre. Dir. Robert Young. Perf. Samantha Morton, Ciaran Hinds, Gemma Jones, Rupert Penry-Jones. A&E, 1997. Film.

LaMonaca, Maria. "Jane's Crown of Thorns: Feminism and Christianity in *Jane Eyre*."

Studies in the Novel 34.3 (2002): 244-263.

Landow, George. "The Doctrines of Evangelical Protestantism." *Victorian Web*. 7 June 2007. Web. 24 Oct. 2013. <http://www.victorianweb.org/religion/evangel2.html>.

Right Obedience and Milton's Abdiel in *Jane Eyre* _____

Jonathan Kotchian

The goal of this essay is to better understand how obedience works in *Jane Eyre*. Appearing below is John Milton's 1667 epic poem *Paradise Lost*—a work Charlotte Brontë draws upon regularly. Here, it is used as a lens through which to examine the various acts of obedience and disobedience in the 1847 novel. In particular, one Miltonic character—Abdiel, the only angel in Satan's ranks to reject sin and remain faithful to God—seems to serve Brontë as a touchstone, helping her to organize and articulate *Jane Eyre*'s stance on the morality of submission and rebellion. Milton's Abdiel is, arguably, the model in *Jane Eyre* for right obedience, a superior form of obedience that is paradoxically achieved only through revolt.

Why does Brontë need Abdiel, and why do readers need this analysis? Without them, *Jane Eyre*'s treatment of obedience is difficult to apprehend coherently. On the one hand, much of the novel's action is built around Jane's revolt against various tyrannies; on the other, the book sometimes extols proper Christian obedience. Sandra M. Gilbert and Susan Gubar's influential reading invites us to credit the novel with "rebellious feminism" (338), and it is hard not to cheer for Jane whenever she refuses patriarchal submission, as when she finds her station at Thornfield too confining:

> Women are supposed to be very calm generally: but women feel just as men feel […] they suffer from too rigid a restraint, too absolute a stagnation, precisely as men would suffer; and it is narrow-minded in their more privileged fellow-creatures to say that they ought to confine themselves to making puddings and knitting stockings, to playing on the piano and embroidering bags. (93)

Then again, another critic warns us *against* reading *Jane Eyre* "as a novel of rebellion" or as a "legitimate assertion of the sovereignty of the self" (Beaty 491), asking us to notice instead its frequent praise of Christian duty, as when Jane decides she must leave Rochester: "Laws and principles are not for the times when there is no temptation: they are for moments such as this, when body and soul rise in mutiny against their rigour; stringent are they; inviolate they shall be" (270). Is obedience, then, a virtue or a vice? Is rebellion sinful or salutary?

Of course, sometimes Brontë clearly signals that obedience depends on circumstances; surely, we are not meant to fault Jane for resisting the brutality of John Reed, or for obeying Rochester's orders as his employee. But other instances elude a simple solution. Consider, especially, the strange case of *Jane Eyre*'s final two paragraphs. After committing herself and Rochester to a cozy happily-ever-after, Jane's thoughts turn finally to St. John Rivers, expressing more longing than seems appropriate. She seems to admire, and even yearn for, not only St. John's missionary life, but for qualities of her former suitor's character that she previously disdained. Her earlier distaste for his "despotic nature" and his desire to "coerce [her] into obedience" (349) is replaced in the final chapter by this:

> He may be stern; he may be exacting; he may be ambitious yet; but his is the sternness of the warrior Greatheart, who guards his pilgrim convoy from the onslaught of Apollyon. His is the exaction of the apostle, who speaks but for Christ when he says—'Whosoever will come after Me, let him deny himself, and take up his cross and follow Me.' His is the ambition of the high master-spirit, which aims to fill a place in the first rank of those who are redeemed from the earth. (385)

Jane here excuses and praises those qualities in her cousin that once frustrated and repelled her into disobedience, and her praise is given pride of place at the very end of her story. She sounds quite envious of St. John's "place in the first rank," and we might even suspect that Jane regrets rejecting her cousin and choosing Rochester.

I suggest that we can explain this strange turn, and indeed the seeming ambivalence toward obedience throughout *Jane Eyre*, by attending to Milton's revolutionary model for what I will call *right* obedience: the seraph Abdiel. The Abdiel model places several *disobedient* qualities (pride, independent thought, scorn, defiance of hierarchy, aggression) under the aegis of ultimate obedience to *valid* authority. Above all, Milton presents in Abdiel a model for *active* virtue, godly virtue defined by trial, struggle, and even rebellion; this active virtue, like St. John's above, is stern, exacting, and ambitious. In appropriating this model, Brontë offers to resolve the tension between self-actualizing feminist rebellion and abject obedience to patriarchal orders. She shows up the binary of Jane's usual approach to commands—"I know no medium: I never in my life have known any medium in my dealings with positive, hard characters […] between absolute submission and determined revolt. I have always faithfully observed the one, up to the very moment of bursting, sometimes with volcanic vehemence, into the other" (341)—as incomplete and lacking. Read this way, *Jane Eyre* leads its protagonist and reader not simplistically toward submission or toward revolt, but rather toward right obedience, submission *through* revolt.[1]

While Abdiel's name appears nowhere in *Jane Eyre*, scholars have long acknowledged Milton's centrality in Brontë's moral imagination. She loved Milton's poetry as a child, and critics list Milton (along with John Bunyan and the Bible) among the authors and works Brontë knew thoroughly and quotes most frequently (Betsinger 112, citing Smith viii). *Jane Eyre* criticism has, however, ignored Abdiel as a model, preferring other Miltonic influences. Gilbert and Gubar applaud Eve's (and Satan's) "rebellion against the hierarchical status quo" (202), finding in Milton's fallen characters the roots for Jane as an "emblem of passionate, barely disguised, rebelliousness" (337), who strives against patriarchy toward equality and liberty. But readings in this tradition fail to account fully for Brontë's praise of obedience. A competing tradition links Jane instead to Milton's pure and unfallen characters. Connie L. Eberhart uses the Lady in Milton's *Comus* to highlight Jane's "insistence upon pristine truth" and "[a]bsolute allegiance to timeless values," crediting her with "a traditional idea of religious duty" (80-81). Likewise, Clay Daniel tries to explain Jane's adherence "to divine law" by suggesting that she "takes over the role of unfallen Adam in

Paradise Lost" (95). But Jane's "determined revolt" fits uneasily into such readings. Though critics in both traditions often acknowledge the problematics of obedience in *Jane Eyre*, their Miltonic models for it are incomplete.[2]

The above description of St. John helps us complete Brontë's Miltonic model. Jane envies St. John's obedience because it is the obedience of a hero, of an exalted, superhuman spirit driven by service to a greater cause; in short, a figure almost *angelic* in his active obedience. By examining the two confrontations between Abdiel and Satan in *Paradise Lost*—the first incurred by Satan's proposal of revolution against God, the second by Satan's appearance on the heavenly field of battle, before his defeat and descent into Hell—we can see the ideal of *active* obedience most clearly.[3] Abdiel's right obedience emerges only through his virtuous disobedience and rebellion, and this paradoxical ideal assists in re-reading *Jane Eyre* more comprehensively, so it is possible to more fully understand its treatment of submission through revolt.

Abdiel honors God in *Paradise Lost* not abjectly, but in an active and unexpected rebellion against Satan's seemingly legitimate authority. Satan's initial address to his host—one-third of all heaven's angels—is tempting because it directly *opposes* honor to abject submission, as he tries to convince his troops to rebel against God. He rejects subservience to God's Son as "knee-tribute" and "prostration vile" (5.782), insisting that these violate the angels' exalted liberty:

> Will ye submit your necks and choose to bend
> The supple knee? Ye will not if I trust
> To know ye right or if ye know yourselves
> Natives and sons of Heav'n possessed before
> By none, and if not equal all, yet free,
> Equally free, for orders and degrees
> Jar not with liberty but well consist. (5.787-93)

Satan, though he disobeys and asserts equality with God, nevertheless maintains hierarchy in his army, adducing their "orders and degrees," their "imperial titles," as evidence that they are "ordained to govern, not to serve" (5.801-02). Ironically, all of Satan's angels obey him without dissent or dispute; all except Abdiel, who insists that obedience need *not* be dishonorable and that the angels ought therefore to see, "of our dignity / How provident [God] is, how far from thought / To make us less, bent rather to exalt / Our happy state under one head more near / United" (5.827-831). In Abdiel's view, service elevates rather than degrades, and God has exalted the angels' honor and dignity by giving rule to the Son, as "all honor to Him done / Returns our own" (5.844-45).

Abdiel acts and speaks on his own, disdaining hierarchical authority, even though Satan is his commanding officer. He insists on the power of his own reason to refute Satan's "argument blasphemous" (5.809). Although Abdiel's speech is thought "singular or rash" (5.851) by all the other angels, he sternly insists, "fearless though alone, / Encompassed round with foes" (5.875-76) that he is right and they wrong. In fact, his rebellion merits Milton's highest praise because it is so proudly and scornfully self-insistent:

So spake the seraph Abdiel faithful found
Among the faithless, faithful only he
Among innumerable false. Unmoved,
Unshaken, unseduced, unterrified
His loyalty he kept, his love, his zeal.
Nor number nor example with him wrought
To swerve from truth or change his constant mind
Though single. From amidst them forth he passed
Long way through hostile scorn which he sustained
Superior, nor of violence feared aught
And with retorted scorn his back he turned
On those proud tow'rs to swift destruction doomed. (5.896-907)

Brontë's readers may recognize this self-insistent rebellion in some of *Jane Eyre*'s greatest moments of moral crisis, moments that are so satisfying because they paradoxically resolve the tension between submission and revolt.

Echoes of Abdiel's right obedience are especially loud when Jane refuses St. John's demand that she marry him. When she offers instead to accompany him to India only as his sister and fellow missionary, he tries to force on Jane a model of passive obedience, but Jane insists scornfully on an active one:

> 'Do you think God will be satisfied with half an oblation? Will he accept a mutilated sacrifice? It is the cause of God I advocate: it is under his standard I enlist you. I cannot accept on His behalf a divided allegiance; it must be entire.'
> 'Oh! I will give my heart to God,' I said. '*You* do not want it.'
> I will not swear, reader, that there was not something of repressed sarcasm both in the tone in which I uttered this sentence, and in the feeling that accompanied it. [...] He had held me in awe, because he had held me in doubt.
> [...] The veil fell from his hardness and despotism. [...] I was with an equal—one with whom I might argue—one whom, if I saw good, I might resist. (346)

Jane, like Abdiel, rebels in service to God, and such resistance is enabled only by obeying individual conscience and right reason. Only by privileging themselves, understanding their own liberty to act independently, can Abdiel and Jane escape passive submission to hierarchy. We might expect Abdiel to bow to his commander, and Jane to submit to St. John as pupil to teacher and woman to man. However, both Abdiel and Jane militantly and heroically insist on insubordination, on the right to obey God on their own, even (and especially) in their sarcasm and scorn.

Too, Jane's tortured decision to leave Rochester and Thornfield is best read as a conflict not only between love and duty, but also between right obedience and abject submission. When Rochester pleads that "'[i]t would not be wicked to love me,'" Jane replies that "'[i]t would to obey you'" (269). Brontë suggests that Jane's love for him is more dangerous because it is submissive and self-denying, as it shouts to her, "'[o]h, comply! [...] tell him you love him and will be his. Who in the world cares for *you*?'" Jane's right obedience emerges in her revolt against this submission: "'*I* care for myself.

The more solitary, the more friendless, the more unsustained I am, the more I will respect myself. I will keep the law given by God'" (270). Here, the Abdiel model helps us understand the insistence on Jane's *solitude*, which otherwise seems odd. When one is tempted to submit to invalid authority, one's resistance is more heroic if it emerges in opposition to the easy road taken by the multitude. Virtue is deemed worthier when single, when isolated.

The importance of the Abdiel model becomes clearer when we consider how Brontë appropriates Milton's view of Christian obedience as necessarily militant, emerging through trial and victory. Right obedience is *superior*, and it elevates its adherents as superior also. "I cannot praise a fugitive and cloister'd virtue, unexercis'd & unbreath'd, that never sallies out and sees her adversary," writes the poet in a prose tract. "He that can apprehend and consider vice with all her baits and seeming pleasures, and yet abstain, and yet distinguish, and yet prefer that which is truly better, he is the true warfaring Christian" (*Areopagitica* 1006). By comparison, Milton scorns untried virtue as repulsively abject; it generates only "obedient unanimity" (1016) and a "grosse conforming stupidity," "forc't and frozen together" (1022). Jane's mental struggles against temptation likewise distinguish her from those who submit out of weakness.

Without the Abdiel model, readers might be tempted, for instance, to view Helen Burns, Jane's friend at Lowood, as rightly virtuous in her passivity, especially as she cites scriptural authority for her submission. When Jane says she could not bear being flogged, Helen tells Jane that "it would be your duty to bear it" (47) and that Jane should "observe what Christ says […] [l]ove your enemies, bless them that curse you; do good to them that hate you and despitefully use you" (49). Jane listens to Helen,

> with wonder: I could not comprehend this doctrine of endurance; and still less could I understand or sympathise with the forbearance she expressed for her chastiser. Still I felt that Helen Burns considered things by a light invisible to my eyes. I suspected she might be right and I wrong. (47)

If we do not acknowledge Brontë's distinction between right and wrong obedience, we might agree with Helen that Christian duty requires abject submission to worldly authority, a view vexingly incompatible with our cheers for Jane's later revolts. But if we see Abdiel as Brontë's model, we can see how rejecting Helen's passive obedience is, in fact, proof of Jane's superior virtue. Moreover, Jane's wish to grab Miss Scatcherd's rod and "break it under her nose" (46) is not merely childish petulance, but also laudable rejection of illegitimate authority. Abdiel does not love or forgive Satan; rather, when the two meet for the second time (on the field of heavenly battle), Abdiel strikes the first blow of the great war, smashing Satan's "proud crest" and forcing him into a meeker posture: "Ten paces huge / He back recoiled, the tenth on bended knee" (6.191-194). A true warfaring Christian, far from submitting to his enemies, is ambitious to prove his right obedience in combat.

Reading for right obedience, we can better see why Jane chafes under St. John's yoke as a member of his household. When she consents to learn "Hindostanee" under his command, she says she "fell under a freezing spell. When he said 'go,' I went; 'come,' I came; 'do this,' I did it." Passive obedience to his (seemingly innocuous) commands is figured as self-destroying enslavement, as St. John "acquired a certain influence over me that took away my liberty of mind [...]. I could no longer talk or laugh freely when he was by" (339). When Rivers praises Jane as "docile, diligent, disinterested" (344), Abdiel helps us see why Jane ought to reject these qualities in herself. True virtue is made of sterner stuff.

Jane's most noteworthy trial comes a few pages later, as St. John disguises his command as solicitous entreaty; he lays his hand on Jane's head, speaking "earnestly, mildly," his look "that of a pastor recalling his wandering sheep—or better, of a guardian angel watching the soul for which he is responsible" (356) as he again tries to coerce her into service as his wife. Again, Jane's struggle is against abject submission that would surrender her individual reason: "I was tempted to cease struggling with him—to rush down the torrent of his will into the gulf of his existence, and there lose my own" (356). Crucially, this surrender masquerades as a Christian submission to the divine:

> All was changing utterly, with a sudden sweep. Religion called— Angels beckoned—God commanded—life rolled together like a scroll—death's gates opening, showed eternity beyond; it seemed, that for safety and bliss there, all here might be sacrificed in a second. (356-57)

However, merited reward in *Jane Eyre* is not won through surrender, but through the *right* obedience of Abdiel; not through meekness, but through individual strength. When Jane hears the cry "Jane! Jane! Jane!" (357), she remembers *herself* and is able to reject the visions of obedience that would make of her a mere sheep: "I broke from St. John, who would have detained me. It was *my* time to assume ascendancy. *My* powers were in play, and in force. I told him to forbear question or remark; I desired him to leave me: I must, and would be alone" (358).

Jane's self-insistence might seem a touch too proud here. However, we can see, through the Abdiel model, how even the most self-insistent pride and ambition are excused, and indeed lauded, under the aegis of right obedience to ultimate authority. Charles W. Durham shows how Abdiel is rewarded for insisting on his own power to disobey, noting that "the reception he gets from God when he returns to the fold of the good angels makes clear that his actions are worthy of emulation" (15). Upon his return from his first defiance of Satan, he is "high applauded" (6.26) and elevated by God, whose praise centers on Abdiel's warfaring self-distinction: [...] "well hast thou fought / The better fight [...]. For this was all thy care: To stand approved in sight of God though worlds / Judged thee perverse" (6.29-37). Remarkably, just before the heavenly battle is joined, Satan calls out Abdiel for daring to step forward and challenge him: "But well thou com'st / Before thy fellows ambitious to win / From me some plume that thy success may show / Destruction to the rest" (6.159-62). Ambition briefly seems as though it might be a bad thing; perhaps Abdiel is overreaching? But in fact, Abdiel backs up his boast by staggering Satan with a mighty blow; ambition turns out to be praiseworthy, as long as it is ambition in the service of God.

Satan mocks the good angels for their base "servility," preferring "freedom," but Abdiel's response sets the reader right by re-interpreting both terms:

> Unjustly thou deprav'st it with the name
> Of servitude to serve whom God ordains
> Or Nature: God and Nature bid the same
> When he who rules is worthiest and excels
> Them whom he governs. This is servitude:
> To serve th' unwise or him who hath rebelled
> Against his worthier as thine now serve thee,
> Thyself not free but to thyself enthralled [...]. (6.169-181)

In other words, Abdiel's service is freedom, and Satan's freedom is slavery. Jane's moment of power and glory is fitting, not unseemly, because in elevating herself, she serves a legitimate higher power who brings Rochester's words to her. Jane's insight that the voice crying "Jane!" is "not [superstition's] deception, nor [its] witchcraft: it is the work of nature" (358) reminds us that individuals may discern between right and wrong authority.

Jane Eyre's strange concluding turn repositions St. John as an Abdiel, rather than a tempting Satan, by casting him as God's subordinate rather than Jane's commander. St. John has previously confessed to a problematic desire for glory: "my ambition is unlimited; my desire to rise higher, to do more than others, insatiable. I honour endurance, perseverance, industry, talent; because these are the means by which men achieve great ends and mount to lofty eminence" (320). But the end of Brontë's novel shows how his ambition can fit within right obedience: he merely wishes, like Abdiel, to "stand approved in sight of God," as he "aims to fill a place in the first rank of those who are redeemed from the earth." His "stern" (an adjective Milton applies to Abdiel at 6.171) and exacting mastery is likewise properly positioned as paradoxical service to God; an apostle or a Greatheart may take liberties as long as he serves a higher purpose.

Jane reluctantly admires this warfaring spirit when she first senses it in St. John, opposing it to the passivity of domestic affairs.

'This parlour is not his sphere,' I reflected; 'the Himalayan ridge, or Caffre bush, even the plague-cursed Guinea Coast swamp, would suit him better. Well may he eschew the calm of domestic life; it is not his element; there his faculties stagnate—they cannot develop or appear to advantage. It is in scenes of strife and danger—where courage is proved, and energy exercised, and fortitude tasked—that he will speak and move, the leader and superior.' (335)

This need for "strife and danger" raises a difficulty when read against Jane's eventual happy marriage to Rochester; the "calm of domestic life" is no sufficient trial for right obedience. Jerome Beaty tries to soothe this annoyance by claiming that Jane merely has a different "way to salvation." St. John's path may "lie through self-denial, self-sacrifice, martyrdom," but Jane's "lies through everyday, domestic life" (499-500). But reading through Abdiel makes clear that Brontë praises in St. John not his abject self-denial, but his aggressive self-insistence in obedience to God, and furthermore shows that women, "just as men do," suffer if they lack such vigorous trials.

Indeed, Jane's description of her marriage seems almost to highlight the lack of exercise for virtue; once Jane ceases her rebellions, her liberty seems almost empty, and the "perfect concord" (384) between her and Rochester substitutes poorly for right obedience. Milton reminds us that "that which purifies us is triall, and triall is by what is contrary," while virtue without trial "is but a blank virtue, not a pure" (*Areopagitica* 1006). Jane's obedience is too easy after her marriage; "[n]ever did I weary of reading to him," she protests, "never did I weary of conducting him where he wished to go: of doing for him what he wished to be done" (384). Her service tends to erase her individuality, not exalt it; as "[n]o woman was ever nearer to her mate than I am; ever more absolutely bone of his bone and flesh of his flesh" (384). Compare that self-abnegation to Jane's earlier pride in her ability to separate herself from her employer's authority:

'I like to serve you, sir, and obey you in all that is right."
'Precisely, I see you do. I see genuine contentment in your gait and mien, your eye and face, when you are helping me and pleasing me— working for me, and with me, in, as you characteristically say, *"all that is right"*: for if I bid you do what you thought wrong [...] [you] would then turn to me, quiet and pale, and would say, "No, sir; that is impossible: I cannot do it, because it is wrong;" and would become immutable as a fixed star.' (185)

Here, to reject patriarchal authority in the service of God is "characteristically" Jane; she maintains her character only by right obedience, submission through rebellion. Nancy Armstrong makes a valid point when saying that *Jane Eyre*'s seeming marital bliss is best read as "claustrophobic," as a "gated community" that shuts out danger by embracing gender roles (535-536), and it is possible that the concluding turn to St. John's Indian mission reveals Jane's longing and appreciation for a moral warfare no longer available to her.

Of course, it might be argued that Milton's model of the warfaring Christian denies right obedience to Jane and all her gender from the very beginning, given the poet's description of Adam and Eve:

> [...] both
> Not equal as their sex not equal seemed:
> For contemplation he and valour formed,
> For softness she and sweet attractive grace:
> He for God only, she for God in him.
> His fair large front and eye sublime declared
> Absolute rule [...].
> [. . . . .]
> [Eve's somewhat disheveled hair] implied
> Subjection [...]. (4.295-308)

In this passage, Adam alone has the reason to distinguish between valid and invalid authority, and the valor to withstand trial; Eve, meanwhile, has to approach God through a human intermediary and seems predisposed to a very un-Abdielian meekness (she later says to Adam, "God is thy law, thou mine. To know no more / Is woman's happiest knowledge and her praise" [4.637-38]). But we can productively read Brontë as revising Milton's model and defending women's capacity for right obedience. James Diedrick persuasively argues that *Jane Eyre* articulates Mary Wollstonecraft's revolutionary "wish that women 'may every day grow more and more masculine,'" here meaning more *rational* (Diedrick 24, citing Wollstonecraft 11). Indeed, the ideas of Wollstonecraft's 1792 *A Vindication of the Rights of Woman* help Brontë build a heroine who connects directly to God through her own reason. Wollstonecraft wishes women were less like "the brutes who are dependent upon the reason of man," calling for them to "attain conscious dignity by feeling themselves only dependent on God" (40). Just so, Brontë's Jane attains a hard-fought dignity by breaking free of masculine reason to insist on her own *direct* right obedience, becoming "immutable as a fixed star" in the face of invalid and intermediate authority.

If we are convinced, finally, that Abdiel serves as *Jane Eyre*'s model for right obedience, we may laugh at the irony of Jane's response to Rochester when he looks forward to their honeymoon.

'I shall revisit [Europe] healed and cleansed, with a very angel as my comforter.'
I laughed at him as he said this. 'I am not an angel,' I asserted; 'and I will not be one till I die: I will be myself. Mr. Rochester, you must not want or expect anything celestial of me—for you will not get it, any more than I will get it of you: which I do not at all anticipate.' (221)

The angelic and celestial are here figured as mirages of fairy-tale perfection; Jane is accusing Rochester of a reality-defying and self-deluding flattery. On the same page, she scolds him for offering to over-dress her in satin and lace and for ignoring the likelihood that his passion for her will fade. She thus rejects the temptations of perfection, choosing to face the world honestly. It is heartbreaking to realize that the married Jane at the novel's end lacks the opportunity to make any such distinction, for her happiness *is* perfect. Unlike St. John, she has no cause for struggle, no means of trial, no strife or danger against which to rebel in right obedience. She has become a vision of celestial joy: safe, contented, pleased to "yield" to her husband, forever allowed to "indulge [her] sweetest wishes" in serving him (384), angelic indeed. Abdiel, by contrast, seems almost human.

Notes

1.   Scholars too often dichotomize self-actualization and Christian obedience in *Jane Eyre*. John Maynard reads too much "irony" and "ambivalence" into the final tribute to St. John, suggesting that Jane tries to "dethron[e] masculine religion" in order to privilege her own "self-realization" (204), but I think attending to the Abdiel model reveals how self-realization can occur even under divine authority. David Jasper helpfully points out the "daring exchange of religion and Romanticism" (221) that allows Jane rightly to obey *her own* vision of God. This liberty lets Jane submit to the "Mother" spirit, who tells her to "flee temptation" (272) as she leaves Thornfield, and also to the "work of nature" (358) that brings Rochester's cry of "Jane!" to Moor House.

2.   See Carol Blessing for how Gilbert and Gubar's reading spawned a scholarly war over Milton's supposed misogyny (or his proto-feminism); intertextual critics may have overlooked Abdiel simply because Eve and her fraught interactions with Satan and Adam fit better into that conflict. For example, Jeffrey Cass finds that Jane "constructs her own identity" (197) by following the feminist pattern of Eve's "fiercely independent" separation from Adam. Eberhart does glimpse in Jane "a recurrent figure in Milton's poetry—the single, uncorrupted chaste spirit among the throngs of fallen humanity" (81), but turns to *Comus's* Lady, not Abdiel, for her model.

3.   A full treatment of obedience, or even of Abdiel, in *Paradise Lost* is beyond the scope of this essay, but see especially Michael Schoenfeldt's discussion of how Milton ties "the achievement of liberty to the performance of obedience" (366) through Abdiel's "active, willed, rational choice" (376). See also Margaret Olofson Thickstun on Abdiel's rejection of conformity (53-70).

Works Cited

Armstrong, Nancy. "Gender Must Be Defended." *The South Atlantic Quarterly* 111.3 (2012):529-47.

Beaty, Jerome. "St. John's Way and the Wayward Reader." *Jane Eyre*. Ed. Richard J. Dunn. New York: Norton, 2001. 491-503.

Betsinger, Sue Ann. "*Jane Eyre* and the Orphan's 'Mother.'" *Brontë Studies* 29 (2004): 111-23.

Blessing, Carol. "Gilbert and Gubar's Daughters: *The Madwoman in the Attic*'s Spectre in Milton Studies." *Gilbert and Gubar's* The Madwoman in the Attic *After Thirty Years*. Ed. Annette R. Federico. Columbia, MO: U of Missouri P, 2009. 60-75.

Brontë, Charlotte. *Jane Eyre. An Autobiography*. Ed. Margaret Smith. Oxford: Oxford UP, 1980.

_____. *Jane Eyre*. Ed. Richard J. Dunn. New York: Norton, 2001.

Cass, Jeffrey. "Miltonic Orientalism: *Jane Eyre* and the Two Dalilas." *Dickens Studies Annual* 33 (2003): 191-213.

Daniel, Clay. "Jane Eyre's *Paradise Lost*." *Dickens Studies Annual* 38 (2007): 93-114.

Diedrick, James. "*Jane Eyre* and *A Vindication of the Rights of Woman*." *Approaches to Teaching* Jane Eyre. Eds. Diane Long Hoeveler and Beth Lau. New York: MLA, 1993. 22-28.

Durham, Charles W. "'To Stand Approv'd in Sight of God': Abdiel, Obedience, and Hierarchy in *Paradise Lost*." *Milton Quarterly* 26.1 (1992): 15-20.

Eberhart, Connie L. "Jane Eyre—A Daughter of the Lady in Milton's *Comus*." *The University of Mississippi Studies in English* 8 (1990): 80-91.

Gilbert, Sandra M. and Susan Gubar. *The Madwoman in the Attic: The Woman Writer and the Nineteenth-Century Literary Imagination*. New Haven: Yale UP, 2000.

Jasper, David. "Religion." *The Brontës In Context*. Ed. Marianne Thormählen. Cambridge, UK: Cambridge UP, 2012. 217-23.

Maynard, John. "The Brontës and Religion." *The Cambridge Companion to the Brontës*. Ed. Heather Glen. Cambridge, UK: Cambridge UP, 2002. 192-213.

Milton, John. *Areopagitica. The Riverside Milton*. Ed. Roy Flannagan. Boston: Houghton Mifflin, 1998. 997-1024.

_____. *Paradise Lost*. Ed. Gordon Teskey. New York: Norton, 2005.

Schoenfeldt, Michael. "Obedience and Autonomy in *Paradise Lost*." *A Companion to Milton*. Ed. Thomas N. Corns. Oxford: Blackwell, 2001. 363-79.

Thickstun, Margaret Olofson. *Milton's* Paradise Lost*: Moral Education*. New York: Palgrave, 2007.

Wollstonecraft, Mary. *A Vindication of the Rights of Women*. Ed. Deidre Shauna Lynch. New York: Norton, 2009.

Abrupt, Absurd, Unconventional: Jane and Rochester Against the Victorian Conversational Landscape _____

Cala Zubair

Jane Eyre is an unconventional heroine who finds herself drawn to her unconventional employer, Mr. Rochester. Charlotte Brontë constructs their eventual, transgressive union through transgressive conversation and the shared style they adopt: frank, sincere, and on equal footing. This comes, however, at the cost of much discursive work. During their first few interactions, Jane and Rochester negotiate the terms of their talk, often dispensing with formalities, foregoing conventional niceties, and battling over "abrupt" and "absurd" tones. This essay examines the way each character regulates the other's language in order to agree upon an egalitarian style. This unconventional style secures the bonds of their relationship, defying rigid Victorian class boundaries, in contrast to Brontë's depiction of divisive, non-egalitarian styles of conversation.

The study of discourse, and specific types of discourse such as conversational interaction, has long garnered attention from linguists interested in studying spoken language, beginning with studies in the 1960s and 1970s (Garfinkel; Goffman; Sacks, Schegloff, and Jefferson). While few linguists have applied the analytical tools developed for spoken language and the field of linguistics to analyses of language used in creative fiction, careful attention to dialogue in fiction involves treatment of many of the same linguistic variables studied during spoken interaction: speaker turn-taking, control over topic of conversation, repetition in sentence structure, and self-interruption or self-repair. This essay builds on linguists' attention to spoken language by analyzing some of these aspects of conversation, while paying specific attention to typification and metalanguage. Using the research of linguists Agha and Jaworksi, Coupland, and Galasinski, this essay will explore the ways Jane and Rochester frame and provide commentary on each other's conversational styles ("typification") through explicit labels and descriptive terms (otherwise known as "metalanguage," or language describing types of language and its function within the discursive context). Considering this within the broader scope of Victorian models of social class equality, this essay also argues that through her characters, Brontë reveals her own ideologies about agreeable versus disagreeable conversational styles and the importance of developing shared, egalitarian styles of talk.

Rochester as Changeful and Abrupt

After Jane's first official meeting with Mr. Rochester, the first informal meeting having happened by accident when Mr. Rochester's horse slipped on ice in the vicinity of Jane's nightly wanderings, Jane comments to Mrs. Fairfax, Thornfield's housekeeper and manager: "'He is very changeful and abrupt'" (Brontë 129). She asserts this analysis in response to Mrs. Fairfax's assessment that "'Mr. Rochester is not strikingly peculiar'" (Brontë 129). On the contrary, through Jane's description, Brontë presents an opportunity for readers to notice a pronounced markedness in Mr. Rochester, ·emplified in his early interactions with Jane.

~hester initiates their first official meeting through his "Let Miss Eyre be seated'" (Brontë 122). He then orders ʒ is asked to serve. When Rochester's ward, Adèle, ‿..t, Rochester suggests with "dark, irate, and piercing" ↳ that Jane perhaps wanted a gift: "'Did you expect a present, Miss Eyre? Are you fond of gifts?'" (Brontë 123). When Jane is not baited into expressing offense or contempt at the assumption, Rochester "takes his tea in silence" with a "'humph!'" (Brontë 223). He then proceeds to lead an interrogation of Jane and her past, asking questions that range from Jane's parents and relatives, to the specifics of her stay at Lowood School, to her experience in society. Jane's metalinguistic labels "changeful" and "abrupt," therefore, follow a conversation amongst Jane, Mrs. Fairfax, Adèle and Mr. Rochester, in which Rochester asserts his authority by dominating the conversation. He maintains control of the topics and turns of their conversation, alternating between command and question. He offers explicit assessments of Jane and her background, and he frames the structure of the interaction to elicit the information he desires.

The overall structure of their first meeting, in fact, can be divided into three parts. The first part of the interaction includes Adèle and Mrs. Fairfax, though Rochester speaks with Jane briefly. He then pauses and drinks his tea and begins a longer conversation, ending this by ordering Jane to the piano and offering a critique of her art. Finally, Rochester closes the long exchange by noticing that Jane has failed to put Adèle to bed, wishes everyone good night, and makes "a movement of hand towards the door," indicating he is tired of their company (Brontë 129). Table 1 below breaks up the interaction into three parts to better observe the different functions of the interaction. First, Rochester is simply becoming acquainted with his guests after returning from his journey. Once he takes his tea, though, he switches to a verbal interrogation of Jane, ending with his command for her to perform and display her artwork. Line numbers below count each time a character speaks, beginning with Rochester's opening command for Jane to sit and ending with his dismissal of his interlocutors. Note that part two of the interchange consists of a verbal appraisal through Rochester's numerous questions and is thus labeled "interrogation." Part three consists of a more physical assessment through Jane's piano recital and drawings and is labeled "evaluation."

Table 1. Interactional Structure of First Official Meeting

(Bronte 122-129)	Part I	Part II	Part III
	Lines 1-14	Lines 15-61	Lines 62-89
Primary participants	Rochester, Adèle, Mrs. Fairfax, Jane	Jane and Rochester	Rochester, Adèle, Mrs. Fairfax, Jane
Primary function & topics	Introduction: discussion of gifts	Interrogation: Jane's background	Evaluation: Piano recital and art critique

Table 2 builds from Table 1 by providing a more quantifiable understanding of Jane's typification of Rochester as changeful and abrupt, focusing solely on part two of their long interchange, the interrogation (lines 15-26). Exclusively involving Jane and Rochester taking short successive turns in speaking, the documented segment gives a closer look at the function of their talk. Each sentence a speaker utters is marked by a new line number and tagged with descriptors, such as "command," "question" (a request for information), "answer," and "evaluation" (where two labels may apply, both are listed). These labels characterize the illocutionary force (the function or contextual effect) of a speaker's utterance, chosen after carefully considering the functional range of sentences' structure in the dialogue.

Table 2. Rochester's Interrogation

Line number	Speaker	Function of sentence	Text (Brontë 124)
15	Rochester	command	Come to the fire.
16	Rochester	question	You have been resident in my house three months?
17	Jane	answer	Yes, sir.
18	Rochester	question	And you came from?
19	Jane	answer	From Lowood school, in—shire
20	Rochester	evaluation & question	Ah! a charitable concern. How long were you there?
21	Jane	answer	Eight years.
22	Rochester	evaluation	Eight years! You must be tenacious of life…
22 (cont.)	Rochester	question	Who are your parents?
23	Jane	answer	I have none.
24	Rochester	evaluation & question	Nor ever had, I suppose: do you remember them?
25	Jane	answer	No.
26	Rochester	evaluation	I thought not.

The question and answer sequence shown in Table 2 resembles an interrogation. Rochester, as the dominant speaker, asks questions and offers evaluation, and Jane, as the non-dominant speaker, answers. Indeed, Jane's sole role here is respondent, while Rochester cross-examines his witness, wavering between question and evaluative statement. In two subsequent segments from part two of their interaction (lines 30-37 and lines 42-48), listed in Table 3 below, Brontë's dialogue similarly places Jane in the role of respondent and Rochester in the role of interrogator.

Table 3. Interrogation Continued

Line number	Speaker	Description of sentence	Text (Brontë 124-125)
30	Rochester	question	Well....if you disown your parents, you must have some sort of kinsfolk: uncles and aunts?
31	Jane	answer	No: none that I ever saw.
32	Rochester	question	And your home?
33	Jane	answer	I have none.
34	Rochester	question	Where do your brothers and sisters live?
35	Jane	answer	I have no brothers and sisters.
36	Rochester	question	Who recommended you to come here?
37	Jane	answer	I advertised, and Mrs. Fairfax answered my advertisement.
42	Rochester	question	Miss Eyre, have you ever lived in a town?
43	Jane	answer	No, sir.
44	Rochester	question	Have you seen much of society?
45	Jane	answer	None but the pupils and teachers of Lowood; and now the inmates of Thornfield.
46	Rochester	question	Have you read much?
47	Jane	answer & evaluation	Only such books as came in my way; and they have not been numerous, or very learned.
48	Rochester	evaluation	You have lived the life of a nun...

Table 3 exhibits a similar question-answer sequence as in Table 2. In lines 30-37, Jane answers Rochester's questions tersely, as in lines 15-26 (Table 2). By lines 42-48, though, her responses both become lengthier and more evaluative. In line 45, Jane's phrase detailing her inexperience in society to include "the inmates of

Thornfield" is obvious and therefore unnecessarily detailed (Brontë 125). Then, in line 47, her response includes an evaluation. She states that the books she has read are not "numerous" or "very learned" (Brontë 125). As if anticipating Rochester's evaluative comment, Jane inserts one of her own. Forty-eight lines into an eighty-nine line dialogue and Rochester's abrupt questioning has perhaps had an effect on Jane. This section of the interrogation ends with Rochester's heuristic summation: "You have lived the life of a nun" (Brontë 125).

In addition to evaluations made during the interrogation sequences above, elsewhere Rochester doles out his opinion freely. He offers additional assessments of Jane such as: "'you have rather the look of another world,'" "'you are very cool,'" and "'that sounds blasphemous.'" Moreover, he inserts several commands into the conversation. He ends his verbal investigation (part two of this first interaction) by telling Jane to "'go, then, into the library; take a candle with you; leave the door open; sit down to the piano, and play a tune'" (Brontë 126). Without softening words such as "please" or phrasing his commands as requests, Rochester's "go," "take," leave," "sit," and "play" make him master to Jane's puppet (Brontë 126). He decides her course of action: when she should perform, when she should end her impromptu concert, and what the value of it is: "'like any other English school girl: perhaps rather better than some, but not well'" (Brontë 126).

Similarly, Rochester examines Jane's artwork. Beginning once again with an order for Jane to "'fetch'" her portfolio, he expresses doubt that the contents are original work, and warns her that he "'can recognize patchwork'" (Brontë 126). After "deliberately [scrutinizing] each sketch and painting," Rochester decides that Jane has "secured the shadow of her thought; but no more" (Brontë 126). Not only assuming superior insight in regards to art, Rochester here also assumes superior insight into Jane, her intentions and visions when creating the work. He concludes dismissively by telling Jane she has "'not enough of the artist's skill and science'" (Brontë 126). Then, as if Jane were in control of the situation, Rochester ends their exchange with a reprimand for keeping Adèle awake too long.

After such a prolonged, variegated interaction, even orphaned, inexperienced Jane is able to notice that Rochester is "changeful" and "abrupt." He asserts control over conversational topics and dominates through his commands and evaluations.

Considering the power structure implicit in Jane's position as a young female employed as a governess by an older male, one might be tempted to think that Rochester's insolent style is not uncommon for an employer conversing with his ward's governess; and perhaps Jane refrains from harsher descriptions because of their societal positions. Jane's situation does not require particular respect or deference. Indeed, Jane herself expresses surprise at a later meeting when Rochester shows concern over how his style affects her ("very few masters would trouble themselves to inquire whether or not their paid subordinates were piqued or hurt by their orders" (Brontë 136). Yet, as described in the following section, Rochester himself indicates, at various points in his discourse, that despite the tacit power of his position, his way of questioning, commanding, and scrutinizing is in need of alteration.

Rochester's Repairs: Against the Backdrop of Victorian Conventions

Rochester's metalinguistic assessments of his own style, which occur when he interrupts himself mid-thought or mid-sentence, indicate that his manner of address should be corrected. His self-interruptions and self-repairs, notated in the text with parentheses, commas, and dashes, are a common feature of spoken language (Fromkin; Schiffrin), used by speakers as a means to evaluate themselves in accordance with politeness standards (Brown).

In the following example, Rochester's self-interruption begins with the phrase "'excuse my tone of command,'" evaluating his own tone as potentially offensive, though the apologetic nature of the utterance is then diminished by his lack of intention to alter his tone: "'—(Excuse my tone of command: I am used to say "Do this," and it is done: I cannot alter my customary habits for one new inmate.'" (Brontë 126). He utters this phrase during his first meeting with Jane, discussed above, extending an explanation of his tone after he produces a long string of questions ("'what age were you when you went to Lowood,'" "'and you stayed there eight years...,'" "'And now what did you learn at Lowood,'" "'can you play?'") and commands ("'come to the fire,'" "'go into the library'") (Brontë 124-126). Separated from the surrounding text with both dashes and parentheses, this statement's larger contribution is to hint that Rochester's style is unacceptable. The indirect apology tempered by the lack of intention to change, of course, is more related to Rochester's contradictory, divided character. Nonetheless, combined with Jane's observations of the peculiarity of his style, Rochester's interruption simultaneously reinforces his unconventional style and provides clues about the type of language Brontë favors. Instead of abrupt tones of command, Rochester should use inviting phrases.

In the discourse immediately preceding Rochester's above listed commentary on his own conversational style, he utters what is a more stereotypical self-repair in spoken language—that is, he re-phrases and changes the structure of his words: "'Go into the library – I mean, if you please –'" (Brontë 126). Surrounded by dashes, Rochester's self-repair of "I mean, if you please" changes his sentence from a command, where he used the imperative form of the verb "go," to a request, where the inclusion of the softening phrase "if you please" makes his sentence more polite (Brontë 126). This rephrasing shows readers how Rochester is beyond the bound of convention, additionally informing readers about Brontë's perception of Victorian politeness standards. Commands, which index unequal power structures and promote class divisions, are harsh and noticeable. Requests with the added use of "please," which make room for the other interlocutor's voice and preferences, are more agreeable.

During their second extended conversation, where Rochester attempts to draw Jane out by making her talk, Rochester also engages in revealing metacommentary and self-repair. He stops himself after two consecutive commands of "speak" and one assessment of Jane as "dumb" (here, he means something more akin to silent) and admits to Jane that he frames his requests in an "absurd, almost insolent form" (Brontë 135). He begs her pardon. By their second interaction, then, Rochester resorts to a truer apology (a request for forgiveness without a promise not to change), and readers witness the negotiation of style between the two interlocutors. But if Rochester's imperatives are abrupt, his questions absurd, and his insults insolent, he alone earns these titles, against the grain of conventional standards.

Jane, Jane, Not Too Plain

Jane's conversational style, unlike Rochester's in his early interactions, rests on the precept that she wishes to be respectful and polite, even if she is direct, unconventional, and inexperienced. Her position as governess is Jane's first attempt at independence and self-sufficiency, and Brontë writes her in her new role with the self-conscious unassuredness a reader might expect of an eighteen-year-old orphan as she first comes into her own. As Jane embarks on her journey from Lowood, she describes herself as "an inexperienced youth…quite alone in the world…cut adrift from every connection, uncertain whether the port to which it is bound can be reached" (Brontë 95). Jane's reflection of her naïveté spills over into her interactions, characterizing her own awkward style through moments where she checks herself against the normative style she fails to achieve.

When she first meets Mrs. Fairfax, Jane stops herself from satisfying her curiosity about her new pupil, Adèle Varens, telling readers, "I should have followed up my first inquiry by asking in what way Miss Varens was connected with her: but I recollected it was not polite to ask too many questions" (Brontë 98). Additionally, she is cautious over how to respond to Rochester during their second meeting. Despite his constant goading, Jane does not want him to think her own inquiries rude (Brontë 134). When she feels she has erred in giving a quick reply of "No, sir" to his question of whether or not he is handsome, she tells readers in her own internal dialogue that she should have deliberated more carefully before answering (Brontë 133). Had she done so, she may have arrived at a rejoinder she was more satisfied with, one that was "conventionally vague and polite" (Brontë 133). Thus in this interactive moment, Jane expresses a desire to speak respectfully by being "conventionally vague and polite" (Brontë 133).

At this point, Rochester stubbornly clings to his own insolent manner by dwelling on Jane's point that he is not handsome, but Jane still shows a desire to follow politeness conventions. She begs Rochester's pardon and offers him an apology for being "too plain": "'Mr. Rochester, allow me to disown my first answer: I intended no pointed repartee: it was only a blunder'" (Brontë 133). Her use of the modal verbs (verbs that express alternate meanings and intentions apart from the occurring reality of a situation) "should" and "ought to have" point towards uncertainty and different possibilities (Brontë 133). They indicate that Jane's candid response to Rochester comes from inexperience, which she is quick to take responsibility for. Rochester, though, interested in her unconventional response, refuses to take her apology as an opportunity to move on. After noting she is "if not blunt...at least brusque" he seems more enraged by her attempt at "softening the previous outage," at trying to make amends by aligning herself with politeness standards (Brontë 133).

Later, during their second arranged encounter (accidental meetings discounted), Rochester asks Jane, "will you consent to dispense with a great many conventional forms and phrases?" (Brontë 137). Though Jane admits to rather liking "informality," she tempers Rochester's expectations by expressing dislike for "insolence" (Brontë 137). A jab at Rochester's admittedly "absurd, almost insolent form" of conversing, Jane's regulatory stance in response to Rochester's request separates agreeable from disagreeable (Brontë 135). Jane lacks convention, but still wishes to be respectful. As Rochester tells readers, the "substance of her speech" is something "ones does not often see" (Brontë 137). It is peculiar in being "frank," but it is still "sincere" (Brontë 137). Jane is unconventional, but in an admirable way. Her politeness and desire to avoid offense contribute to a transgressive style that is liberating in the way it champions fairness.

Unpleasant Styles and the Victorious Jane

Miss Blanche Ingram, on the other hand, an accomplished, high society lady and the would-be future wife of Rochester, has no interest in fairness or equality. Just as Brontë characterizes the positive aspects of Jane's direct, open, and uncensored speech, she uses Blanche to demonstrate a disagreeable style that is restricted, elitist, and non-egalitarian. As Poovey's 1984 study of Victorian women writers—specifically, Mary Wollstonecraft, Mary Shelley, and Jane Austen—indicates, "doubling" of female characters was a common technique. Two women characters, portrayed as opposites, are placed in contexts where the author uses them to reveal and challenge normative ideological continuums (Poovey 43). Brontë does precisely this with Jane and Blanche.

Brontë hints at what a non-egalitarian discursive style might entail early on, when Rochester is describing what Jane is not: a woman whose speech demonstrates "affectation, or coldness, or coarse-minded apprehension of one's meaning" (Brontë 137). These are descriptors for a style Jane is not proficient in, but which Miss Blanche Ingram is perfectly fluent, making her an exemplary foil for Jane's frankness and sincerity. Blanche embodies coldness with her "spiteful antipathy" to Adèle, and the way she scorns to touch Jane with "the hem of her robes," making every attempt to withhold her gaze and attention from the young governess (Brontë 188). She disguises her own coarse-mindedness with conversational tricks, which Jane easily recognizes as the "vernacularly termed trailing," or playing on another's ignorance of a chosen topic to seem clever (Brontë 175). She uses words and put on airs "intended to excite" (Brontë 182). Rather than being commanded to play the piano, as Rochester commands Jane, Blanche commands Rochester to sing, so she might impress her audience with her playing (Brontë 182). Her coarse-minded affectation embodies the distastefulness of class-based interactional styles, as do Jane's conversational mêlées with Rochester.

During their second meeting, Brontë contrasts Jane's style with Rochester's insolence. Her eventual victory is a win for equal opportunity speech. Several times throughout their second interaction, Rochester orders Jane to speak: "'It would please me now to draw you out—to learn more of you—therefore speak'" (Brontë 135). Rochester's order expresses the trope that talk is connection, but Jane's response indicates that she thinks certain types of talk do not necessarily foster connection. Talk that presupposes conversational affectation should be avoided: "If he expects me to talk for the mere sake of talking and showing off, he will find he has addressed himself to the wrong person" (Brontë 135). Jane reports these words in her inner dialogue, choosing to remain silent in the face of Rochester's command to speak. She would rather bear his insults of being dumb than fall victim to ostentatious speech.

Jane also refuses to accept Rochester's "masterful" and "abrupt" style (Brontë 136). In a conversational duel akin to a physical altercation, Jane uses silence and terse answers in response to Rochester's commanding tone until her style causes him to reflect on his words, realize he is outmaneuvered, and then make forbearance so as to start conversing on shared, equal terms. The duel begins when Rochester asks Jane to agree that he may converse in a manner "a little masterful, abrupt: perhaps exacting" (Brontë 136). Jane retorts, "do as you please, sir" (Brontë 136). Her response is not an affirmation that Rochester may use a distasteful, insolent tone due to his age and experience. Rather, it puts the burden on Rochester to reflect on and account for his style. By offering a minimal response and retracting the access Rochester seeks to her opinion, Jane's brevity suggests disapproval. It also leaves Rochester unsatisfied. He calls her answer "no answer," "irritating," and "evasive" (Brontë 136). When she concedes to offer a more clear answer, her retort is a chastisement for his tone: "I don't think, sir, you have the right to command me, merely because you are older than I, or because you have seen more of the world than I have" (Brontë 136). Her disagreement with Rochester causes him to quickly lose his footing. Despite his superior status as Jane's employer, and the relative newness of their acquaintance, Rochester's commands give way to Jane's composure. Transgressing normative boundaries, Jane will speak with Rochester only when treated as an equal.

Rochester later makes a request: "you must still agree to receive my orders now and then...will you?" (Brontë 136). He begins this phrase with the use of "must," implying he may give Jane another order. His order is retracted when he again expresses a need for Jane to agree, turning his command into a request with "will you?" Rochester seeks common ground by conceding that he will only give orders "now and then," other times Jane might expect a question, request, or discussion, against the grains of an authoritarian employer-employee, class-differentiated relationship. Jane has turned Rochester's abrupt style into a more accommodating discourse.

Nor will Jane rest easy in her unconventional style if it at all resembles Rochester's often assumed absurdity. Above all else, Jane values "no snivel! –no sentiment!—nor regret! ...only sense and resolution" (Brontë 163). She ends her second exchange with Rochester when his language becomes "enigmatical," explaining that she has "no wish to talk nonsense," "deeming it useless to continue a discourse which was all darkness" (Brontë 140-1). Later in the text, when Rochester dresses as a gypsy and "talks nonsense," once again attempting to draw Jane out, Jane's primary worry is that she may have fallen into absurdity. At this point in Jane's narrative, Rochester has very nearly done away with commands, and though offering few apologies elsewhere in the text, he seeks to make amends for tricking Jane into thinking he was a gypsy. But she will only forgive him "if, on reflection...[she finds she has] fallen into no great absurdity" (Brontë 205). Young, inexperienced, and unconventional she may be, but Jane is, as Rochester observes, no "talking fool" (Brontë 153). Jane's lack of convention is positive, powerful, and fairness-affirming.

Conversational Equality and Brontë's Positive Unconventional

Despite the way Jane and Rochester's early interactions typify the importance of avoiding certain conversational styles (Rochester's abruptness, insolence, and absurdity, and Miss Ingram's coarse-minded ostentation), Brontë does not necessarily propose a dislike for talk in general. Towards the novel's end, Jane begins to recover from her failed attempt at marriage through talk. Staying with Diana and Mary Rivers, Jane finds "a reviving pleasure" of intercourse (Brontë 355). She takes "full satisfaction to discuss with them during the evening" what she had read during the day (Brontë 356). She delights in "their discourse, witty, pithy, original" (Brontë 401) and prefers "listening to, and sharing in it [their discourse], to doing anything else" (Brontë 401).

Talk is moreover the primary way Jane and Rochester form a close relationship. In their second conversation, rather than ordering Jane to leave to put Adèle to bed, this time Rochester keeps her from her task, hoping for the future days when Jane will be able to speak freely, and confessing delight that he finds "'it impossible to be conventional'" with Jane (Brontë 141). He later admires her "'peculiar mind; it is a unique one,'" appreciating that Jane listens quietly to his secrets (Brontë 146). As the two become intertwined, Jane depicts their attachment through talk—not cold, insolent talk that differentiates the status of the speakers, but sincere and meaningful talk that promotes uniform speaker standing.

As stated above, after Jane's victory in several interchanges of their second meeting, Rochester has understood that his harsh style will not work with Jane. Instead, during later encounters, he seeks her out as confidante, discussing his past with Céline Varens, Adèle's mother, and his experiences and travels in the world. He cultivates an "ease of manner" that frees Jane from "painful restraint" (Brontë 149). "The friendly frankness, as correct as cordial," draws Jane to him (Brontë 149). Rochester determines that Jane's "gravity, considerateness, and caution were made to be the recipients of secrets" and creates a bond with her through this new style of conversing (Brontë 146): "The more you and I converse, the better; for while I cannot blight you, you may refresh me" (Brontë 146). And Jane does not grow weary of playing agent of salvation by listening to Rochester's confessions and stories, but rather relishes in them as an affirmation of her self-restraint: "The confidence he had thought fit to repose in me seemed a tribute to my discretion" (Brontë 148). She takes "keen delight in receiving the new ideas he offered, in imagining the new pictures he portrayed" (Brontë 149).

Thus to succeed in transgressing the social boundaries that might keep them apart, Jane and Rochester must also succeed in transgressing the boundaries of normative speech styles. After engaging in her conversational duels with Rochester to achieve a shared style, Jane describes how her interactions with him blossom into a more "uniform" deportment and a closer relationship:

> He did not take fits of chilling hauteur; when he met me unexpectedly, the encounter seemed welcome; he had always a word and sometimes a smile for me: when summoned by formal invitation to his presence, I was honored by a cordiality of reception that made me feel I really possessed the power to amuse him. (Brontë 149)

Though at this early point in their relationship Jane "talked comparatively little" (Brontë 149), after they are married, their conversations are an even better model of relational equality: "We talk, I believe, all day long: to talk to each other is but a more animated and an audible thinking" (Brontë 459). Rochester's changed style signifies the importance of conversational styles in interpersonal relationships. In conversation, as in their lives, Jane and Rochester learn to communicate "not through the medium of customs, conventionalities," but as equals (Brontë 257). To reach such relational equality and create a bond of friendship and love, Jane and Rochester had to connect in talk, which like their marriage, violated the margins of conventionality.

In painting Jane and Rochester against the backdrop of convention, Brontë provides commentary on the function of speech and communication in Victorian England. From Rochester's early conversational style, readers learn that ideal conversational partners do not give orders over requests, or make abrupt judgments on their interlocutor's personality, tastes, or background, or even sit for long periods in silence drinking tea while others await their company. From Jane, we learn that the unconventional can be admirable, so long as it lacks ostentation and demonstrates the sort of earnest intelligence that places speakers in equal standing. The two together show the power of talk in breaking rigid social boundaries to create lasting bonds.

Works Cited

Agha, Asif. *Language and Social Relations*. Cambridge: Cambridge UP, 2007.

Brontë, Charlotte. *Jane Eyre*. New York: Signet, 1997.

Brown, Penelope. *Politeness: Some Universals in Language Usage*. Cambridge: Cambridge UP, 1987.

Fromkin, Victoria. "The Non-Anomalous Nature of Anomalous Utterances." *Language* 47.1 (1971): 27-52.

Garfinkel, Harold. *Studies in Ethnomethodology*. New Jersey: Prentice Hall, 1967.

Goffman, Erving. "The Interaction Order: American Sociological Association, 1982 Presidential Address." *American Sociological Review* 48.1 (1983): 1-17.

Jaworksi, Adam, Nicholas Coupland, and Dariusz Galasinski. *Metalanguage: Social and Ideological Perspectives*. Berlin: Walter de Gruyter, 2004.

Poovey, Mary. *The Proper Lady and the Woman Writer: Ideology as Style in the Works of Mary Wollstonecraft, Mary Shelley, and Jane Austen*. Chicago: U of Chicago P, 1984.

Sacks, Harvey, Emanuel Schegloff, and Gail Jefferson. "A Simplest Systematics for the Organization of Turn-Taking for Conversation." *Language* 50.4 (1974): 696-735.

Schiffrin, Deborah. *In Other Words*. Cambridge: Cambridge UP, 2006.

Jane Laughs Last: Developing Feminist Humor in Charlotte Brontë's *Jane Eyre*

Amanda T. Smith

Charlotte Brontë's *Jane Eyre* is not a funny novel, at least not in the way we are accustomed to encountering humor. It seems odd to call a character like Jane funny when she spends the majority of the novel struggling through physical abuse, encounters with a madwoman, and a shocking nuptial interruption. Humor, however, plays a predominant role in her development. Jane uses humor throughout her life as a means to an end as she advances from a silent, self-defensive sense of irony to a controlled use of competitive wit and, eventually, public expression. In an era in which feminine perfection was synonymous with shrinking, both the literal corseting of waistlines and the metaphorical biting of tongues, Brontë provides a heroine who grows stronger and louder with each page. In forming Jane, Brontë anticipates Virginia Woolf's notion that humor serves as "a knife that both prunes and trains" (60). Instead of cutting herself down to size in acquiescence to societal imperatives, she wields wit against Victorian social and literary conventions. Her humor ties her to Bertha Rochester, whose laughter marks her presence in the novel and provides a disruptive escape from containment. While Bertha's lack of control ultimately confines her within patriarchal fears of the feminine hysteric, Jane presents an alternative vision of a laughing woman in control, one who gains the critical distance necessary to question the validity of those forces controlling her life.

Jane Eyre's anger and passion—traits that modern feminist critics celebrate—caused some of Brontë's contemporary reviewers to recoil. In the *Quarterly Review* of 1848, Elizabeth Rigby calls Jane, "a decidedly vulgar-minded woman—one whom we should not care for as an acquaintance, whom we should not seek as a friend, whom we should not desire for a relation, and whom we should scrupulously avoid for a governess" (qtd. in Allott 110). Modern critics view Jane's aggression more positively, as representative of systemic, but often silenced, outrage experienced by repressed women. Sandra M. Gilbert and Susan Gubar, for instance, read Jane's development as "a story of enclosure and escape" and "a distinctively female *Bildungsroman* in which the problems encountered by the protagonist … are symptomatic of difficulties Everywoman in a patriarchal society must meet and overcome" (339). However, these critics overlook the ways Jane learns to use humor to sustain her in these "female realities" (339). Mikhail Bakhtin describes humor as holding "the remarkable power of making an object come up close, of drawing it into a zone of crude contact where one can finger it familiarly on all sides … dismember it, lay it bare and expose it" (23). Traditionally, the humorist is in a dominant position; however, as Bakhtin, Regina Barreca, Nancy Armstrong and several other humor theorists have noted, when the marginalized appropriates the privileges of laughter, revolutionary social critique can occur. By the end of the novel, Jane discovers not only the private pleasure her wit can afford, but also how to use humor to expose artifices propping up Victorian society. Jane's transition from vulnerable blankness to crafted identity is punctuated by developmental stages: from untrained impudence to self-defense, aggression, seduction, and, eventually, fully-realized pleasure and public impact.

Impudent Humor: Jane's Childhood at Gateshead

Creating a new story for women begins with reading the old ones at a slant. Young Jane embodies this first stage of rebellion as she effortlessly reads ironic subtexts that those in positions of authority fail to see. Jane's talent for spotting absurdity surfaces early as a means of coping with traumas at Gateshead. Brontë sets the stage for tragedy by emphasizing Jane's "physical inferiority" and Mrs. Reed's enforcement of feminine silence: "until you can speak pleasantly, remain silent" (3-4). Like that impossible walk that begins the novel, Jane's life begins in negation and confinement. In her article, "The Goblin Ha-Ha: Hidden Smiles and Open Laughter in *Jane Eyre*," Robin Jones describes the crippling effect of this hostile environment on humor and self-expression: "[Jane's] abused childhood at Gateshead allows for no laughter and its infrequent smiles are subdued or hidden" (202). Silent though she may be,

---

Jane puts her marginal position to good use as a critical observer. Just before John Reed strikes her, Jane recalls, "I mused on the disgusting and ugly appearance of him" (7). Instead of succumbing to a paralyzing fear that would push a weaker heroine to hysterics, Jane *muses* on the flaws of her oppressor. Regina Barreca suggests that it is "[b]ecause she originates from a position handicapped by poverty and neglect" that "Jane Eyre learns to feed off an instinctive and unbridled intelligence" (61). This instinct allows Jane to observe the comic subtext and distance herself from traumatic situations. In his work on the psychological components of humor, *Jokes and Their Relation to the Unconscious*, Sigmund Freud explains that tendentious humor serves to make "our enemies small [or] inferior," which allows a cathartic release of tension (102). Freud shares a kinship with Thomas Hobbes, who claims that humor is the experience of "'sudden glory'" in the "'apprehension of some deformed thing in another' that, through comparison, suddenly reveals some eminence in the self'" (46). Though Jane does not humiliate John, she responds to his attacks with a mental triumph, albeit a fleeting one, over this first representative of masculine dominance. Jane's observations allow her to experience her anger, prevent her submission, and form the foundation for the aggressive humor she will develop as a woman.

In her initial interview with Mr. Brocklehurst, the stern headmaster of Lowood School, Jane advances from silent observation to expression. When he asks her how she intends to avoid going to hell, rather than supplying the scripted response to his catechism, Jane replies, "I must keep in good health, and not die" (34). Though still merely a child, Jane humorously cuts through the rhetoric of religious authority and reveals a subtext. Nancy Armstrong explains that the ability to read these subtexts "always identifies the female as the one with the power to determine the meaning of words and things, a power capable in certain instances of changing the nature of the words and things themselves" (205). Jane's unanticipated yet valid response exchanges the practical for the pious, thereby revealing a viable alternative narrative. Brocklehurst, unable to interpret this subtext, responds, "How can you keep in good health?

Children younger than you die daily" (34). Jane realizes that she is not "in a condition to remove his doubt," and, rather than continue the exchange, she discloses, "I only cast my eyes down … and sighed" (34). What Brocklehurst interprets as a sigh of repentance seems more like frustration at his misreading. Frances Gray argues that this type of humor arising from incongruity "may shatter our view of accepted reality, suddenly de-familiarizing a political or social system (such as patriarchy) and allowing us to perceive flaws" in what must be presumed to be infallible (32). By unintentionally undermining Brocklehurst's authority, Jane reveals an alternate text running alongside the dominant one. Though her laughter remains unexpressed, Jane's precocious responses to those dominating forces of her youth serve as effective self-preservation and signal the beginnings of transgression.

Self-Defensive Humor: An Education in Female Options at Lowood

Jane's budding ability to maintain critical distance enables her to survive the struggles that consume girls like Helen Burns at Lowood. Jane looks on as Helen numbs herself to the harsh punishments she receives, noticing, "[T]o my surprise she neither wept nor blushed: composed, though grave, she stood, the central mark of all eyes" (61). Elaine Showalter calls Helen "The Angel of Lowood" who represents "the perfect victim and the representation of the feminine spirit in the most disembodied form" (72). Jane documents this angel's worsening condition as she "was talking to herself now: she had forgotten I [Jane] could not very well understand her" (65). Helen's reactions are symptomatic of a retreat into the mind, rendering her passive in the face of oppression—an example against which Jane will define herself.

Fortunately, Miss Temple provides Jane with an alternative way of coping with patriarchal regulations. Brocklehurst scolds Miss Temple for allowing some of the girls to have, what he considers, an "excrescence of curled hair" (73). Jane focuses on Miss Temple during his tirade, noticing, "Miss Temple passed her handkerchief over her lips, as if to smooth away the involuntary smile that curled them" (73-74). Jane also conceals her own amusement at

Brocklehurst's behavior as she states, "while seeming to be busy with my sum … [I] held my slate in such a manner as to conceal my face" (75). Brocklehurst is fodder for a joke that Jane silently shares with Miss Temple. Freud describes the triangulation of two people who share a joke at a third person's expense in his analysis of tendentious joking. He explains that tendentious jokes demand three participants: the person telling the joke, the object of the joke, and a third party who laughs with the joke teller (95). The example he introduces to illustrate this point involves two men laughing at a woman. The first person thus uses humor to "strip the woman naked before the third" (95). When Miss Temple and Jane laugh at Brocklehurst's expense, they turn this triangle on its head and expose the tenuous foundations of the patriarchal restrictions he represents. Jones explains the impact of this reversal: "[I]n their cultural roles as nurturers, [women] are the repositories of aggression, not the instigators. Laughter in women is unexpected because the incongruous or the marginal aren't expected to laugh at the dominating force" (202). Jane defends herself against Brocklehurst's indoctrination by joining with another woman in questioning the validity of social mandates for feminine self-abnegation.

As promising as these reversals of power are, Miss Temple and Jane's concealed laughter renders feminist social progress incomplete. Jones characterizes Miss Temple's reaction as an instance of Jane learning "how *not* to laugh or smile" (202). Jane does observe a woman's obligation to conceal laughter; however, she also witnesses Miss Temple's defiance, particularly in terms of feeding the girls. Her performance of obedience facilitates these quiet yet vital rebellions. Through Miss Temple, Jane learns to protect herself by appearing to function within restrictive paradigms while indulging in the amusing recognition of inherent faults. Lisa Sternlieb describes this technique as Jane's "calculated harmlessness," a trait that "works as a weapon of self-defense" (471). The nourishment that Miss Temple provides and the education Jane receives at Lowood is a better understanding of the humor that comes naturally to her. This newfound knowledge enables Jane to assert what kind of woman she will be. If Helen's resignation into spiritual invisibility and Miss Temple's clever insurrection are the options available to her, Jane declares, "I was no Helen Burns" (75).

Aggressive and Seductive Humor: Jane Becomes Her Own Mistress

Humor that was once carefully concealed becomes outspoken when Jane achieves personal and financial independence as a governess at Thornfield. Jane notes the irony in her "new servitude," claiming, "There is something in that … I know there is because it does not sound too sweet; it is not like such words as Liberty, Excitement, Enjoyment, delightful sounds truly; but no more than sounds for me; and so hollow and fleeting that it is a mere waste of time to listen to them. But Servitude! That must be a matter of fact" (102). Jane's remarks smack of sarcasm, but truly the closest she can get to agency is as a servant. Mary Poovey supplies an historical perspective on this social role in her article, "The Anathematised Race: The Governess and *Jane Eyre*," explaining that the governess "was meant to police the emergence of undue assertiveness" in the children of the upper crust while not displaying "willfulness or desire herself" (170). Though denied equal freedom and class status, the governess did gain a level of access to the family usually denied to other servants. Jane's position at Thornfield, therefore, provides her with a privileged vantage point as the unobserved observer. Her name, Eyre, could signal her air-like invisibility, but it might more accurately suggest her willing (and eventually willful) transparent honesty. Brontë reverses class privilege by "allowing the codes of accepted behavior to be satirized by one who by rights should be envious, not contemptuous, of them" (Barreca 66). Suspended between family and servants, Jane is close enough to these aristocratic "codes of accepted behavior" to critique them.

Though Jane eventually privileges her romance over her career, the relationship she pursues facilitates her independence. The reciprocity between Jane and Rochester encourages her to speak what she once stifled. Readers of the novel may have found Rochester's candor with Jane surprising, but even more shocking are Jane's unflinching responses to him (Richetti 357). Jane notes, "his manner freed me from painful restraint" (180). Rochester may be another "master," but he not only offers Jane a forum for expression, he incites her aggression and desire. At first, Jane's biting candor seems as unpremeditated as it was in her childhood. She surprises Rochester and herself with her response when he asks her if she finds him handsome: "the answer somehow slipped from my tongue before I was aware: -- 'No, sir.'" (160). Rochester engages her all the more for her unusual frankness. His encouragement gives her the opportunity to express her private wit, a crucial step in realizing that she "really possessed the power to amuse" (180). Though a masculine authority sanctions this power, Jane defies the boundaries of the typical Victorian heroine by using her wit to attract her hero. Conduct book writers like James Fordyce, a contemporary of Brontë's, express the popular concern about witty women: "[N]eed I tell you, that men of the best sense have been usually averse to the thought of marrying a witty female?... we cannot be easy where we are not safe. We are never safe in the company of a critic; and almost every wit is a critic by profession" (191). However, Rochester pursues Jane *because* their relationship is more "a fencing match than a waltz" (Barreca 62). While Rochester maintains the authority of both class and gender to elevate her to his level, it is Jane's sharp wit that compels him to do so.

Even as she builds her relationship with Rochester, Jane approaches the romance plot with the same skepticism with which she views Brocklehurst's catechism. When Rochester, disguised as a fortuneteller, asks "What tale do you like best to hear?" she wryly responds, "Oh, I have not much choice! They generally run on the same theme—courtship; and promise to end in some catastrophe—marriage" (249). As marriage is traditionally the goal for nineteenth-century women, the equation of it to a catastrophe might seem incongruous until we note the irony that this institution often further confined women and spelled the ending of their story in novels (unless death provided an untimely ending). Of course, even as Jane criticizes this traditional plot, she is well on her own path to that "catastrophe." This courtship may conform to the marriage plot as delineated by Rachel Brownstein in that it "is about finding validation of one's uniqueness and importance by being singled out among other women by a man" (xv); however, by casting Jane as the romantic heroine, Brontë privileges wit over the feminine pretenses and class privilege that Blanche Ingram so masterfully performs. Brontë extends her humorous twist on the marriage plot by playing with the romantic climax as Jane spars instead of swooning during Rochester's proposal: he asks "Do you doubt me, Jane?" and she replies, "Entirely" (320). He continues, "You have no faith in me?" and she matches him: "Not a whit" (320). Brontë jars romantic expectations as she casts the hero as the straight man in Jane's joke. Just as young Jane proves that there are multiple ironic responses to Brocklehurst's catechism, mature Jane shows us that there is more than one way to receive a proposal.

Jane's playful sparring turns into real aggression when romance threatens her independence. Some critics see Rochester's teasing as "a source of power, and therefore … an evasion of that equality in which he claims to believe" rather than playful reciprocity (Gilbert and Gubar 354). Mary Poovey paints Jane as a victim that "Rochester wantonly taunts … with his power" (181). Rochester clearly teases Jane; however, these assessments fail to consider Jane's maturing skill in taunting him right back. Jane's humor becomes most aggressive when Rochester attempts to doll her up as his bride. Refusing both the bridal costume and the "bathos of sentiment," Jane exposes her "hard—very flinty" side and skillfully tests her "needle of repartee" (Brontë 344).

Well before feminist critic Judith Wilt asserted, "comedy allows [a woman] to show the occasional flash of steel under the yarn, needling while knitting" (176), Jane realized the power of anger edged with wit. Rather than submerging her identity in her fiancé, she challenges Rochester's romantic casting. When he suggests that she will be his "angel," she snaps, "I am not an angel … and I will not be one till I die: I will be myself" (327). Despite loving him, Jane responds to Rochester with the same irreverence with which she told Brocklehurst she would avoid hell—by not dying. Nettled by this fraught pet name, Jane deflates Rochester's sentimentality with logic, the antithesis of romance, as she cleverly reminds him that death is the prerequisite to becoming an angel.

Jane succeeds in making Rochester "cross and crusty," but is rewarded for her insolence because "a lamb-like submission and turtle-dove sensibility, while fostering his despotism more, would have pleased his judgment, satisfied his common-sense, and even suited his taste, less" (345). While Jane consistently expresses aggression through humor, she now realizes the seductive power of her wit. Some critics cast Jane's taunts as ultimately conservative. Patricia Meyer Spacks, for instance, claims, "[S]he delights in manipulating him, teasing him to the point of anger because she thus maintains his interest and suits his taste," thereby expressing "desperation," not power (63-64). Heather Glen acknowledges the irreverence of Jane's wit, but reads the sparring as more combative than romantic: "The love between Jane and Rochester is portrayed less as a growing concord than as a continual struggle for dominance" (55). However, Jane does not torment Rochester solely to beguile or defeat him; she pleases herself as she "laughed in [her] sleeve at his menaces" (345). Exchanging slates for sleeves, Jane conceals her laughter just as she did at Lowood, but she is enjoying herself at his expense, not forcing her foot into an ill-fitting glass slipper in order to secure a husband.

Unbridled Laughter: Jane Meets Bertha
While Jane's relationship with Rochester emboldens her, she does not laugh out loud, thereby denying herself bodily pleasure. Rochester notices Jane's refusal to laugh and asks, "Do you never laugh, Miss Eyre?" (170). When Jane remains silent, Rochester decides, "I see, you laugh rarely; but you can laugh very merrily" (170). Rochester's acknowledgment of Jane's private pleasure validates its existence, but, by withholding her laughter, Jane publicly denies what she privately enjoys. As Audrey Bilger explains in *Laughing Feminism*, this self-censorship had practical roots in nineteenth-century tenets of feminine propriety that linked laughter with sexuality. Bilger explains, "Suspicions regarding laughter's sexuality led John Gregory, in his extremely popular conduct book, to advise that

young women beware of getting carried away in group laughter" because "'she is then believed to know more than she should do'" as "laughter reveals an active understanding that belies innocence" (23). When she refuses to laugh, Jane denies her knowledge and desire. Jane eventually describes the destructive consequences of this self-denial, a source of intense frustration, claiming, "[W]omen feel just as men feel; they need exercise for their faculties...they suffer from too rigid a restraint, too absolute a stagnation, precisely as men would suffer.... It is thoughtless to condemn them, or laugh at them, if they seek to do more or learn more than custom has pronounced necessary for their sex" (133). As long as Jane restrains herself, she suffers this stagnation and endures an internal conflict between her private and public identity.

Bertha Rochester's loud, pervasive laughter strikes a sharp contrast with Jane's silenced laughter. Whether as emotion to Jane's intellect, passion to Jane's love, or body to Jane's spirit, Bertha serves as Jane's double to most critics. Gilbert and Gubar read Bertha as Jane's "truest and darkest double: she is the angry aspect of the orphan child, [Jane's] ferocious secret self" (360). They claim that Bertha represents Jane's repressed anger and desire in action. However, by ignoring humor as a component of Jane's development, these assessments deny the possibility of Jane's self-expression. Barreca considers the relationship between Jane and Bertha in terms of humor by suggesting, "Jane makes the joke and Bertha laughs" (64), but suggests that "it is reductive to say that the split between Jane's dryly ironic humor and Bertha's thickly loud laughter is simply … an unbridgeable gap between a woman who can only manufacture the cause and one who can only offer the effect" (64). Considering Jane's encounter with Bertha as a stage in her development of distinctly feminist humor bridges this gap.

Laughter announces Bertha's existence in the narrative. On hearing this laughter Jane describes it as "distinct, formal, mirthless" (122), as well as "tragic" and "preternatural" (123). As Jane perceives it, Bertha's laughter is disconnected from amusement, mental process, or natural explanation; instead, her "low, slow ha! ha!" signals her madness (133), which is distinctly tied to her sexuality. Elaine Showalter makes this link explicit by referring to Dr. William Acton's 1857 study of female insanity, *The Functions and Disorders of the Reproductive Organs*, which reports, "Sexual appetite was considered one of the chief symptoms of moral insanity in women" ("Charlotte Brontë" 73). Rochester also connects Bertha's outbursts with her "giant propensities" and "intemperate and unchaste" nature (391). Bertha's laugh isolates the quality of humor that Jane denies herself, that which "validates the body and its needs" (Wilt 177), but it lacks the intellectual force of Jane's wit. Therefore, Bertha also falls short of complete, rebellious humor and remains cast in masculine fears about uncontrollable women. This fear runs beyond the sanctity of the individual household, and, as John Richetti explains, "Bertha becomes the image of desire ungoverned, of sexuality outside the domestic sphere and the law, terrorizing the order of the family and thus the nation" (370). However, while Bertha might seem to escape her restraints through untamable laughter, she is ultimately as restricted if not more so than Jane. Bertha is both an aberration of the Victorian ideal and an embodiment of another equally stultifying construct: the monstrous, hysterical woman. Whereas Jane can use her wit constructively to effect real change, Bertha, cast in this "hysteric" role, can only be destructive.

Bertha disrupts contrived domestic peace and unsettles convention, but she also destabilizes Jane's sense of identity. If this Mrs. Rochester exists, who is she? Can the controlled witty woman and the laughing woman occupy the same space? In coping with this identity crisis, Jane confines herself even more securely in her intellect: "I shut myself in, fastened the bolt that none might intrude…. And now I thought: till now I had only heard, seen, moved—flowed up and down where I was lead or dragged—watched event rush on event, disclosure open beyond disclosure: but *now I thought*" (373). Despite the calculated decisions Jane has made, she represents her experience as similar to Bertha's, all instinct and reaction; however, Jane regains the critical perspective that she has learned to harness through humor. Barreca notes that her "wit is a fence against encroachment; it will guarantee distance and thereby permit perspective on the relationship" (62). Jane might flirt with Bertha's madness and pure reaction; however, she ultimately returns to her most powerful trait, her wit, and her best option, rejecting Rochester by declaring, "I will *not* be yours. *I* care for myself" (403).

Jane's Marriage of Wit and Laughter

Refusing the role of Rochester's silent second wife is an act of self-preservation; however, Jane risks losing another part of herself with St. John Rivers, who tries to redefine her as his religious "helpmate." In her new position within the Rivers' household, Jane attempts the banter she mastered with Rochester. When St. John offers her a position as a teacher in a village school, he asks, "What will you do with your accomplishments?" (453). Jane quips, "Save them till they are wanted. They will keep" (453). St. John, however, does not appreciate her humor. He is a man of marble who would transform Jane into a missionary wife, and "the glad tumult, the garrulous glee of reception" that drives her "irked him" (503). Despite this disconnect between them, it appears that Jane, now rendered financially dependent and vulnerable, will succumb to these attempts to set her on the conventional wifely path; however, she again replaces the scripted response with sarcasm. St. John earnestly warns her, "Will He [God] accept a mutilated sacrifice? ... I cannot accept on His behalf a divided allegiance: it must be entire" (519). Jane replies, "Oh! I will give my heart to God! ... *You* do not want it" (519). Just as she did with Brocklehurst, Jane deflates this man who would coerce her into what he has determined as her appropriate course and, by extension, religious institutions that reduce women to supporting roles. In so doing, she maintains her autonomy and leaves him wondering, "Is she sarcastic, and sarcastic to *me*?" (519).

The path that Jane chooses leads her back to Rochester and to a satisfying bond of mind and body, wit and laughter—an optimistic new kind of marriage. Sandra Gilbert addresses this decision when she revisits the novel in her article, "*Jane Eyre* and the Secrets of Furious Lovemaking." She states, "In fact, what Jane discovers through this climax of impassioned epiphany is that the paradise for which she longs is not St. John's heaven of spiritual transcendence but rather an earthly paradise of physical fulfillment" (367). When Jane returns to find a wounded and subdued Rochester, she is compelled to rescue him, an impulse that resurrects the image of Jane as the archetypal angelic figure. Rochester certainly expects her to play the angelic role when he asks her, "You are altogether a human being, Jane?" (559). However, now that she is truly her "own mistress" (556), both personally and financially thanks to a lucky inheritance, rather than inspiring this salvation through scripture, she uses humor. She replies, "I conscientiously believe so, Mr. Rochester" (559).

Jane's practical answer creates incongruity that renders such romanticism (and the position in which it places a heroine) a little silly. Refusing to play the doting nurse, Jane mends him by mocking him: "It is time some one undertook to rehumanize you … for I see you are being metamorphosed into a lion or something of that sort … whether your nails are grown like birds' claws or not, I have not yet noticed" (558). Initially, Rochester undercuts her taunts with the bleak reality of his lost vision and hand. He meekly asks, "Am I hideous Jane?" but she sustains her strategy, responding, "Very sir: you always were, you know" (560). Eventually, Rochester begins to jab back, "you mocking changeling…. You make me feel as I have not felt these twelve months" (561).

The jest that fully revives him is a twist on a joke he played on her during their courtship. Just as Rochester incited Jane's jealousy and desire by pretending to woo Blanche, Jane uses St. John to rouse him. When she hears the jealousy in Rochester's questions about her experiences with St. John, Jane realizes that her tactics have been successful in reviving Rochester, and she has reversed the power that he previously held over her. Esther Godfrey explains that this exchange "completes the power reversal brou Goffman, Erving ght about by Rochester's loss of his estate, his social position, and his eyesight" (866). Gilbert and Gubar also mark this exchange as a shift in power and see Jane's return to Rochester as an opportunity for her to teach him in "a school of life where Rochester must learn those lessons Jane herself absorbed so early" (369). Jane craftily mimics the tactics Rochester once used to provoke her. Her mastery goes beyond their early exchanges as she has usurped the dominant role, proving that this role is not inherently linked to gender or class. She no longer merely reacts to him, but instigates and controls the repartee. By appropriating the traditionally masculine privilege, Jane reveals these roles to be social constructions. This role reversal is evidence of her development beyond conventional feminine options throughout the novel.

Now in command, Jane experiences the physical pleasure of humor that she witnessed in Bertha. She proudly exclaims, "I laughed and made my escape, still laughing as I ran up the stairs. 'A good idea!' I thought, with glee. 'I see I have the means of fretting him out of his melancholy for some time to come" (561). Not only is Jane laughing out loud, she is presumably laughing all the way to the bedroom. Critic Robin Jones speculates, "Jane will end her life in Ferndean, no doubt happily, but one wonders with what kind of laughter" (211). Considering Jane's triumphant experience in this instance alone, we can assume it will be with a fully expressed laughter with all the pleasure that provides. Jane exalts not only in personal pleasure but also social defiance. Audrey Bilger puts the social impact of feminist humor in perspective as she states,

> Considering that the potency of female laughter made conduct writers condemn it as unfeminine and that a sense of humor was denied the ideal domestic woman, it follows that if we can catch women laughing, we will hear the echoes of a defiance of this rule and of a reclamation of their right to humor. (25)

By the end of her development, we do hear Jane laughing. While she marries Rochester, she does not forfeit her wit or restrict her laughter and, therefore, paves the way for a new heroine both within and beyond marriage.

Several critics point to Jane's marriage and Bertha's death as ultimately conservative gestures. Along with making way for the felicitous conclusion, however, Brontë extends her critique of restrictive feminine paradigms through the demise of Bertha's hysterical laughter. If we view Bertha as a manifestation of the patriarchal fears of the laughing, physical woman, Brontë rejects and destroys this misrepresentation along with the greatest symbol of Rochester's inherited dominance, his mansion. With these patriarchal constructs debunked and removed, Jane can embody both rational wit and laughter without forfeiting her identity and self-control. Gilbert ultimately decides that Jane's purpose "will not be to eradicate but to accommodate and decriminalize this fiery and desirous animal self that marks her as a most unusual Cinderella" (362). The marriage of Jane's wit and laughter is her method for achieving this goal. The assumption that defiant female laughter, and, therefore, the untamable aggression and desire that accompany it, dies with Bertha is a critical misreading. This perspective fails to take the arc of Jane's development into consideration and denies the sound of her own rebellious, albeit sane, laughter pealing through the halls of Ferndean.

The Humorist Heroine Goes Public: Jane as Author

To further combat the notion that Jane's story concludes in her marriage or reaches its climax in saving Rochester, Brontë's title page credits Jane, suggesting that she sets aside her domestic "needle of repartee" and picks up the pen as a critically witty autobiographer. Recent criticism has turned to Jane's authorship as an outlet for her outrage. Glen suggests that "this sense of the narrator as artist carries with it suggestions of her superior, visionary power" (57). Sternlieb also makes the crucial point that "[b]y reading Bertha as the instrument of Jane's suppressed anger, feminist critics have tended to neglect readings of the novel that allow for the actual expression of that anger … they erase Jane's narrative agency" (468). Sternlieb stresses the often-ignored fact that Jane controls the representations we read. Both Glen and Sternlieb, however, overlook the way in which Jane uses critical humor as part of her craft. Jane's authorial quips permeate the novel. For instance, while reflecting on her ruined wedding, Jane writes, "The morning had been a quiet morning enough—all except for the brief scene with the lunatic" (373). The biting social critique of institutions like Lowood also surfaces in Jane's sarcastic asides to the reader about the starvation the girls endured. When she retorts,

"Thanks being returned for what we had not got" (51), for instance, she calls attention to the irony of having to thank God despite being denied everything of substance. Showalter explains that starvation was part of the effort to "create the intensely spiritualized creature the Victorians idealized as the Angel in the House," because it emphasized the religiously demarcated spirit over the earthly person (*Literature* 117-18). Jane, as author, sardonically derides one of the most fundamental Victorian ideals for women and creates a public record of the repercussions of such ideals.

Jane proudly directs the reader's attention to her own sarcasm at St. John's implication that she must resign herself to wifely duty. Considering her refusal, she states, "I will not swear, reader, that there was not something of repressed sarcasm both in the tone in which I uttered this sentence, and in the feeling that accompanied it" (519). The sarcasm Jane repressed in the moment finds expression in her writing. Jane's wit has serious implications in that it "transgresses even the most sacred territories" and "Jane wields her words like weapons, especially towards religious men" (Barreca 65-66). Returning to Freud's theory of tendentious humor, as an author, Jane often explicitly involves the reader as the second point in her triangular ridicule, consistently positioning oppressive institutions as the objects of her derision. In this and several other direct addresses, Jane couples with the reader in the same way that she once did with Miss Temple, thereby encouraging readers, as she once was encouraged, to embrace autonomy. Marriage is far from the end of Jane's narrative; her writing, complete with a public record of her cutting humor, is the beginning of feminist instigation.

Rachel Brownstein, a critic who writes extensively about the evolution of the heroine, praises that fact that "*Jane Eyre* ends in a marriage that defiantly affirms not the heroine's transformation but her remaining herself" (156). However, Jane progresses well beyond this marriage with a sense of humor that surpasses mere expression of the instinctive sense of irony she relished as a child. Through humor, she develops a complex and critical awareness of the expectations and conventions affecting women and aggressively challenges them. Jane's development of humor from its modest beginnings as a coping device to fully-expressed wit and laughter supplies her with an alternative way to handle the abuse of Gateshead, the paralyzing edicts of Lowood, the destructive romance of Thornfield, and the religious expectations of Moor House. Jane's humor also provides a critical commentary on the confinement of women within conservative literary frameworks. Through Jane's development into a humorous heroine and author, the reader laughs along with Jane at the incongruities of patriarchal constructs that constrict the lives of women and, consequently, questions their efficacy. To overlook Jane's anger, desire, and the humor through which she experiences and expresses herself is to deny her defiant last laugh.

Works Cited

Allott, Miriam. *The Brontës: The Critical Heritage*. Boston: Routledge & Kegan Paul, 1974.

Armstrong, Nancy. *Desire and Domestic Fiction: A Political History of the Novel*. New York: Oxford UP, 1987.

Bakhtin, Mikhail. *The Dialogic Imagination*. Ed. Michael Holquist, Trans. Caryl Emerson and Michael Holquist. Austin: U of Texas P, 2000.

Barreca, Regina. "'I'm No Angel': Humor and Mutiny in *Jane Eyre* and *Villette*." *Untamed and Unabashed: Essays on Women and Humor in British Literature*. Ed. Regina Barreca. Detroit: Wayne State UP, 1994. 61-79.

Bilger, Audrey. *Laughing Feminism*. Detroit: Wayne State UP, 1998.

Brontë, Charlotte. *Jane Eyre*. Oxford: Clarendon Press, 1969.

Brownstein, Rachel M. *Becoming a Heroine: Reading About Women in Novels*. New York: Viking, 1982.

Freud, Sigmund. *Jokes and Their Relation to the Unconscious*. New York: Penguin, 2003.

Gilbert, Sandra M. and Susan Gubar. *The Madwoman in the Attic*. New Haven: Yale UP, 1979.

Gilbert, Sandra M. "*Jane Eyre* and the Secrets of Furious Lovemaking." *Novel* (1998): 351-372.

Glen, Heather. *Charlotte Brontë: The Imagination in History*. New York: Oxford UP, 2002.

Godfrey, Esther. "*Jane Eyre*, from Governess to Girl Bride." *Studies in English Literature* 45.4 (2005): 853-71.

Gray, Frances. *Women and Laughter*. Charlottesville: UP of Virginia, 1994.

Hobbes, Thomas. *Human Nature and De Corpore Politico.* Ed. and Transl. by J. C. A. Gaskin. New York: Oxford UP, 1999.

Hunt, Linda C. "Charlotte Brontë and Women's Culture." *A Woman's Portion: Ideology, Culture, and the British Female Novel Tradition.* New York: Garland, 1988. Jones, Robin. "The Goblin Ha-Ha: Hidden Smiles and Open Laughter in *Jane Eyre.*" *New Perspectives on Women and Comedy.* Ed. Regina Barreca. Philadelphia: Gordon and Breach, 1992. 201-12.

Poovey, Mary. "The Anathematised Race: The Governess and *Jane Eyre.*" *New Casebooks:* Jane Eyre. Ed. Heather Glen. New York: St. Martin's Press, 1997. Richetti, John. "Speak what we think': Women Writers." *The Columbia History of the British Novel.* New York: Columbia UP, 1994. Showalter, Elaine. *A Literature of Their Own: British Women Novelists from Brontë to Lessing.* Princeton: Princeton UP, 1977.

———. "Charlotte Brontë: Feminine Heroine." *Jane Eyre.* Ed. Heather Glen. New York: St. Martin's, 1997. 68-77.

Spacks, Patricia Meyer. *The Female Imagination.* New York: Alfred A. Knopf, 1975. Sternlieb, Lisa. "*Jane Eyre*: 'Hazarding Confidences.'" *Nineteenth-Century Literature* 53.4 (1999): 452-479.

Wilt, Judith. "The Laughter of Maidens, the Cackle of Matriarchs: Notes on the Collision Between Comedy and Feminism." *Gender and Literary Voice.* Ed. Janet Todd. New York: Holmes & Meier, 1980.

Woolf, Virginia. "The Value of Laughter." *The Essays of Virginia Woolf: Volume I 1904-1912.* Ed. Andrew McNeillie. New York: Harcourt Brace, 1987. 58-61.

Playing with Dramatic Adaptations: Charades as an Approach to John Brougham's 1849 Adaptation of *Jane Eyre* _____

Mary Isbell

The third act of John Brougham's *Jane Eyre* (1849) opens with two servants, John and Robert, conversing as they arrange curtains in the Thornfield Hall drawing room for an evening of charades. When Robert inquires as to the reason for such elaborate preparations, John replies:

> Bless your unsophisticated ignorance, these are the games that shuts up theatres; this is for domestic play acting – what with charades, as they call them, tableauxes, and fancy performances, in drawing rooms, the bread is fairly taken out of the poor people's mouths as they makes it a purfession. I once had some hambition to be a player myself, but since the quality has taken it up, I've altered my mind. (Brougham 87)

In Brontë's novel, Jane is too unfamiliar with the notion of "playing charades" to see in them any threat to professional actors. As Jane Austen did with the scandalous private theatricals in *Mansfield Park* (1814), and as George Eliot would do in her depiction of Gwendolen Harleth's extended tableaux in *Daniel Deronda* (1876), Brontë presents domestic entertainments as a frivolous pastime of the wealthy. John's more pointed suggestion is that the trend of charades is taking bread from the mouths of those in the theatrical profession; since "the quality" has taken up this habit of domestic entertainments, John explains, they are less likely to purchase tickets to the professional theater. This is one of a number of class-conscious features in Brougham's novel adaptation that will be explored in this essay. Hopefully, it will encourage more analysis of *Jane Eyre* in light of the eight dramatic adaptations recovered and reproduced by Patsy Stoneman in her 2007 illustrated compilation, titled *Jane Eyre on Stage: 1848-1898*. I propose a methodological approach to these dramatic adaptations, one that is inspired by the resonances between playing charades and making sense of a theatrical adaptation. The acting charade, a game in which a specific word or phrase is represented by a series of complex scenes constructed by actors who are not allowed to speak, provides a useful approach to adaptation by emphasizing the role of spectator recognition and interpretation in the success of the performance event. Argued in what follows is that twenty-first century readers, who study nineteenth-century theatrical spectators and the adaptations they watched, become participants in a game of charades themselves. As this essay's title suggests, playing with dramatic adaptations is encouraged.

To provide evidence of the way charades were played in the nineteenth century, the famous Bridewell charade in *Jane Eyre* is analyzed. However, what is first important to note is the considerable scholarly attention the game has received as an important metaphor in the novel. Joanne E. Rea argues that, "In the solution of the charade in which Mr. Rochester is a participant lies an important thematic and onomastic key to the novel as a whole" (75). Rea explains that the performance representing "Bride" as "an ironic allusion to Mr. Rochester's legal wife, Bertha, as well as to the forthcoming marriage that Jane (who knows nothing yet of the mad Mrs. Rochester) envisions between Mr. Rochester and Blanche Ingram" (75). She also explains that, "the tableau foreshadows the mockery of a marriage that Rochester is prevented (by his brother-in-law, Richard Mason) from carrying out with Jane as the innocent "bride" (76). In their classic work of feminist criticism, *The Madwoman in the Attic: The Woman Writer and the Nineteenth-Century Literary Imagination*, Sandra M. Gilbert and Susan Gubar point to the charade as relaying "a secret message: conventional marriage is not only, as the attic implies, a 'well' of mystery, it is a Bridewell, a prison" (350). They also play with the figurative meaning of "charade" as something false, writing, "The charade of courtship in which Rochester engages [Blanche] suggests a grim question: is not the game of the marriage 'market' a game even scheming women are doomed to lose?" (350). In *Caught in the Act: Theatricality in the Nineteenth-Century English Novel* (1992), Joseph Litvak ably demonstrates that Jane's lack of attention to the meaning of the charade "deflects attention from any similarity between that nonresponse and the 'dumb show' [the charade] enacted before our eyes" (54). Litvak builds his analysis by articulating what Jane is doing when she resists involvement in the game of charades.

These readings provide tremendous insight into the complexity of Brontë's narrative depiction of performance, but this scene should not be approached only as a metaphor to be interpreted. Instead, it can be seen as evidence of the way charades were played in the nineteenth century. I draw on the particular features of nineteenth-century charades to articulate a model for playing with dramatic adaptations. We often play charades today with the hurried goal of representing as many words or phrases as possible in a fixed amount of time, but in the nineteenth century, the game was often approached with all the elaborate preparation of a small theatrical production. At Thornfield Hall, servants are tasked with removing the tables from the dining room to clear a space for the makeshift theater, and Mrs. Fairfax is "summoned to give information respecting the resources of the house in shawls, dresses, draperies of any kind" to be used for costumes (182). The emphasis on scenes carefully prepared to represent syllables of one word as opposed to the speedy progression through as many words as possible places more emphasis on the meaning of the performance. As Dorothy Noyes points out, the performed charade allows multiple levels of communication between participants, and this is certainly the case with Rochester, who acts as the stage manager of the evening's first production (Noyes 221). He chooses which guests he will include in his acting company (he asks Jane to play, but accepts her refusal without insisting) and selects the word that will be hinted at by his troupe of actors: "Bridewell." Given the anticipated engagement between Rochester and Blanche, it is a rather cheeky decision to represent a word that calls for staging a mock wedding. Brontë encourages us to interpret this in a number of different ways as the novel progresses. While at first it seems like he is flirting with Blanche by creating a situation in which the two must pretend to be married, this changes when we learn that Rochester intends to marry

Jane, not Blanche. This information makes his decision seem more likely motivated by a desire to make Jane jealous or at least see how she reacts to such a scene. In either case, the game creates a space, in which roles assumed create powerful resonances with the situations of the characters performing in them.

To understand this resonance, we need to understand how charades and dramatic adaptations tell stories in similar ways. Both use human beings—actors—to represent a story or a sequence of stories. When the word "story" appears in this essay, it refers to something very specific. As H. Porter Abbott explains in *The Cambridge Introduction to Narrative*, "When in casual conversation, English speakers say they've heard a 'good story,' they usually aren't thinking of the story as separate from the telling of it" (18). When the term "story" is used in this essay, however, it refers to the definition Abbott offers: "a chronological sequence of events involving entities" (Abbott 241). In other words, a story is raw material that can be spun in different ways. A narrative is the tale plus the telling. Brontë's novel *Jane Eyre*, then, is a narrative made up of the story of Jane's progress from childhood to adulthood and Brontë's narration of that story (conveyed through Jane's first-person narration); narratologists like Abbott refer to the second component of a narrative as "narrative discourse" or, "the story as narrated" (Abbott 238). The fact that a story is separable from the way it is told is what enables adaptation, particularly adaptation across different media. The eight dramatic adaptations of Brontë's *Jane Eyre* reproduced by Stoneman in *Jane Eyre on Stage* are wildly different, but they all contain certain core features of the Jane Eyre story that are recognizable no matter how they are told or even how much they alter events or entities in the story.

Both charades and dramatic adaptations rely on spectator recognition of their stories' core features. An adaptation is most pleasurable when one recognizes the story from the source text, but anyone who has watched a film version of a classic novel instead of reading the book knows that one can still enjoy an adaptation without having read the source text. The point here is that one will not be successful *playing with* an adaptation if one does not recognize the story. It should perhaps go without saying that an evening of charades is not an occasion to represent something one's spectators have never seen before, as doing so would make it nearly impossible to guess the necessary word. In the charades at Thornfield Hall, the first story represented is that of a man and a woman getting married. Rochester assumes the role of the bridegroom and casts Blanche as his bride, and together they mime a wedding story wearing makeshift wedding attire on a make-believe altar. Spectators have no trouble recognizing the story that is unfolding, however. Jane reports on the game from her "usual seat" in the shadow provided by the window seat (she was almost invited to participate as one of the spectators, but Lady Ingram deemed her "too stupid for any game of the sort" – she had previously refused Rochester's invitation to act) (182). Jane plays the game quite well, however, from her position on the periphery. In the first scene she explains that it was "easy to recognize the pantomime of a marriage" (183).

Recognition is equally important for dramatic adaptations. The first recognizable element of the Jane Eyre story in Brougham's adaptation occurs in the first scene of the play. The curtain opens to find Miss Gryce and Miss Temple in "a very plain chamber in Lowood academy." The action begins with the entrance of Miss Scatcherd, who says, "Here's a fine to do! Who do you think is coming here directly?" When Miss Temple cannot guess, Miss Scatcherd responds: "The veritable Mr. Brocklehurst himself. The generous endower of this most benevolent institution for the confusion of intellect and suppression of liberty" (Brougham 74). The elements of the Jane Eyre story set in Lowood academy are recognizable here, though they are presented very differently from Brontë's novel. Instead of Jane's first-person narration, we have the frustrated thoughts of Lowood teachers shared in private. The sarcasm is thick in Miss Scatcherd's reference to "the generous endower" and the "most benevolent institution," which spectators familiar with the story will recognize as the school where students are served burnt porridge and subjected to floggings and other forms of public humiliation.

Recognition is only one step in a game of charades. One must also guess the word being represented with each scene. In the Thornfield version of the game, each scene illustrates one syllable of a whole word that is also enacted in a concluding scene. Brontë describes the act of guessing as "divining" the word or syllable illustrated by the scene, and this verb is telling. "Divine" has a number of meanings as a verb, but the closest to Brontë's use is this: "To make out by sagacity, intuition, or fortunate conjecture (that is, in some other way than by actual information); to conjecture, guess" ("divine"). The charade is an enigma, after all. One must apply one's wits to solve it. The lack of "actual information" is what presents the challenge to "the divining party" at Thornfield Hall. The fact that the story of Eliezer and Rebecca presents more of a challenge than the story of the wedding invites us to consider the effort that went into divining the first word of the game. Jane's narration demonstrates the complexity of the scene:

> Ere long, a bell tinkled, and the curtain drew up. Within the arch, the bulky figure of Sir George Lynn, whom Mr. Rochester had likewise chosen, was seen enveloped in a white sheet: before him, on a table, lay open a large book; and at his side stood Amy Eshton, draped in Mr. Rochester's cloak, and holding a book in her hand. Somebody, unseen, rung the bell merrily; then Adèle (who had insisted on being one of her guardian's party) bounded forward, scattering round her the contents of a basket of flowers she carried on her arm. Then appeared the magnificent figure of Miss Ingram, clad in white, a long veil on her head, and a wreath of roses round her brow: by her side walked Mr. Rochester, and together they drew near the table. They knelt; while Mrs. Dent and Louisa Eshton, dressed also in white, took up their stations behind them. A ceremony followed, in dumb show, in which it was easy to recognize the pantomime of a marriage. At its termination, Colonel Dent and his party consulted in whispers for two minutes, then the colonel called out, - "Bride!" Mr. Rochester bowed, and the curtain fell. (182-3)

We don't know what the party whispered to one another because Jane, our narrator, is not officially participating in the game. They likely were attempting to settle on which of many components in the scene to use. Even when excluding words with more than one syllable, they might have selected "church," "groom," "aisle," "veil," or many others. That the party has no trouble deciding that bride was the most important element of the scene suggests that the "magnificent figure" of Blanche as the bride was the most striking feature the performance.

For the second scene at Thornfield Hall, the story shifts from a generic wedding ceremony to a particular story from the Bible, increasing the difficulty for the "divining party" (184). Jane describes the scene in detail, and her narration invites the reader to guess at the story being mimed:

> Seated on the carpet, by the side of this basin, was seen Mr. Rochester, costumed in shawls, with a turban on his head. [...] Presently advanced into view Miss Ingram. She, too, was attired in oriental fashion [...] She approached the basin, and bent over it as if to fill her pitcher; she again lifted it to her head. The personage on the well-brink now seemed to accost her; to make some request: -- "She hasted, let down her pitcher on her hand and gave him a drink." From the bosom of his robe, he then produced a casket, opened it and showed magnificent bracelets and ear rings; she acted astonishment and admiration; kneeling, he laid the treasure at her feet: incredulity and delight were expressed by her looks and gestures; the stranger fastened the bracelets on her arms, and the rings in her ears. It was Eliezer and Rebecca: the camels only were wanting.

Jane immediately recognizes this as the story of Eliezer and Rebecca, so clearly that she sees certain movements directly representing the story as it appears in the Bible. The quotation in Jane's narration is from The Book of Genesis, the source of the story being represented on the stage. One might also draw useful parallels between Jane's narration and the wide variety of visual representations of Rebecca at the well. We do not know whether the divining party recognize the story or not, because Jane is not privy to their private deliberations. What we do know is that they decide not to offer a word for the second scene and instead request that Rochester's cast of characters proceed with "the tableau of the whole."

I would like to propose that this strategy of play—a process of divining the intention behind individual scenes where possible and combining them to understand the whole—is similar to our process of making sense of dramatic adaptations. What one would have recognized after watching the first scene of Brougham's adaptation that the play begins with Lowood instead of Gateshead, and that it places much more emphasis on laughing at Mr. Brocklehurst as a fool than on fearing him as a villain. I want to push the comparison between charades and dramatic adaptations a bit further here to suggest that the restriction on speech in the game of charades is similar to the absence of a narrator's commentary in a dramatic adaptation. The story of Jane Eyre is a much simpler thing than the first-person narrative Brontë uses to tell it. Consider how Jane relates her first impressions of Brocklehurst in the novel:

> *He*, for it was a man, turned his head slowly towards where I stood, and having examined me with the two inquisitive-looking grey eyes which twinkled under a pair of bushy brows, said solemnly, and in a bass voice, "Her size is small: what is her age?"
> "Ten years."
> "So much?" was the doubtful answer; and he prolonged his scrutiny for some minutes. Presently he addressed me—"Your name, little girl?"
> "Jane Eyre, sir."
> In uttering these words I looked up: he seemed to me a tall gentleman; but then I was very little; his features were large, and they and all the lines of his frame were equally harsh and prim. (Brontë 31-32).

Without having our attention directed by the thoughts of a heroine who has experienced terrifying hell-fire interrogation from Mr. Brocklehurst, we are more likely to see him as ridiculous instead of scary. His first entrance onto the stage in Brougham's adaptation is framed by the covert insubordination of his policies by the Lowood teachers. Miss Scatcherd is in the middle of describing how she plans to give Mr. Brocklehurst a piece of her mind when he enters, and she fumbles to come up with something else to say (Brougham 74). The entrance is deliberately comic and undermines any sense of authority Brocklehurst attempts to establish throughout the scene.

This absence of written narrative also makes it challenging to convey on stage Jane's many incisive criticisms of Brocklehurst and the snobbish aristocrats at Thornfield Hall. Faced with this restriction, Brougham decides to have Jane articulate, through asides, soliloquies, and direct confrontations, things that Brontë's Jane does not say aloud in the novel. I discuss below one of the most striking examples of this through Brougham's addition of direct interaction between Jane and Lord Ingram. Charades silence actors to make guessing the word harder, but the incompatibility of written narrative with a theatrical production is simply a feature of dramatic representation. These are different restrictions on speech, in other words, but they nevertheless have a tremendous impact on the resulting performance event.

As mentioned above, one can simply consume an adaptation as its own story, but for the purposes of this essay, it is necessary to play with adaptations—a process that asks us to divine the meaning of the adaptation. In the novel, when the spectators have trouble divining the word represented by the second scene, they postpone making their decision until they have seen the "tableau of the whole." Likewise, it is often difficult to make sense of an adaptation until one has experienced the whole thing. I draw this parallel between the challenging work of guessing syllables in a charade and divining the meaning of the adaptation to emphasize the creativity each undertaking requires. There are at least two levels on which we can play with adaptations. First, we can play in our analysis of adaptations we experience today, and second, we can engage the even trickier task of analyzing nineteenth-century adaptations of the novel, which requires that we divine how spectators in the nineteenth-century theater might have interpreted the adaptation.

An important part of this second way of playing with dramatic adaptations involves the analysis of performance events readers will never be able to see. To recreate something ephemeral, it is necessary to examine available material traces of that event. This often begins with the dramatic text, but also includes attention to playbills, play reviews, and information on the performers playing the roles. Brontë provides some of these traces in her novel for the ephemeral performance event created through the game of charades. Though Jane is excluded from explicit participation in the game, she does interpret the resonances created by the performance. Her narration of the scene constructs an account of the performance event that locates the recognizable story and notes the particular way Rochester staged it. Jane focuses especially on the persona and appearance of the performers inhabiting roles in the stories, noting what makes them successful in representing those characters. When describing the scene of Rebecca at the well, Jane explains that Rochester's "dark eyes and swarthy skin and Paynim features suited the costume exactly: he looked the very model of an eastern emir, an agent or a victim of the bowstring." She also lingers on the fact that Blanche's "cast of form and feature" and her "general air" make her representation of Rebecca effective (183).

Though play reviews offer a limited perspective on productions seen by many spectators, they offer invaluable insight into the reception of a play. I approach Jane's reflections on the supposed engagement of Rochester and Blanche, prompted by the charades, as a performance review. Her primary criticism in this review is that while Blanche might make a believable wife for Rochester, their performance does not represent Jane's ideal marriage story. She begins this review by acknowledging her own bias (she does love Rochester), but then makes a persuasive case for her disappointment in the performance event:

> I saw he was going to marry her, for family, perhaps political reasons; because her rank and connexions suited him; I felt he had not given her his love, and that her qualifications were ill adapted to win from him that treasure. This was the point—this was where the nerve was touched and teazed—this was where the fever was sustained and fed: *she could not charm him*. (186)

Jane not only believes she has divined Rochester's reason for enacting a wedding story, she interprets his performance as disturbing because it only fuels her belief that Blanche is not right for him.

It is possible to consult published play reviews of dramatic adaptations to get the same sort of insight presented by Jane's thoughts on the game of charades in Brontë's novel. Stoneman has done the hard work of locating reviews of many of the nineteenth-century productions of *Jane Eyre* adaptations. The only review of Brougham's 1849 production of *Jane Eyre* at the Bowery Theatre reveals the sort of plays that were popular with the Bowery's working class audience:

> At the Bowery, a drama by Mr. Brougham – one of his series, evidently, of dramatic versions from popular novelists – has been produced with marked success. The novel of 'Jane Eyre' presents many incidents of a strikingly dramatic character, and there is scarce a personage in the entire work who could not be made to appear advantageously on the stage. The more prominent of these Mr Brougham has taken hold of and worked into a composition of much interest and dramatic merit. Still he labors under the disadvantage of being confined to the present time, and deprived of an opportunity of reveling in that richness of costume and scenery which forms so strong an ingredient in all pieces written for the Bowery stage. Could 'Jane Eyre' be carried back to the Middle Ages and honored by those nondescript dramas in vogue on the stage, the enthusiasm of the audience would have known no bounds. (Stoneman 72)

It is useful here to return to the distinction between the story and the story as narrated. This review suggests that the working-class spectators at the Bowery were less interested in story than in medieval costumes and scenery. One gets the sense that this reviewer is a bit frustrated with this predictable desire of the Bowery audience. The use of "nondescript" to describe the dramas "in vogue" at that time is telling. If only Brougham's *Jane Eyre* weren't burdened with such a rich story, the reviewer seems to say, the playwright might have been more successful with Bowery audiences, who seem only to crave spectacle. When considering the richness of Brougham's dramatic text, it is important to note that it might not have been appreciated at the Bowery.

As mentioned above, the first scene of Brougham's play opens with teachers at Lowood academy complaining about Brocklehurst. The second scene of the play opens on the drawing room at Thornfield Hall. Rochester's guests fill the room, discussing him as a "half-savage, whole-riddle of a fellow" in his absence (77). Brougham then directs us to deride these guests by introducing likable servants who mock the aristocrats' pretensions. When the servant John first enters the drawing room, he addresses the audience to describe the Dowager Lady Ingram and her daughters as "the old tabby and the young kittens," who treat all of the female characters of their acquaintance as mice to be played with (78). When Lady Ingram summons John, he answers, "Yes, my lady," but then aside to the audience calls her a "mouser" (79). He then tells the audience he's going to "tease her a bit." She wants to know who has just arrived at Thornfield Hall, but she wants him to volunteer the information. Importantly, the comic exchange pivots on his control over the situation:

Dow: Was that Mr. Rochester who arrived just now?
John: No, my lady. Now I'll tease her a bit; she won't like to ask me who it is. I know she'll have to though.
Dow: Not Mr. Rochester?
John: No, my lady.
Dow: More friends, I presume.
John: No, my lady.
Dow: I certainly heard a carriage stop.
John: Yes, my lady.
Dow: I thought I couldn't be mistaken.
John: No, my lady.
Dow: A stranger?
John: Yes, my lady.
Dow: Indeed – a gentleman?
John: No, my lady.
Dow: A lady?
John: No, my lady.

Dow: Neither a gentleman or a lady? How stupid you are; who can it be?

John: Only the new governess, my lady.

Not only has Brougham masterfully brought his spectators into allegiance with the servants in the mockery of Rochester's guests, he has also introduced Jane as a governess, not a lady. Brougham draws here on the discussion about insufferable governesses that occurs within Jane's hearing in Brontë's novel, but he makes Lady Ingram absurdly disturbed by even the word "governess." This prompts Lord Ingram, her son, to ask John to "Bring some liqueur and trot out the new governess" so they can have a "prime lark" (79). When Jane enters, the Dowager screams and Jane *"recoils timidly at first but rapidly collects herself"* (80). Jane attempts to excuse herself, assuming some mistake has been made, but Lord Ingram insists she stay. Brougham's Jane is bold and self-assured in the unfriendly situation, holding her own when Lord Ingram tries to have a laugh at her expense. He begins by asking her name, to which she responds,

Jane: Jane Eyre – you are? –

Lord Ing: Theodore, commonly called Lord Ingram – and so you are – aw – Jane Eyre. Yes, delighted – do you know, Jane, that you're devilish pretty?

Jane: My Lord!

Lord Ing: Upon my life you are – eh, Dent?

Col Dent: Undoubtedly.

Jane: Sir, your sisters, I believe, are in the room – were any one toaddress either of them as you have now addressed me, what would be the result?

Lord Ing: Positively I don't know, I can't imagine; it's a very different thing – they are –

Jane: Made of a different clay: their hearts are more sensitive, their feelings more refined perhaps. Reverse the picture, my Lord, and you will be nearer to the truth. In the school of poverty is oftener found that intuitive delicacy which fears to wound – inured to suffering themselves, they know and feel for that in others.

Lord Ing: A regular sermon, by Jupiter; quite Addisonian. Did you get that out of the Spectator? (80)

Here is all of the sentiment Jane expresses in Brontë's novel, but spoken directly to one of Rochester's guests, who has insulted her. One wonders, however, how this exchange appealed to working-class (primarily male) spectators at the Bowery. These spectators have been directed earlier in the scene to see snobbish aristocrats mocked by a male servant, but now they see one soundly conquered by a woman with only her principles of respectability. Did they cheer Jane or laugh at her sense of propriety? Does this parody the central values of Brontë's novel or strengthen them?

There is evidence from later in the play that Brougham was specifically interested in commenting on Jane's principles as expressed earnestly in the novel. The exchange takes place between Rochester and Lord Ingram, as Rochester attempts to extricate himself from his engagement to Blanche by pretending that he has no money. After announcing that he is penniless, he looks at Blanche and, noticing her changed demeanor towards him, says "By heavens, her features are as calm as marble. What are promises and protestations, gentle looks and whispered sentences – all hollowness, pretence, and lies" (99). Lord Ingram responds with this:

Come, come, Rochester, this is a most unimaginative age; that sort of talk reads tolerably well in novels, but sounds somewhat impertinent in real life. Your paper heroes are privileged individuals, but flesh and blood people don't feel inclined to listen to such improbable mouthing. (99)

Brougham has positioned one of his most unsympathetic characters as a critical voice on the kind of sentiment one might find in a novel. Was he anticipating that his spectators would cheer the sentiments of Lord Ingram, the dastardly (but decidedly comic) insulter of Jane's honor?

Explained in this essay is how one might approach a dramatic adaptation as though it were a charade. Before closing, it is necessary to consider Brougham's adaptation of the charade scene for his play. That Brougham adapts Brontë's depictions of performance in the novel for his play is noteworthy; most other adaptations of the novel ignore these moments of performance, but he combines the charades and the gypsy scene into one performance-filled evening (and a meta-theatrical Act). This essay opens with the beginning of this scene, which uses a conversation between the servants John and Robert to present the game of charades as evidence of excess that is hurting the lower classes by keeping the elite from buying theater tickets. Because in Brougham's telling, both Jane and Rochester disapprove of the frivolities of the wealthy, neither participates in the game; it is entirely the doing of the guests. Rochester invites Jane to observe them, saying "I presume you care as little as myself for those frivolous pastimes, and yet they may amuse you" (89). Rochester then reveals in an aside to the audience that he has a scheme in the works that requires her presence in the drawing room. John then delivers the fake letter that calls Rochester away so he can assume the gypsy costume.

The depiction of the charades and the gypsy scene (which Brougham uses to allow Rochester to propose to Jane) are themselves fascinating, but there is an oddity at the start of the scene, one that indicates once again that Brougham is calling attention to the possibilities and limitations of adapting a novel for the stage. To understand this scene, one must know that John Downey, the comic servant, has a crush on Grace Poole and is fascinated by her secrets. Once John and Robert finish their work on the curtain for the charades, they decide to see if the mechanism will work. As the stage directions describe, *"Curtain drawn discovers Grace Poole with her cake and pint of beer."* John calls Robert over to have a look and explains, "look, Bob. that's what the gentry calls a tabloo." What John references here is quite complex. The tableau usually occurs at the conclusion of a scene, when characters hold their positions to add emphasis to a key moment in the story. It is both a key component of spectacular representations on the nineteenth-century stage and also a domestic entertainment, like charades and private theatricals, that is popular with the upper classes. Stoneman describes the tableau as a common feature in *Jane Eyre* adaptations, noting in her introduction that one scene in T.H. Paul's *Jane Eyre* concludes with "the 'Maniac' on the parapet of Thornfield against a background of flames, while Jane points to her, naming Rochester's duty: 'save your wife!'" (Stoneman 5). Like the charade in Brontë's novel, the surprise appearance of Grace Poole on the makeshift stage, and her refusal to move when the guests arrive to undertake their performance, are ripe with potential thematic resonances for Brougham's play. Instead of offering us a dramatic tableau of the shocking appearance of Bertha Mason, Brougham creates a tableau of Grace Poole, guarding her secrets. She is discovered doing something mundane; as Robert notes, "Why, there's half-witted Grace, with her everlasting pint of beer" (87). The intended effect is not to astound, but to conjure a laugh. The tableau becomes much more meaningful, however, if spectators recognize Grace Poole's role in the Jane Eyre story. Surprising us with Grace Poole in an accidental tableau seems a decidedly self-reflexive move; a comment to his audience on the sort of play he might have created instead.

Argued here is that the game of charades played at Thornfield Hall provides an exciting approach to dramatic adaptations. Several scenes from Brougham's dramatic adaptation of the novel have been analyzed. To use Brontë's term, readers of this essay have become members of the "divining party" and engaged in making sense of the 1849 production at the Bowery Theatre. Many questions have been posed and speculative guesses made because there are many things we will not ever know for certain about the theatrical past. Of course, theater historians have also amassed a tremendous amount of "actual information" about the nineteenth-century stage. Books like Jim Davis and Victor Emeljanow's *Reflecting the Audience: London Theatregoing, 1840-1880* (2001) and Rosemary K. Bank's *Theatre Culture in America, 1825-1860* (1997) tell us a great deal about audience experiences in nineteenth-century theaters. By studying Patsy Stoneman's collection of reviews in *Jane Eyre on Stage*, it is possible search for play reviews in nineteenth-century newspaper databases, which are developing all the time. This is not to mention the playbills, images, and diary accounts of experiences in the theatre available in physical and virtual archives. When faced with the enigma of *Jane Eyre* on stage, one should have fun playing the game.

Works Cited

Brontë, Charlotte. *Jane Eyre*. Oxford: Oxford UP, 2000.

Brougham, John. *Jane Eyre (1849)*. *Jane Eyre on Stage, 1848-1898: An Illustrated Edition of Eight Plays with Contextual Notes*. Ed. Patsy Stoneman. Aldershot: Ashgate, 2007. 65-108.

"Divine" Def. 2. *Oxford English Dictionary Online*. Oxford English Dictionary, n.d. Web. 18 Nov. 2013.

Gibert, Sandra M. and Susan Gubar. *The Madwoman in the Attic: The Woman Writer and the Nineteenth-Century Literary Imagination*. New Haven: Yale UP, 2000.

Litvak, Joseph. *Caught in the Act: Theatricality in the Nineteenth-Century English Novel*. Berkeley: U of California P, 1992.

Noyes, Dorothy. "Enigma, Folk." *Folklore: An Encyclopedia of Beliefs, Customs, Tales, Music, and Art, Volume 1*. Santa Barbara: ABC-CLIO, 2011.

Rea, Joanne E. "Brontë's Jane Eyre." *Explicator*. 50.2 (1992): 75-78.

Stoneman, Patsy. Ed. *Jane Eyre on Stage, 1848-1898: An Illustrated Edition of Eight Plays with Contextual Notes*. Aldershot: Ashgate, 2007.

'A Solemn and Strange and Perilous Thing': Rereading a Reading of *Jane Eyre*

Meghan Sweeney

"I know what I feel, and how averse are my inclinations to the bare thought of marriage."

(*Jane Eyre*)

When I was in high school, I had a slightly crazed English teacher who delighted in giving us pop quizzes on relatively obscure moments from the novels we were reading. It was, he insisted, to get us to focus on details, but it made us resentful. By asking questions such as "What color are Jane Eyre's eyes?" he almost ruined *Jane Eyre* for me, even though it was a novel that I had read and loved before. (The answer he wanted: Jane's eyes are green, but Rochester, in his passion, thinks they're hazel. I got it wrong.)

Despite my teacher's attempts to reduce our reading experience to a handful of mundane questions, I still liked the book. It had much to recommend it: cruel relatives, orphans, a mansion, a mystery. *The Secret Garden* for adults! I did think that Jane should have stayed with Rochester rather than listening to the moon and running away (surely marriage, bigamist or no, had to be better than half-dying on the moors and then, post-rescue, listening to the notorious bore St. John day after day), but it was still a thrilling read.

The next time I read it, I was five years wiser, a senior in college taking a "British Women Writers" course, with a professor who didn't care about eye color. She emphasized details, too, but not just for the sake of knowing them. Instead, we used textual details to formulate nuanced opinions about the many issues that *Jane Eyre* raised. When we discussed the novel as a class, I refined my position on Jane's escape from Rochester. I began re-reading sections of the book, observing connections and contradictions. Sure, Jane was impetuous. But there were, it now seemed to me, many good reasons for her to flee from Rochester.

Now, years later, I return to *Jane Eyre* as an English professor who studies Anglo-American stories about weddings. In particular, I explore the ways that texts, including picture books, novels, toys, and films are adapted for, marketed to, and consumed by children and young adults. Although I do not usually focus on the nineteenth century, I continue to be fascinated by Jane Eyre (whom we meet as a child and later as a young adult), and the novel, which begins its dénouement (or decline, depending on your perspective) with the famous line "Reader, I married him."

The more pressing question for me now is not why would Jane leave Rochester, but why would she return to marry him? By the final chapters, Jane has gained a family and a fortune as well as valuable teaching experience in a school of her own. Rochester does not fare so well, physically or emotionally. As an article at the online magazine *Slate* humorously puts it: "Reader, I married him" may be the most puzzling lines of the novel "given that *I* is a wealthy young woman and *him* is a one-eyed, one-handed, pushing-40 grump who proposes to a nanny half his age only to admit[1] at the altar that he's already got a wife and she's locked in his attic. Dreamy!" (Winter). Nevertheless, as this same writer observes, "in a 2009 poll by British romance publisher Mills and Boon, readers voted Edward Rochester the 'most popular hero in literature'" (Winter).

What is it about Rochester that enchants so many readers? In a more scholarly—but still somewhat wry—article, critic Sandra Gilbert suggests that *Jane Eyre* offers us "the archetypal scenario for all those mildly thrilling romantic encounters between a scowling Byronic hero (who owns a gloomy mansion) and a trembling heroine (who can't quite figure out the mansion's floor plan)" (780). So many stories have used similar themes (such as Daphne DuMaurier's *Rebecca*) that this romantic archetype may seem hard-wired, a universal story of passion, rather than a culturally constructed template.

Moreover, so many movie versions, in which otherwise rather beautiful actresses play the "plain Jane" role by pursing their lips and wearing frumpy frocks, emphasize the thrill of Jane's return, depicting it as a reunion of two soul mates after a gruesome tragedy.

The story seems to have what we commonly refer to as "a fairy tale ending," but we may not be attuned to the ways that this ending is also part "Bluebeard," with a hint of "Rapunzel"[2]—fairy tales, but not of the unequivocally happy sort. When we attend to the language of the book itself, though, we can see how ambivalent it is about the happily-ever-afters of marriage.

In my class as an undergraduate, I wrote papers in order to explore this ambivalence. As is so often the case with critical writing, I didn't come up with ideas about *Jane Eyre* and marriage on my own; rather, ideas emerged from conversations I had with other students and with my professor. In particular, an inquiry paper prompt helped me organize my thoughts. In it, my professor asked us to "compare the imagery of 'fetters' and chains in the Bridewell charades (chapter eighteen) with the imagery of bracelets, rings, and silken threads described in chapter 24. What connects these two moments in the novel? What insight does this give you into both Jane's and Rochester's views of marriage?"

On my own, I wouldn't have thought to link these two chapters, but as I reread, I began to see connections. I remember the thrill of confronting unfamiliar ideas about love and death, power and subservience as I prepared to address the prompt. I jotted down notes in the margins: "part of [Jane] wants to be subservient," "would have arm broken b/c wouldn't be a sacrifice to her emotional self," "Love as physical annihilation," and, finally, "Yes to marriage is the clincher." I was shocked to see how Jane's "yes" to Rochester's marriage proposal drastically changed their power dynamic.

When Jane runs away from Rochester, it is, as we know, because he has another wife living in the attic. But it's important to trace Jane's uneasiness about marrying him back (at least) to their engagement scene. Once she agrees to marry him, he becomes possessive and condescending.

As I wrote my first inquiry paper, I was concerned with this marked transformation in Rochester. By chapter twenty-four, he is, I wrote:

no longer the agitated, tormented Rochester with flushed face and "strange gleams in the eye"' (Brontë, Bantam 242). He no longer overflows with ardent emotion begging, "Jane accept me quickly" (242). He has become, beginning the morning after the passionate proposal night, a much more complacent Rochester who is content to play games, with Jane as the pampered purpose of these games. He is a Rochester who, as Jane says, "fretted, pished and pshawed" (259), who desires to dress her up in fine clothing, and refers to her consistently in diminutive terms: "little sunny faced girl" and "little elf" (245). The sense of urgency of the night has given way to an affectionate tyranny of the day. (Sweeney)

What caused this shift? I soon found that a five hundred-word paper was not enough to explore such complicated emotions and shifts in power. As the semester went on, I developed a seven-page paper and then a twelve-page paper, arguing that the charade scene of chapter eighteen "provided clues to Rochester's shifting self" and emphasized the performative nature of gender roles.

Years later, I still find some of my arguments in this paper to be persuasive, although there are moments I'd want to rework or expand; there are also sections that could have used additional research. In particular, I have two crucial suggestions for my undergraduate self. First, I'd want to explore the imperialist implications of the scenes I discuss. Second, I'd critique more strenuously the notion of companionate marriage—marriage for affection and love—that the novel (at times) embraces. I suggested that Rochester was torn by contrary impulses: the desire for a marriage of equals and the belief (bolstered by law and convention) that women were men's inferiors. Now, I'd argue that nineteenth-century companionate marriage itself needs to be interrogated for the ways that it confers privilege on the wedded couple as it isolates them from a broader community.

By including excerpts from my undergraduate paper below, as well as my thoughts on it now, I hope to emphasize that every analysis might be productively revisited—even many years later.

"Charadized"

In my undergraduate essay I coined a somewhat infelicitous term to describe the power dynamic between Jane and Rochester: "Charadized Relationships." With that term, I hoped to emphasize the way that the multiple performances of the charade scenes are mirrored in Jane and Rochester's own relationship, particularly after they become engaged.

I began by reading the charade scene of chapter eighteen closely, keeping in mind what we had learned in class about England in the 1840s. I wrote that the first charade is a fairly stock representation of marriage, with its:

> "magnificent figure, clad in white" as well as wreath of roses, a jubilant flower girl, and a dutiful bridal party (Brontë, Bantam 171). Despite the exuberance of Adèle the flower girl, it has a dignified air to it, as Rochester and Blanche kneel and the attendants take "up their stations behind them" (171): it is, Jane says, "easy to recognize the pantomime of a marriage" (171). Yet although the word being mimed is "Bride," it is Rochester who dramatically takes control of the stage at the end: "Mr. Rochester bowed, and the curtain fell" (171). Even in the voiceless "Bride" charade, Rochester's presence weighs heavily. In a larger context, "Bride" as a charaded word reveals women's role as a supplementary accessory to the man. (Sweeney)

As my paper indicated, the bride charade is notable for many reasons. Before it begins, Jane states her "ignorance" of the term "playing charades," suggesting that the pageantry and performances of the charade are foreign to her. However, she does find it "easy to recognize the pantomime of a marriage" when she sees it (Brontë, Bedford 185). Although she stands apart from such performances, she is also subject to social rules governing the "performance" of marriage, as her acceptance of Rochester's proposal later in the book makes clear.

By the time *Jane Eyre* was published, the ideal of the companionate marriage had firmly taken root in England: as one writer observes, "Once it was doubted that affection could and would naturally develop after marriage, decision-making power had to be transferred to the future spouses themselves" (Stone 218). This had an effect of "equalizing relationships between husband and wife" as early as the seventeenth century (218). However, such "equalizing" is relative. Even though marriage for love seemed an obvious improvement, women's economic, cultural, and political inequalities were often obscured within the institution.

In my paper, I did observe that it wasn't until 1870 that the Married Women's Property Act was passed in England, allowing women to own their own property. Yet, it's also important to emphasize that the Matrimonial Causes Act, a law that enabled women to retain their own earnings when separated from their husbands, wasn't passed until 1857. Moreover, until 1839—just a few years before the publication of *Jane Eyre*—a woman had no claim on her own children. As one saying (attributed loosely to eighteenth-century British politician William Blackstone) went: "husband and wife are one and the husband is that one" (qtd. in Stone 218).

Thus, the three charades are particularly interesting, since they make these power imbalances manifest in a figurative way. While the first charade presented a conventional nineteenth-century marriage, the second presents an Orientalist view of the male-female relationship, featuring Rochester and Blanche dressed as Eliezer and Rebecca from The Book of Genesis. In this story, Eliezer, a servant, is sent to select a wife for his master's son, Isaac. He devises a test, in which the woman who offers water to him and his camels will be deemed a suitable bride. The virtuous Rebecca passes the test, and Eliezer presents her with beautiful jewels. In the charade itself,

> Rochester is once again a domineering figure; this time "he looked the very model of an Eastern emir" (172). Blanche's role in the charade is to be the alluring, yet chaste (as is emphasized in the Biblical tale) woman with "beautifully-moulded arms bare" (172). She is the "Israelitish princess," notably of the "patriarchal days" (172). Although she seems to be in power, for she stands poised above the male figure, her power has actually been created and defined by the male, who has chosen to kneel at her feet, chosen

her to be the recipient of his treasures. He has, moreover, "accost"ed her to make his request, suggesting not mutual respect, but a more violent spirit. By bestowing treasures upon her, despite her delight, he has made her his, has made her a character in his drama, as he "fasten[s] the bracelets on her arms and the rings in her ears" (172).

There are stunning similarities between this charade and Rochester's treatment of Jane, particularly in chapter twenty-five, after they are engaged. Jane's reflection: "I thought his smile was such as a sultan might in a blissful and fond moment, bestow on a slave his gold and gems had enriched" (255) recalls the charade and reveals Rochester's dark desire to control and manipulate. He will bestow upon her not just his smile but literal jewels as well: "I wrote to my banker in London to send me certain jewels he has in his keeping.... I hope to pour them into your lap" (245). He will afford Jane every attention "that [he] would accord a peer's daughter" (245).

At this point, I would want to observe the ways that the language of the novel reflects and even helps create imperialist ideology. This is a topic taken up by many critics, including Gayatri Spivak, in her article "Three Women's Texts and a Critique of Imperialism," which begins: "It should not be possible to read nineteenth-century British literature without remembering that imperialism, understood as England's social mission, was a crucial part of the cultural representation of England to the English. The role of literature in the production of cultural representation should not be ignored" (243). In these two scenes, the novel draws on ideas about the East—which are not ideas about an actual East, but a Western ideal, shaped by a sense of entitlement—in order to obliquely critique patriarchy. Here, and at other moments throughout the novel, Brontë suggests that removing problematic "Eastern" elements would lead to more equitable relations between men and women. Such a view, common among nineteenth-century feminist writers, furthers imperialist ideologies even as it attempts to break down patriarchy, since it enables "British readers to contemplate local problems without questioning their own self-definition as Westerners and Christians"

(Zonana 593). Brontë's problematic use of imperialist tropes notwithstanding, the charade scene provides a pointed critique of wedlock. With the third charade, the critique is complete and the "secret message" (as Sandra Gilbert puts it) is revealed:

> "conventional marriage is not only...a 'well' of mystery, it is Bridewell, a prison" (Gilbert 789). Marriage, intimately linked to Bridewell prison, famed for incarcerating prostitutes, is also linked to prostitution. This third tableau presents, then, a stark picture of marriage as mystery, prison, and prostitution. It elaborates, furthermore, what is missing in the first two charades, illuminating aspects of character that the first two charades obscured. (Sweeney)

In this third charade, "Only a portion of the drawing-room was disclosed, the rest being concealed by a screen, hung with some sort of dark and coarse drapery" (Brontë, Bantam 172). The rest of the lavish Thornfield drawing room, which featured prominently in the last two charades, has been obscured. As the curtain rises, Jane notes that the 'stage' has been stripped of all embellishments and most customary props. The excess of the two previous charades— the embroidery, the ornaments, the flowers, the marble basin—are gone and only very rudimentary furniture remains. Rochester is the lone figure in a "sordid" scene where all is not revealed, and what is revealed is seen dimly (172). Like the stark scene itself, Rochester has been stripped of the shawls he wore as emir, symbolically stripped of his emblems of power. Acting as a prisoner, an outcast on the fringe of society, Rochester is alone on stage without others as foils to his power. His fearful portrayal of a prisoner is very unlike his usual erudite, independent self. He is acting without prop, unkempt and with "desperate and scowling countenance" (173). This description is remarkably like that of his wife Bertha: "It was a discolored face--it was a savage face" with "fearful blackened inflation of the lineaments" (269). The "quantity of dark, grizzled hair, wild as a mane" (278) on Bertha's head is not unlike Rochester's "rough bristling hair."

The scene is a grim reminder that marriage, when stripped of its stabilizing accoutrements (like the props of the first two charades), can be a psychosexual power play in which the masculine seeks dominion over the feminine. This darker Dionysian side of marriage threatens the order, stability, and seeming immutability of the marriage paradigms represented in the first two charades. (Sweeney)

This third charade—the tableau of the whole—is "Bridewell," which, it seems worth noting, is not just "Bridewell, a prison," but Bridewell, an orphanage: Bridewell Palace was given by Edward VI to the City of London in 1553 for use as both an orphanage and a place of punishment. This may serve as a reminder to us that Jane, as an orphan, has been imprisoned before, and will be so again, if she succumbs to the fantasy of the charade.

The third charade also provocatively links Bertha and Rochester. While I allude to this in my paper, I would explore their connection even more, in particular looking at the important final chapters of the novel.

In her article on *Jane Eyre* and disability Elizabeth Donaldson argues that, "at her death, Bertha's disabling mental illness is transferred to the body of her husband as physical impairment and blindness, which, in turn, are deployed by Brontë to depict melancholic madness" (108). Yet, she cautions, the two experiences are quite different: Bertha's madness is "congenital and chronic" while "Rochester's is coincidental and curable" (109). His vision is restored in time for him to recognize his son as his own; Bertha remains an almost inhuman Other, who dies a brutal death. The very fact of Bertha's existence "is a condemnation of the marriage glorified by the Victorians as the private paradise, a configuration of the scandalous, ugly history involving upper-class familial betrayal and warfare caused by patrimony" and by "British colonialist activities" (Huang 110). The final chapters of the novel attempt to remove all traces of Bertha, except insofar as she has been a catalyst for Rochester's reformation. And although, as the novel has made clear, Brontë is aware of the dangerous power men held in marriage, she ultimately reproduces the language of colonizer/colonized and master/servant when she describes Jane and Rochester's reunion.

As an undergraduate, though, I was more troubled by the punishments that Brontë lavishes upon Rochester at the end of the novel. I found it peculiar that she could so expertly critique gender roles in the charade scene and then succumb to what I thought of as essentialist thinking. Why, I wondered, is "the maiming of Rochester"—a symbolic castration/literal loss of vision and a loss of his hand—"a necessary prelude to the lovers' reunion"? (Boone 97). Now, however, I'd suggest that Rochester's disfigurement (brutal, perhaps, but nothing compared to Bertha's ghastly death) is a violent physical revolt against his fearsome phallic power and the legal, social, and sexual benefits that manhood conferred. It can be read as a kind of acknowledgement, however inchoate, that these injustices have a palpable effect on the body. The physical and emotional razing of Rochester at the end *should* trouble us as readers, not because we find it unpleasant, but because Brontë had good reasons for it in her attempt to create her "final union of relative parity" (97).

The ending also demonstrates that Jane is complicit in perpetuating the same psychosexual power plays as Rochester. With Bertha conveniently out of the way and Rochester thus reduced, Jane has her moment of triumph. Throughout chapter thirty-seven, she is coy without somehow being coquettish. (The image of Jane, "pertinaciously perched" (Brontë, Bedford 432) on Rochester's knee, may call to mind the flirtatious little Adèle scrambling onto laps). Although Jane still manages to be scrupulously honest, she nonetheless, as one critic says, "teases and manipulates, arouses his jealousy and bestows little endearments": "the truant Cinderella returns a little queen" (Huang 114). Her gentle sadism scans (for many readers) as titillating courtship practice.

Whereas Rochester once teased her by allowing her to believe he loves Blanche, now she torments him by suggesting that she cares for St. John Rivers, telling him that St. John is "an accomplished and profound scholar" and "a handsome man: tall, fair, with blue eyes, and Grecian profile" (Brontë, Bedford 430). Jane insists that she allows the jealousy to sting Rochester because it is "salutary," giving him respite from his melancholy, but it is clear that she takes pleasure in her newfound power. Before, his age, class, and sexual experience conferred greater power; now she, with her youth and physical ability, has the upper hand, and Rochester worries that he will be seen as fatherly. In this reversal, the servant is now the master, although she still, cheekily, calls him master.

Despite this power reversal, Rochester retains (Jane makes sure to emphasize), a significant portion of his manly strength:

> He groped: I arrested his wandering hand, and prisoned it in both mine.
> "Her very fingers!" he cried; "her small, slight fingers! If so, there must be more of her."
> The muscular hand broke from my custody; my arm was seized, my shoulder—neck—waist—I was entwined and gathered to him. (422)

His "muscular" hand does not stay "prisoned" by hers for long and soon Rochester (here a force that seizes, entwines, and gathers) makes clear that he still has Jane in his clutches. Her power has its limits.

I realize now that, as an undergraduate, I was invested in seeing Jane as a kind of love-warrior. She was idiosyncratic, complex: sometimes fiery and sometimes cold. When she says, "Reader, I married him" I saw it as Jane asserting her power as an active subject: "the tacit message being that 'I' married 'him'—not that 'he' married 'me' or even that 'we were married' (Oates 202). The statement seemed appropriately fierce: Jane was choosing her fate. And, she assures us again and again, she and Rochester are blissfully happy: she tells us (not *quite* gloating) that "no woman was ever nearer to her mate than I am" (Brontë, Bedford 439). Even at the time, though, I felt that the conclusion was over-hasty. Within the space of a few pages, the problematic master and servant games (apparently) dissolve, the baby shows up, Rochester regains his sight, and they live happily ever after in "perfect concord" (439).

And what, I ask now, is the nature of this perfection? It is predicated not only on our acceptance of Jane's subordinance to

Rochester—for, despite her masterful games, she has accepted that her job is "doing for him what he wished to be done" (439)—but also on the exaltation of couplehood at the cost of almost all else. The novel's final chapter emphasizes the solitary existence the couple leads. It is true that they do see Jane's cousins a few times a year, and a much-reformed (that is to say, more fully British) Adèle is a "pleasing and obliging companion" when she's not away at school (439). For the most part, though, they live alone, in shadowy Ferndean, in relative isolation. Such an existence reflects the nineteenth-century imperative of domestic bliss. According to popular media of the day, home was not a house, but a 'sanctuary of domestic love,' an 'oasis,' a 'hallowed place,' a 'quiet refuge from the storms of life" (Coontz 164). The motto of the periodical "*The Magazine of Domestic Economy*, which began publishing in London in 1835," was: "The comfort and economy of home are of more deep, heartfelt, and personal interest to us, than the public affairs of all the nations of the world" (qtd. in Coontz 164); Rochester and Jane (now Mr. and Mrs. Rochester) exemplify this ideal. They create an insular world in which they become everything to each other: "I know no weariness of my Edward's society: he knows none of mine, any more than we each do of the pulsation of the heart that beats in our separate bosoms; consequently, we are ever together" (Brontë, Bedford 439).

In his history on marriage in Britain, John R. Gillis emphasizes that the conjugal bond has not always been seen as "the only possible relationship capable of fulfilling the human need for companionship, intimacy, and love" (12). Although the ideal of a companionate marriage had been in place for generations, during the nineteenth century, "young people started to believe that love was far more sublime and far less reasoned than mutual esteem" (Coontz 178). The mid-nineteenth century was also a time of increased sexual and marital conformity (Gillis 231), when the conjugal couple was hailed as the primary model for opposite-sex relations and a sign of what seemed inevitable progress in male-female relationships. A profusion of images and texts idealized them. In 1847 (the same year that *Jane Eyre* was published), the poet Alfred, Lord Tennyson wrote, "seeing either sex alone/Is half itself, and true marriage lies/ Nor equal, nor unequal. Each fulfills/Defect in each" (qtd. in Gillis 232).

Such a sentimental view of the married couple had an effect on honeymooning, which (for those who could afford it), was often a family affair before the middle of the century. Friends and family might accompany the couple on post-nuptial travels, emphasizing the communal nature of the conjugal bond. In fact, "it was not until 1846 that an upper-class marriage manual commented, as a relative novelty, that 'the young couple take their journey, as is now the fashion, in a tête-à-tête'" (Stone 225). In *Jane Eyre*, Rochester suggests that his life with Jane itself will itself be an extension of the honeymoon: "our honey-moon will shine our life-long: its beams will only fade over your grave or mine" (Brontë, Bedford 438). The extended honeymoon at Ferndean thus reflects the trend toward exclusionary couplehood and also, as with any powerful and popular literary text, plays a role in its construction.

Despite its very real images of servitude, despite its image of a sequestered couple (who would probably be accused of suffocating co-dependence if transferred to modern times), the ending appeals to many readers. In what Gillis calls our "conjugal age, when the couple has become the standard for all intimate relationships, the unmarried and the married," (3) Rochester and Jane's "perfect concord" (Brontë, Bedford 439) can seem tantalizing. At a time when physical appearance often trumps emotional connection, the bond between these two, fostered by scintillating conversation, seems a good model. Add to this a supernatural intervention that seems to preordain their reunion, and the tug of this marriage plot is hard to resist.

Still, I have suggested that by looking more carefully at the language of the novel and reading it within its historical context, we might be more cautious about celebrating the ending. Rather than accepting Jane's vision of blissful union, we can continue to ask questions. Do we have evidence that the imperious Rochester could be rehabilitated? Is nuptial isolation a satisfactory model of male-female relations? What does the novel encourage us to forget or deny in order to see the ending as a happy one?

Had I been a more intrepid researcher as an undergraduate, I might have come across a letter that Brontë wrote to a good friend on her own honeymoon in 1854, in which she acknowledged her own ambivalence about marriage: "It is a solemn and strange and perilous thing" she says, "for a woman to become a wife. Man's lot is far—far different" (qtd. in Moglen 235). Like Jane, Brontë was conflicted about marriage. Her letter suggests anxiety about the gender divide, her own inability or unwillingness to speak about the benefits marriage conferred to men, and the loneliness of the "honeymooning" woman. Brontë wasn't married when she wrote *Jane Eyre*, nor should *Jane Eyre* be read as her autobiography, despite its original subtitle.[3] Still, it's hard not to think of just how perilous marriage was for Brontë and how a difficult pregnancy may have led to her early death less than a year after her wedding. Her own life and the life of her heroine demonstrate that, despite the rise of companionate marriage in the nineteenth century, marriage was still a solemn, strange, and perilous thing for women on several fundamental levels: economically, emotionally, and physically.

Thus re-reading *Jane Eyre* today doesn't give me the romantic thrill I once expected, which is, in a sense, a disappointment. In another sense, though, I've come to understand that recognizing the novel's complexities is its own pleasure. I've gained fresh insight into the role of love, courtship, and marriage, not just in this wonderfully conflicted novel, but also in the world beyond the book. When I teach other novels in my college classes, then, I remain mindful of my own encounters with *Jane Eyre*. I don't deny the pull of romance plots, but I encourage students to be aware of what forces sustain these plots, define them, and grant them their power. As they become careful critical readers, students also, I hope, have the chance to experience the particular thrills that this kind of reading (and rereading) can offer.

Acknowledgment

Thanks to my college professor, Maryclaire Moroney, who first guided me down this path.

Notes

1. "Admit" is a bit generous here. He is, rather, forced into confessing.
2. In "Bluebeard," the titular character marries and murders several women and keeps their corpses in a locked room in his castle. Jane herself likens Thornfield to "Blue Beard's castle" in chapter eleven (Brontë, Bedford 114). In "Rapunzel," the prince is blinded when a witch throws him off of a tower and into thorn bushes below; in Jane Eyre, Rochester is blinded by (the fire at) Thornfield. Like the prince, Rochester regains his sight, recovering from his encounter with the "witch," Bertha.
3. Jane Eyre was originally published under the title *Jane Eyre: an Autobiography*.

Works Cited

Boone, Joseph. *Tradition Counter Tradition: Love and the Form of Fiction*. Chicago: U of Chicago P., 1987.

Brontë, Charlotte. *Jane Eyre*. 1847. New York: Bantam Books, 1988.

Brontë, Charlotte. *Jane Eyre*. 1847. Boston: Bedford Books, 1996.

Coontz, Stephanie. *Marriage, a History: From Obedience to Intimacy or How Love Conquered Marriage*. New York: Viking, 2005.

Donaldson, Elizabeth. "The Corpus of the Madwoman: Toward a Feminist Disability Studies Theory of Embodiment and Mental Illness." *NWSA Journal* 14.3 (2002): 99-119. *Project Muse*. Web. 15 Oct. 2013.

Gilbert, Sandra M. "Plain Jane's Progress." *Signs* 2.4 (1977): 779-804. *JSTOR*. Web. 30 Sept. 2013.

Gillis, John R. *For Better, For Worse: British Marriages, 1600 to the Present*. New York: Oxford UP, 1985.

Huang, Mei. *Transforming the Cinderella Dream*. New Brunswick: Rutgers UP, 1990.

Moglen, Helen. *Charlotte Brontë: The Self Conceived*. 1976. Madison: U of Wisconsin P. 1984.

Oates, Joyce Carol. "Romance and Anti-Romance: From Brontë's *Jane Eyre* to Rhys's *Wide Sargasso Sea*." Virginia Quarterly Review (1985): 44-58. VQROnline. Web. 15 Oct. 2013.

Spivak, Gayatri Chakravorty. "Three Women's Texts and a Critique of Imperialism." *Critical Inquiry* 12.1 (1985): 243-61. *JSTOR*. Web. 30 Sept. 2013.

Stone, Lawrence. *The Family, Sex and Marriage in England, 1500-1800.* New York: Harper's Torch Books, 1979.

Sweeney, Meghan. "'Charadized' Relationships in *Jane Eyre.*" Unpublished Undergraduate Paper. John Carroll U, 1997.

Winter, Jessica. "Up in the Eyre." *Slate.* Slate Group, 10 March 2011. Web. 15 Sept. 2013.

Zonana, Joyce. "The Sultan and the Slave: Feminist Orientalism and the Structure of *Jane Eyre.*" *Signs* 18.3 (1993): 592-617. *JSTOR*. Web. 12 Sept. 2013.

Re-Reading *Jane Eyre*: **Not a Romantic Marriage Plot but a Tale of Evolving Feminist Consciousness** _____

Barbara Waxman

I remember well the first time I read Charlotte Brontë's *Jane Eyre* as a teenager in the early 1960s. It was winter break from school, and I devoured the novel in one full day: I took it in as a page-turning, romantic tale of a young, mousy orphan growing into womanhood by means of her intelligence, pertness, and the wit that catches the eye of her employer, the imperious and sexy Edward Rochester. The attractiveness of this Romantic hero overshadowed my moral concerns about wife Bertha, as Edward began a flirtation with Jane that almost led to an act of bigamy.

I noticed the strength Jane had to abandon, on moral grounds, her beloved master and to leave the fraught patriarchal space of Thornfield. But I failed to notice the rebellious tenor of Jane's moral promptings. I noticed her longing to be bodily and emotionally possessed by Rochester, but I did not see that Jane made a *feminist* choice, that is, the choice *for* woman's autonomy and a choice *against* oppression or silencing by a man—a choice insuring that Jane will be her own mistress. She declares, "'Mr. Rochester, I will *not* be yours'" (311). When she is soon sheltered in another patriarchal household, that of St. John Rivers, I did not attend much to this even more imperious man, who wants to suppress half of Jane's nature and impose upon her his evangelical mission and patriarchal will. I simply wanted Jane and Edward to reunite. I didn't appreciate how much emotional independence and moral strength she was developing while apart from Rochester. I also saw Jane learn submission to St. John—but I did not interrogate this lesson of feminine self-suppression. Finally, when Jane is telepathically called back to the Rochesterian space of Ferndean, the reunion of the two seemed a perfect celebration of love. Jane's words, "Reader, I married him," represented the pinnacle of her achievement, the wifely role.

Notice how my first reading—well before I had developed into a feminist reader and literary scholar myself—understates Jane's growing power and does not value the decisions she made to protect her integrity, her autonomy. I was so enthralled by Rochester's charisma that I missed signs of Jane's growing feminist consciousness: her awareness of her own and other women's oppression as well as her increasing strength to resist feminine submission. I missed the development of her gendered activism, registered through Jane's retrospective narrative, which traces her movements into symbolically-resonant spatial settings: from orphaned dependency, yet incipient rebellion, at Gateshead; to years of intermittent resistance and agency at the charity school Lowood; to lesser dependency as governess at Thornfield, where she walked the corridors that taught her about the oppression of married women through the metaphor of Bertha's chains. At Thornfield, she grew in feminist consciousness, but was still reliant on salary and the approval of her master and dreamed of marrying him (it made sense to me in 1960). Marsh End and the school in Morton seemed an insignificant limbo where she awaited reunion with Rochester; I missed the significant work she did as teacher at the girls' school, her agency there, the true significance of her inheritance (I thought it a nice way for her to pay back her cousins for their generosity), and the strength of her resistance to St. John's scheme to colonize her life.

However, this perspective changed when I returned to the book a decade later: I was amazed to learn how different Brontë's novel is from that romantic book. Multiple readings later, having embraced feminism and the tools of feminist literary criticism, I saw the novel's feminist subplot and the growth in the main plot of Jane's feminist consciousness, depicted through the symbolic settings. Finally, 1 could see the novel's closing message of women's empowerment in marriage and beyond. My own feminist consciousness had developed enough for me to observe Jane's resistance to all forms of oppression and her questioning of the practices of patriarchal institutions.

With the help of feminist critics Sandra Gilbert and Susan Gubar in their ground-breaking book *The Madwoman in the Attic*, I now see in Brontë's novel a feminist text way ahead of its time (1848). I learned from Gilbert and Gubar that structurally, the main plot may unfold into happiness within a revised version of the patriarchal institution of marriage, while the subplot tells of the true damage marriage can do to a woman through the madwoman raving against society's incarceration of herself. This subplot joins forces with the narrator's overt feminist musings in the mansion's third story, recalled by an older and stronger Jane, to convey a message of feminist strength and resistance to women's oppression—even if the protesting wife has to be destroyed in a house fire to pacify patriarchal readers. Aided by Gilbert and Gubar's exposure of this subplot's workings and abetted by my own fully-evolved feminist notions, I now see how Jane, with Edward somewhat chastened, is able to use her strength, financial autonomy, and feminist consciousness to form a marriage with a man no longer her master.

Elaine Showalter also enables me to see that the marriage of Jane and Rochester is a marriage of equals because Jane has become mistress of herself emotionally, quelling her own "dark passion" (122, 124) and fully integrating her spirit with her body (113). I see Jane's fully integrated central consciousness—more than Showalter does—as a *feminist* consciousness. Showalter's historicizing discussion of women's literature, *A Literature of Their Own: British Women Novelists from Brontë to Lessing*, argues that British women writers may be grouped in three chronological phases: feminine, feminist, and female. Showalter posits that *Jane Eyre* belongs to the feminine phase, as indicated by the author's use of the male pseudonym (Currer Bell), by the "preaching of submission and self-sacrifice" (21), by the punishment of self-assertion in the heroines, and by projection of their ambitions onto male characters who attain success (28). However, it may be more useful to see Brontë's novel as a radical forerunner of the feminist phase of novels by women, which Showalter characterizes as follows: "The feminists challenged many of the restrictions on women's self-expression, denounced the gospel of self-sacrifice, attacked patriarchal religion, and constructed a theoretical model of female oppression" (29). This feminist novelistic project, as my re-reading of the novel suggests, describes the scope and purpose of Jane's narrative, especially Jane's outcry against the injustices that patriarchal institutions have perpetrated against women. I would just add to Showalter's definition of the feminist novel one notion that fits the adult Jane: *agency*. Jane's narrative reveals how she takes initiatives to direct her own fate. I will argue that the older Jane, married to Edward for a decade, has a fully developed feminist consciousness that colors her retrospective narrative, in which she counsels readers to gender activism and portrays her own self-possession.

My re-reading is also indebted to the feminist methods of Judith Fetterley in *The Resisting Reader*. She applies these to American literature by men, but if we assume that women may be complicit with men in reinforcing patriarchal values in the nineteenth century, we can use Fetterley's method of resistant reading to interpret Brontë's novel by resisting the romantic main plot and Rochester's manipulations of Jane, while also criticizing his destruction of Bertha's spirit (Showalter 122). Fetterley's method rests on her definition of the work of the feminist critic: "the first act of the feminist critic must be to become a resisting rather than an assenting reader and, by this refusal to assent, to begin the process of exorcising the male mind that has been implanted in us" (xxii). To resist the male mind's notions that women are weak and submissive and men are strong and dominant is to question even female authors' traditional characterizations or gender role stereotypes in literary texts. Fetterley thus proposes an activist reading project: "To expose and question that complex of ideas and mythologies about women and men which exist in our society [and the Victorians'] and are confirmed in our literature is to make the system of power embodied in the literature open not only to discussion but even to change" (xx). These words enabled me in re-reading Brontë's novel to question Jane's acquiescence to the charisma, sexy charm, and ruthless power of Edward Rochester and to temper my earlier view of Jane's marriage as happily-ever-after. Because of Fetterley's work, I have a perspective, which "questions . . . [the Victorian patriarchal system's] values and assumptions and which has its investment in making available to consciousness precisely that which the literature wishes to keep hidden" (xx).

I now revisit the novel's architectural spaces, guided by Showalter and other feminist critics to examine how these spaces function symbolically to depict female sexuality and an oppressive patriarchal power (Showalter 113). In these spaces, Jane directly questions patriarchal values and behaviors. With my feminist lenses on, I now observe her questioning and point out the increasing signs of the protagonist's emergent feminist outlook and feminist agency. I resist the novel's surface marriage plot and reinterpret the nature of Jane's marriage to Edward by underscoring Jane's intensifying feminist consciousness, that is, a perspective, which advocates for the empowerment of women and challenges all people and institutions that oppress others.

At Gateshead, Jane's position as a dependent in the Reed household is precarious and marginal; she is excluded from the family circle of her aunt and cousins. She is subjected to bullying and physical assault by cousin John Reed, patriarch-in-training and future owner of Gateshead; she fears him and is "habitually obedient" to the future master (23). When he flings a book at her, however, she rails against him, the first act of rebellion readers see. John is the oppressor, "'a slave-driver. . . .—like the Roman emperors!'" (23). He is described by an older Jane as a male dictator.

Jane is punished for her rebelliousness with confinement in the red-room. In this room, the patriarch of Gateshead had died; it still retains the patriarchal power and presence of Mr. Reed. The red rage of Jane's protest against her oppression—"the mood of the revolted slave was still bracing me with its bitter vigour" (27)—is evident here. When I first read the novel, I thought of Jane as a naughty child, not a repressed slave, but her thoughts about her situation, as voiced by the adult Jane, are expressed in the language of a feminist who feels the slave's injustice, "Why was I always suffering, always brow-beaten, always accused, for ever condemned?" (27). She intends to end her suffering through "insurrection . . . to achieve escape from insupportable oppression" (27-8). When she has a ghostly visitation by her dead uncle, his presence is unnerving to a girl with feminist leanings! Confined in the terrifying space of the red-room, Jane can only submit by losing consciousness. I once dismissed the red-room episode as the performance of a disobedient child. I did not ask why naughtiness was punishable for girls, while Cousin John was surly to his mother, yet still indulged. Now, I see the traditional gender roles at Gateshead and their unfairness to Jane. No wonder she rebels—against both sexism and classism.

Before Jane leaves for Lowood School, she confronts her aunt about their interactions, using language that challenges societal rules (48). She identifies Aunt Reed as her foe (51) because Mrs. Reed is a woman who subscribes to patriarchal institutions and practices. I now see the feminist spirit of the liberator in Jane's celebratory language of self-empowerment: "my soul began to expand, to exult with the strangest sense of freedom, of triumph, I ever felt. It seemed as if an invisible bond had burst, and that I had struggled out into unhoped-for liberty" (48). What I had observed in my early reading of *Jane Eyre* as a triumph in the battle between children and authority figures, I now see as feminist utterance by the adult Jane: she remembers this showdown with Mrs. Reed as one skirmish in the battle against the oppressive Victorian doctrine of The Angel in the House (originally a poem by Coventry Patmore that praises the Victorians' domestic ideology). Jane's confrontation with Mrs. Reed prepares her to resist Lowood School's space of self-repression.

Mr. Brocklehurst, Lowood's male authority figure, seems, in this re-reading, the epitome of both patriarchal imperiousness and evangelical Christianity's doctrine of self-abnegation, at least for lower-class females. I had previously seen that he was peremptory to Jane, but now I see him as bolstered by institutions that attempt to silence rebellious females. Lowood is almost like a convent: "it punishes and starves . . .[the girls'] sexuality" (Showalter 117). Brocklehurst's advocacy of discipline, submission, and spartan fare and dress (72) is evident in the spaces and daily routine of Lowood: burnt porridge; scant meals; severe, brown uniforms; unheated rooms; and nary a "frivolous" curl on feminine heads. Lowood teaches the girls "'to mortify . . . the lusts of the flesh'" (74). Jane resists such education.

Showalter and other critics have suggested that Jane has two female role models at Lowood who reinforce the lessons of femininity as selfless generosity, moderation, spiritualization, and self-repression. These behaviors are embodied in Miss Temple and Helen Burns (344). Miss Temple exemplifies the moderation, gentleness, and intelligence of the female adult. She accepts some patriarchal rules of refined womanhood, but when her pupils are literally starving, she orders a decent lunch for them, challenging Brocklehurst's extreme doctrines. In her friendship with Helen, Jane's budding feminist principles protest against the unjust punishment that Helen meekly endures (62). She watches Helen being beaten by a teacher with twigs and declares that in her place, Jane would break the rod. Helen advises Jane to submit to her duty (65); she quotes a Biblical passage about returning good for evil— teaching submission in the face of abuse of power (65).

Jane would take this Biblical lesson of submission as patriarchal and overpower it. By including it, as an adult, in her retrospective narrative and by questioning the lesson, she could be said to have "engorged the patriarchy" in feminist critic Nina Auerbach's sense of the term. Auerbach says: "'Probably I share the primitive superstition that by writing about the patriarchy, as by eating it, I engorge its power'" (qtd. by Gallop 229). Jane is engorging the patriarchy by denouncing the idea of returning good for evil: "If people were always kind and obedient to those who are cruel and unjust, the wicked people would have it all their own way" (67). To resist injustice and tyranny is, in Jane's view, a way to improve the world: a good feminist principle.

My feminist viewpoint also guides me now to notice the resurgence of Jane's resistant feelings after Miss Temple's departure into matrimony. Jane's state of mind is marked architecturally as she gazes outside a window, seeking a breath of fresh air and a new perspective, specifically the mountain peaks beyond Lowood's "prison" walls. She utters a feminist prayer for liberty, or at least for "a new servitude" (93-4). I resist Jane's self-characterization here;

she thinks she is moving from one kind of servitude to another, but I also see her growth in feminist empowerment and consciousness. At age eighteen, she is autonomous, having earned a teacher's salary for two years, and she is able to take the initiative to leave, using some of her salary to advertise her availability for a position as a governess.

Because governesses are viewed as servants in the Victorian era, we can examine how Jane eventually transgresses this servitude at Thornfield. Jane's emphasis in her narrative on the space of the third story of the house shows us her feminist views in ways I did not notice when first reading the novel; I was so intent on the turns of plot and the evolution of the relationship between Jane and Rochester that I failed to interpret the symbolic significance of this setting and did not examine the interior monologues of Jane that occur in the house's third story and gallery. The third floor acts like a minor character in the narrative, carrying a socially subversive theme about women in Victorian society—in the same way that, as Gilbert and Gubar have famously argued, Bertha Mason and her subplot function in the novel as angry feminist commentary on how the patriarchy constrains Victorian women.

The first-person narrator gives painstaking and lengthy (longer than I had remembered) attention to description of the third story, and this reading invites opportunities to interpret symbolically the objects in the setting symbolically. Well before Rochester enters the plot, this space reveals his patriarchal history and Jane's restlessness, her resistance to the oppression she experiences daily as a poor, single Victorian woman. When Jane recalls her tour of the house with Mrs. Fairfax, she describes the "relics," the carved -wood furnishings of the third story, which make it "a home of the past: a shrine of memory" (113). And some of the furnishings resemble "the Hebrew ark" (113). Having had a Jewish education, unlike Jane, I know the ark would house Torah scrolls, ancient Hebrew scriptures written by generations of male scribes. Perhaps as the daughter of a clergyman, Brontë herself had some lessons in the Hebrew scriptures. In any case, patriarchal Hebrew forefathers hover in the woodwork, so

Jane might be associating the ark-like furnishings with the history of Thornfield's male owners.

The third story contains a staircase that leads up to the attic rooms (one of which houses Bertha) and from there, by ladder and trap-door, to the roof, or "leads." When Jane retraces her steps alone down the ladder and staircase to the dark corridor of the third story, while Mrs. Fairfax latches the trap-door, Jane describes the corridor in sinister patriarchal terms as "a corridor in some Bluebeard's castle" (114). Beth Newman notes that Bluebeard was "a fairy-tale character who married and murdered several women, whose bodies he kept locked in one of the rooms in his castle" (fn 114). This grim characterization of the third story's architectural space alludes to the possibilities of a dangerous violence within the institution of marriage.

Experiencing claustrophobia in the mansion owned by Edward the patriarch, Jane often flees to the leads to seek a larger perspective, "a power of vision which might overpass that limit" (116). She also paces back and forth along the corridor of the third story like a caged beast—like the imprisoned Bertha. Considered from a feminist ideological perspective, what has struck me the most in re-readings of Brontë's text is the overtly feminist language of Jane's narrative as she reminisces about what she thought while walking this corridor (granted, the text is written when she is an older married woman, looking back on her days as a young governess). She remembers meditating on the unfairness of traditional Victorian gender roles:

> Millions are condemned to a stiller doom than mine, and millions are in silent revolt against their lot. Nobody knows how many rebellions besides political rebellions [social or gender rebellions] ferment in the masses of life which people earth. Women are supposed to be very calm generally: but women feel just as men feel; they need exercise for their faculties, and a field for their efforts, as much as their brothers do; they suffer from too rigid a restraint, too absolute a stagnation, precisely as men would suffer; and it is narrow-minded in their more privileged fellow-creatures to say that they ought to confine themselves to making puddings and knitting stockings, to playing on the piano and embroidering bags (116-17).

Jane here protests against the unfulfilling domestic roles assigned to Victorian women. She affirms the equal humanity of women and men, the similarities in their intense feelings, ambitions, and complex intellectual faculties: women yearn for a role and purpose beyond a kind of robotic, gender-role-performance. Jane asserts that women need a societal role and a workplace outlet for their talents and faculties. I am reminded of Florence Nightingale's decrying of women's lack of meaningful work in *Cassandra*. Similarly, the Prelude to George Eliot's *Middlemarch* (1874) bemoans the lack of an outlet for the intellectually and spiritually gifted protagonist Dorothea Brooke; Dorothea has no "coherent social faith and order," no opportunity to lead "an epic life" (3-4). Brontë, many years before Eliot, is voicing similar frustrations through Jane. Marriage is a less-than-satisfactory outlet for an epic life.

In this patriarchal residence, the courtship between Jane and Rochester plays out, conveying not only Rochester's emotional infidelity to Bertha and intention of being sexually unfaithful to her, but also his cruel manipulation of Jane through Blanche Ingram and of Blanche too. As Gilbert and Gubar assert, within Thornfield's thorny patriarchal walls, the "game of the marriage market [is] a game even scheming women [like Blanche] are doomed to lose" (350). In this reading, I resist Rochester's cruel charms as I watch him use Blanche and her marital hopes to create jealousy in Jane's heart. I especially see Rochester's sexually charged interactions with Jane as taking advantage of her powerless position. He exudes "the very essence of patriarchal energy" (Gilbert and Gubar 351)—energy comprised of social power and libido—when he flirts with Jane.

Thus it is possible to interpret Edward's behavior as sexual harassment of Jane because, to win her heart, he uses his position of power as master of Thornfield Hall, as her employer, and as a man twenty years her senior. Jane, however, is complicit in the sexualizing of their relationship, which might compromise her autonomy. In this respect, her feminist consciousness has a blind spot. Or perhaps as a feminist, Jane boldly acknowledges the workings of sexual desire in a young woman. One thing is in any case apparent in Jane and Edward's interactions: they both bemoan the asexuality of Jane's training at Lowood, she criticizing Brocklehurst for cutting the girls' hair off (130)—hair being a symbol of sensuous femininity—and he observing twice that she has been raised to be a nun. He says, "'You have lived the life of a nun'" (129) and calls her a "little nonnette" (137). This patriarch would remove from the Lowood nun the self-repression which, ironically, her patriarchal education has produced in her: "'The Lowood constraint still clings to you somewhat; controlling your features, muffling your voice, and restricting your limbs; and you fear in the presence of a man and a brother—or father, or master, or what you will—to smile too gaily, speak too freely, or move too quickly'" (144). Her conformity to patriarchal rules is evident in her demeanor; he would remove these rules, releasing the "natural" Jane to disobey the doctrine of The Angel in the House and to satisfy her sexual nature.

That their flirtation is physically based is evident in the recollections of the Jane-narrator, who has been Edward's wife for a decade, when she recounts their early conversation by the fireplace. He asks her if she finds him handsome (137), stands by the mantel and reveals to her, somewhat flauntingly, his "unusual breadth of chest" (138), and confesses to her that he is a common sinner. Deftly, calculatingly, he broaches the subject of his desire for pleasure in life. His language implies that this pleasure is sensual: he speaks of "'sweet, fresh pleasure, . . . as sweet and fresh as the wild honey the bee gathers on the moor'" (142). The bee penetrating the flower is certainly suggestive of Rochester's desire to penetrate the nun-like, therefore sweet and fresh, Jane.

The second sign of the dynamic of sexual harassment evident in their interactions is that Rochester uses a peremptory tone in giving Jane orders and expects them to be obeyed (136) ; also, he declares his "right to be a little masterful" with her because he is old enough to be her father (139). Jane, too, knows that she must obey his orders as "a paid subordinate" (140). Yet, she rationally stands her ground within this unequal power situation, denying Edward's right to ascendency over her due to age, "'I don't think, sir, you have a right to command me, merely because you are older than I, . . . your claim to superiority depends on the use you have made of your time and experience'" (140). She also declares that, as a "free-born" person, despite being a paid subordinate, she would not tolerate "insolence" from her master, and she is skeptical of his stated intention not "'to treat . . . [her] like an inferior'" (139). She feels the sexual pressure and resists it.

From this early establishment of Jane's feminist awareness in her fireside chat with her master, the narrative moves to the space of Edward's bedroom when Bertha sets her husband's bed on fire; in this space, at this moment in the plot, readers may question the strength of Jane's feminist consciousness. Jane proactively rescues her sleeping master from the flames, which might suggest that he is in her debt for saving his life, something of a power-equalizer. But if the flames represent Bertha's outrage at her treatment by Rochester—Nina Auerbach calls Bertha "that paradigm of incendiary womanhood that sprang out of the revolutionary [eighteen] forties" (43)—then I regret Jane's collusion with her master over Bertha's oppression. She is willing to keep silent about the partial knowledge she has gained regarding Bertha this night and in the subsequent night, when Bertha wounds her brother Richard Mason (214). Although she has the feminist self-possession not to let Rochester seduce her on the night of the fire, she still displays loyalty to patriarchy by keeping her master's secret about the attack on Richard. (Granted, with full knowledge of Bertha's oppressive situation, she might have exposed Rochester's cruelty.)

Jane's feminist self-possession is demonstrated subsequently and often during the remainder of her time at Thornfield. After a brief fantasy of requited love and marriage to her master, Jane recognizes that her own rank and position within Rochester's household make their marriage untenable; in feminist terms, she acknowledges their unequal power relations:

> "It does good to no woman to be flattered by her superior, who cannot possibly intend to marry her; and it is madness in all women to let a secret love kindle within them, which, if unreturned and unknown, must devour the life that feeds it; and, if discovered and responded to, must lead, . . . into miry wilds whence there is no extrication" (164).

Jane's reference to "miry wilds" foreshadows the moral swamp that she almost advances into with Edward. Before she moves to the brink of marriage, she admits to readers that she has, regrettably, been mastered by Edward; he imposes on her "an influence . . . that took my feelings from my own power and fettered them in his" (177-38). Here are more images of incarceration and chains associated with love in a way that would not have alarmed my romantic, adolescent, reading self (how wonderful to be mastered by love, to be swept away by passion!); yet Jane's imagery of love here mirrors the chained marital condition of Bertha and is cause for resistance in my present feminist reading.

The outdoor space of the arbor makes obvious how close Jane comes to submitting to Rochester's influence, to becoming the fallen woman so vilified and ostracized by Victorian society. She is nearly seduced there, her head turned by that symbol of romantic love, a rose (217), and by his words of affection: he calls her his pet lamb and his friend (217-18). Now I see how Jane is being manipulated into a frenzy of jealousy and fear of losing her lover to Blanche. The "Eden-like" orchard, where the trees are "laden with ripening fruit," now becomes a metaphor for ripe, young Jane, who is waiting to be seduced by a serpent-like (phallic?) master (247). I no longer cheer at the advancement of this scene's romantic outcome because I see his taunting of the governess with news of his marriage to Blanche and his cruel insistence that Jane leave him for a new position with the family "O'Gall of Bitternutt Lodge" (250). His sardonic humor in naming this fictive family so negatively and punnily is missed by Jane and also by me in my earlier readings. I do notice, however, that Jane's feminist consciousness is in operation as she prepares to leave her employer in the orchard, dismissing "the medium of custom [and] conventionalities," while declaring herself his equal and herself as autonomous: "'I am a free human being with an independent will; which I now exert to leave you'" (252).

Nevertheless, he proposes marriage, they kiss, and she consents. The engagement reveals a new fluidity within their power dynamic. Jane pursues her advantage as affianced and claims some feminist power before the wedding. She may master him now, as he confesses, yet he likes her pliancy, suggesting he will afterwards easily bend her to his will. It is perhaps out of a feminist consciousness that Jane alludes to the demonically strong women of antiquity who overpower and destroy Hercules and Samson; and Edward voices some anxiety that she may prove to be the Eve that brings him down (259-60). They are trying out different power relations. What form of marriage awaits them if Rochester is compared to a Turkish sultan and Jane to his slave, even though she derides the comparison (267)? This seraglio reference is cause for resistance in a feminist reader.

Knowing about his treacherous dealings with Bertha, I no longer trust Edward to do right by Jane: while he may have been deceived by his father and brother into marrying Bertha, one wonders if he has driven Bertha mad by withholding affection and chaining her to a loveless existence. Jean Rhys imagined this very dynamic in her novel *Wide Sargasso Sea*. Bertha's visit to Jane's bedroom and her outraged tearing of the bridal veil now elicits my sympathy. Inevitably, Jane's vision of "the paradise of union" (254) is stained by the presence of Bertha. Also alarming is Jane's confession that her man has become her God, her idol (272). Jane's feminist consciousness is napping, though, in retrospect, she seems to regret this idol worship.

At the altar, Jane's feminist consciousness is painfully re-awakened. She gathers the resolve to resist love and curtail worship of her idol, and she ultimately gathers the strength to abandon this patriarch to his own suffering. The feminist *cri de coeur* is Jane's parting declaration: "'*I* care for myself . . . I will respect myself'" (312). But even then, she undermines her self-respect with self-hatred for abandoning her unhappy master: this is the backsliding feminist at her nadir (317).

When Jane flees Thornfield, she reverts to the role of nun, her love frozen; images of winter end this second volume, though it is midsummer: "ice glazed the ripe apples, drifts crushed the blowing roses" (292). Roses of love and apples of temptation are frozen in time. She remains in this state of repressed passion when she is taken in by St. John Rivers and his sister. The "force and fire" of her love for Edward emerge only in her recurring dreams of him (359).

St. John's self-abnegation and restlessness are not so different from Jane's, but unlike Jane, his evangelical beliefs urge self-repression in the service of Jesus (399). Jane criticizes him for his "evangelical charity" toward her as distinct from his sisters' genuine compassion (341-42). He judges Jane as unattractive and intractable (333), yet he chooses her to be "mistress" of the new girls' school in his parish (an interesting word choice in contrast to Edward's desire to make Jane his mistress). Both struggle to "'control the workings of inclination and turn the bent of nature'" (354). Later, St. John asks her to ignore "the mere fever of the flesh" (367) and be his helpmate in his missionary work. Both have loved another person, so marriage would be an act of self-denial for both. Jane describes St. John's struggle against loving Rosamond Oliver as a "despotic constriction" of the heart (357). In this re-reading, I note that Jane portrays repression in marriage as imposed equally on male and female when mutual love is absent; without love as counterpoint to marriage's constraints, the institution founders.

One further observation about Jane's feminist outlook comes with my re-reading. When Jane learns she is an heiress, she is delighted that she need not obtain financial security through the female's usual means, marriage: "independence would be glorious—yes, I felt that—*that* thought swelled my heart" (374). Brontë's use of emphatic italics here underscores Jane's delight in no longer needing to be beholden to a husband for her upkeep. And like a generous man, Jane is subsequently pleased to bestow her largesse on her three cousins.

So heiress Jane declines the proposal to marry St. John. Self-styled as a "'cold, hard, ambitious man'" (367), he does not respect the domestic sphere or love and would not make a good husband. Jane still believes fervently in love, which he does not offer her. In this re-reading, I also see her recoiling from his Christian stoicism and his despotic nature. Jane recognizes him to be "of the material from which nature hews her heroes—Christian and Pagan—her lawgivers, her statesmen, her conquerors" (384). Her words tell that St. John is a lawmaker and a rule-maker, a leader and a patriarch of whatever society he joins. She is prompted by feminist self-possession to resist his mission because his influence stifles her "liberty of mind" (388). He suppresses her warm nature; his icy kiss fetters her, and she is "in thrall" to him (389). This language evokes the world of the slave and recalls Bertha's fetters. St. John would force her to close up half her identity. Jane will not sacrifice her integrity, her belief in love, or her own vitality to marriage's "iron shroud" (394). Urged by a feminist agency and enabled by financial independence, Jane protects her "unblighted self" and insures the freedom of her mind and heart (398).

I cannot say that my negative view of St. John is especially new in this re-reading because the language Jane chooses to portray him is consistently chilling, and I was put off by his iciness in early readings of the text. What this reading yields to me, however, is the intense disapproval in Jane's descriptions of St. John's despotic behavior and the heat of her antipathy to the submissive role he would impose on her. He would have her become the wife who is The Angel in the House; when she refuses, he says that she is selfish—the antithesis of the self-abnegating Angel. This patriarchal stance shakes Jane to the core of her feminist consciousness: "as a man, he would have wished to coerce me into obedience" (400).

As the novel nears its end, I am now struck by the wholeness of Jane's nature, which is nourished by her relationship with Edward, in contrast to the half-existence she would have had as St. John's wife. With Edward, Jane "thoroughly live[s]" (426) because their love is mutual and deeply felt. When the two reunite, they meet on equal terms. Combing his hair, acting as his eyes and hands, Jane clearly has some dominion over him. As many critics have argued, in maiming Edward, Brontë is able to create a more egalitarian marriage for them. Yet his injury does not bring emasculation. His vigorous spirit and virility are fostered in marriage to Jane: he may shed tears at Jane's return, but these roll down a "manly cheek" (433). Jane declares him unlike the lightning-struck chestnut: he is a green and vigorous tree--quite phallic, really (433). And, as the last chapter informs readers, they do have children and he does enjoy partially-restored vision in one eye.

Add to this union the equalizing impact of Jane's inheritance. In their first conversation at Ferndean, she tells Edward: "'I am independent, sir, as well as rich; I am my own mistress'" (423). This language is proudly feminist as Jane asserts her equality with her master. Only, I do wish that Jane had kept at her feminist work as a girls' educator instead of only being "useful" to her husband. Like Katie R. Peel, I would like to resist Jane's submission to the age-old, male-directed institution of marriage. Peel says, "For Jane's story to end in a conventional marriage plot is jarring. Ironically, Jane's reward for all of her hard work and independence is to surrender them both. She forsakes them in order to serve her husband. Her doing so is a disappointment, especially because Jane develops value through her work" (157). A feminist's disappointment is inevitable, but my consolation is Jane's financial independence—the heiress is her own mistress. And perhaps she will raise their son to be a feminist.

This novel is, then, a revised version of the marriage plot. That Jane and Edward are "meant" to be together, as shown in the mental telepathy across time and space that summons Jane to Edward's side, may seem rather sentimental, written to please Victorian readers. Pleasing to a more progressive nineteenth-century reader might have been the message that marital love triumphs at the end when the wife is empowered to become her husband's "prop and guide" (437). Victorians, both male and female, might have been surprised at the positive transformation of the patriarchal Edward.

Jane Eyre has some elements to please and surprise twenty-first century feminist readers as well. Guided by the work of feminist literary critics, we can detect the following: the novel's resistance to patriarchal values embedded in traditional marriage; challenges to traditional gender roles through depictions of bright, capable women and their ambitions; interrogation of the figure of The Angel in the House through the negative aspects of the proposed marriage between Jane and St. John; feminist activism and resistance to societal rules, as modeled by Jane; and finally, the novel's visionary transformation of the patriarchal marriage into an egalitarian institution capable of nurturing love and mutual respect. While there are many ways to interpret *Jane Eyre*, re-reading Brontë's novel has reaffirmed for me the power of the feminist critical lens, and, not coincidentally, the firmness of my own feminist consciousness.

Works Cited

Auerbach, Nina. *Woman and the Demon: The Life of a Victorian Myth*. Cambridge, MA & London: Harvard UP, 1982.

Brontë, Charlotte. *Jane Eyre*. Ed. Beth Newman. Boston & NY: St. Martin's Press, 1996.

Eliot, George. *Middlemarch*. 2nd ed. Ed. Bert G. Hornback. New York & London: Norton, 2000.

Fetterley, Judith. *The Resisting Reader: A Feminist Approach to American Fiction*. Bloomington, IN: Indiana UP, 1981.

Gallop, Jane. *Around 1981: Academic Feminist Literary Theory*. Oxon, England & New York: Routledge, 2012.

Gilbert, Sandra M. and Susan Gubar. *The Madwoman in the Attic: The Woman Writer and the Nineteenth-Century Literary Imagination*. New Haven: Yale UP, 1979.

Peel, Katie R. "The Inadequacy of Closure in Charlotte Brontë's *Jane Eyre*; or, Why 'Reader, I Married Him' Is One of the Most Disappointing Sentences in Victorian Literature." *Critical Insights: Good and Evil in Literature*. Ed. Margaret S. Breen. Ipswich, MA: Salem Press, 2012. 144-58.

Showalter, Elaine. *A Literature of Their Own: British Women Novelists from Brontë to Lessing*. Expanded ed. Princeton, NJ: Princeton UP, 1999.

RESOURCES

Chronology of Charlotte Brontë's Life _____

1812	Patrick Brontë and Maria Branwell marry.
1814	Maria Brontë is born.
1815	Elizabeth Brontë is born. Charlotte Brontë is born in Thornton, Yorkshire, England on April 21. She is the third of six children.
1817	Patrick Branwell Brontë is born.
1818	Emily Brontë is born.
1820	Anne Brontë is born. Family moves to Haworth, where Patrick Brontë is appointed Perpetual Curate of St. Michael and All Angels Church.
1821	Maria Brontë dies on September 15. Children are cared for by her sister, Elizabeth.
1824	Maria, Elizabeth, Charlotte, and Emily attend Cowan Bridge School for Clergy's Daughters.
1825	Maria and Elizabeth die of tuberculosis. Charlotte and Emily return home to Haworth.
1831-1832	Charlotte attends Roe Head School, meets Ellen Nussey and Mary Taylor.
1833	Charlotte writes *The Green Dwarf* novella.
1835-1838	Charlotte teaches at Roe Head School.
1839-1841	Charlotte works as a governess.
1842	Charlotte attends school at the performance, maintained by Constantin and Claire Heger, in Brussels. Aunt Elizabeth dies in October; Charlotte and Emily return to England. Charlotte returns to Brussels to teach.

1844	Charlotte returns to Haworth in January.
1846	Charlotte, Emily, and Anne finance the May publication of a volume of poetry under the names Currer, Ellis, and Acton Bell. Two copies sell.
	Charlotte seeks a publisher for *The Professor*. The publisher Smith, Elder, and Co. encourages her to send a longer work.
1847	*Jane Eyre* is published.
1848	Branwell dies in September. Emily dies of pulmonary tuberculosis in December.
1849	Anne dies of pulmonary tuberculosis in May; *Shirley* is published in October.
1850	Charlotte meets Elizabeth Gaskell.
1853	*Villette* is published.
1854	Charlotte marries Arthur Bell Nicholls in June. They honeymoon in Ireland.
	Charlotte and unborn child die on March 31. Death certificate lists phthisis as cause of death.
1856	*The Professor* is published posthumously; Elizabeth Gaskell's *The Life of Charlotte Brontë* is published.

Works by Charlotte Brontë

Juvenilia
The Young Men's Magazine (with Branwell), 1830
The Green Dwarf, 1833
Tales of Angria (with Branwell), 1839

Poetry
Poems by Currer, Ellis, and Acton Bell, 1846

Novels
Jane Eyre: An Autobiography (as Currer Bell), 1847
Shirley: A Tale (as Currer Bell), 1847
Villette, 1853
The Professor: A Tale (pub. posthumously), 1857
Emma (fragment, pub. posthumously), 1860

Bibliography

Allott, Miriam, ed. *The Brontës: The Critical Heritage*. London: Routledge and Kegan Paul, 1974.

Anderson, Victoria. "Investigating the Third Story: 'Bluebeard' and 'Cinderella' in *Jane Eyre*." *Horrifying Sex: Essays on Sexual Difference in Gothic Literature*. Ed. Ruth Bienstock Anolik. Jefferson, NC: McFarland, 2007. 111-21.

Armstrong, Mary A. "Reading a Head: *Jane Eyre*, Phrenology, and the Homoerotics of Legibility." *Victorian Literature and Culture* 33.1 (2005): 107-32.

Armstrong, Nancy. "Gender Must Be Defended." *South Atlantic Quarterly* 111.3 (2012): 529-547.

Bardi, Abby. "'In Company of a Gipsy': The 'Gypsy' as Trope in Woolf and Brontë." *Critical Survey* 19.1 (2007): 40-50.

Bolt, David, Julia Miele Rodas, and Elizabeth J. Donaldson. *The Madwoman and the Blindman: Jane Eyre, Discourse, Disability*. Columbus: Ohio State UP, 2012.

Borie, Charlotte. "From Shrine to Stage: Inner Space and the Curtain in *Jane Eyre*." *Brontë Studies: The Journal of the Brontë Society* 34.2 (2009): 107-116.

Boumelha, Penny. "'And what do the women do?' *Jane Eyre*, Jamaica and the Gentleman's House." *Southern Review: Literary and Interdisciplinary Essays* 21.2 (1988): 111-122.

Cadwallader, Jen. "'Formed for Labour, Not for Love': Plain Jane and the Limits of Female Beauty." *Brontë Studies: The Journal of the Brontë Society* 34.3 (2009): 234-246.

Eagleton, Terry. *Myths of Power: A Marxist Study of the Brontës*. Basingstoke, England: Palgrave Macmillan, 2005.

Federico, Annette R., ed. *Gilbert & Gubar's* The Madwoman in the Attic *after Thirty Years*. Columbia: U of Missouri P, 2009.

Fisk, Nicole Plyler. "'I Heard Her Murmurs': Decoding Narratives of Female Desire in *Jane Eyre* and *Secresy*." *Brontë Studies: The Journal of the Brontë Society* 33.3 (2008): 218-231.

Garofalo, Daniela. "Dependent Masters and Independent Servants: The Gothic Pleasures of British Homes in Charlotte Brontë's *Jane Eyre*." *Manly Leaders in Nineteenth-Century British Literature*. Albany, NY: State U of New York P, 2008. 137-154.

Gilbert, Sandra and Susan Gubar. *The Madwoman in the Attic: The Woman Writer and the Nineteenth-Century Literary Imagination.* New Haven: Yale UP, 1979.

Glen, Heather, ed. *The Cambridge Companion to The Brontës.* Cambridge: Cambridge UP; 2002.

Griesinger, Emily. *Charlotte Brontë's Religion: Faith, Feminism, and* Jane Eyre. *Christianity and Literature* 58.1 (2008): 29-59.

Hagan, Sandra and Juliette Wells, eds. *The Brontës in the World of the Arts.* Aldershot, England: Ashgate, 2008.

Hope, Trevor. "Revisiting the Imperial Archive: *Jane Eyre, Wide Sargasso Sea,* and the Decomposition of Englishness." *College Literature* 39.1 (2012): 51-73.

Kapurch, Katie. "'Unconditionally and Irrevocably': Theorizing the Melodramatic Impulse in Young Adult Literature through the *Twilight* Saga and *Jane Eyre*." *Children's Literature Association Quarterly* 37.2 (2012): 164-187.

Kaufman, Heidi. "Becoming English: (Re)Covering 'Jewish' Origins in Charlotte Brontë's Jane Eyre." *English Origins, Jewish Discourse, and the Nineteenth-Century British Novel: Reflections on a Nested Nation.* University Park, PA: Pennsylvania State UP, 2009.

LeFavour, Cree. "'Jane Eyre Fever': Deciphering the Astonishing Popular Success of Charlotte Brontë in Antebellum America." *Book History* 7 (2004): 113-41.

Leggatt, Judith. "From the Red Room to Rochester's Haircut: Mind Control in *Jane Eyre*." *English Studies in Canada* 32.4 (2006): 169-188.

Livesey, Ruth. "Communicating with Jane Eyre: Stagecoach, Mail, and the Tory Nation." *Victorian Studies: An Interdisciplinary Journal of Social, Political, and Cultural Studies* 53.4 (2011): 615-638.

Losano, Antonia. "Ekphrasis and the Art of Courtship in *Jane Eyre*." *The Woman Painter in Victorian Literature.* Columbus, OH: Ohio State UP, 2008.

Macedo, Ana Gabriela. "After Mrs. Rochester: Rewriting as Re-Vision." *Journal of Adaptation in Film and Performance* 3.3 (2010): 271-289.

Marcus, Sharon. "The Profession of the Author: Abstraction, Advertising, and *Jane Eyre*." *PMLA: Publications of the Modern Language Association of America* 110.2 (1995): 206-19.

Michie, Elsie. "From Simianized Irish to Oriental Despots: Heathcliff, Rochester and Racial Difference." *Novel: A Forum on Fiction* 25.2 (1992): 125-40.

Milton, Catherine A. "A Heterogeneous Thing: Transvestism and Hybridity in *Jane Eyre*." *Styling Texts: Dress and Fashion in Literature.* Eds. Cynthia Kuhn, Cindy Carlson, and Suzanne Ferriss. Youngstown, NY: Cambria, 2007. 189-208.

Munjal, Savi. "Imagined Geographies: Mapping the Oriental Habitus in the Nineteenth Century British Novel." *Postcolonial Text* 4.1 (2008): [14 pages].

Peterson, M. Jeanne. "The Victorian Governess: Status Incongruence in Family and Society." *Suffer and Be Still: Women in the Victorian Age.* Ed. Martha Vicinus. Bloomington: Indiana UP, 1972. 3-19.

Poovey, Mary. "The Anathematised Race: The Governess and *Jane Eyre*." *Uneven Developments: The Ideological Work of Gender in Mid-Victorian England.* Chicago: U of Chicago P, 1988. 126-63.

Rich, Adrienne. "*Jane Eyre*: The Temptations of a Motherless Woman." *Jane Eyre.* Ed. Richard J. Dunn. New York: W. W. Norton, 2000. 469-83.

Rubik, Margarete and Elke Mettinger-Schartmann. *A Breath of Fresh Eyre: Intertextual and Intermedial Reworkings of* Jane Eyre. Amsterdam: Rodopi, 2007.

Silvey, Jane. "It All Began with *Jane Eyre*: The Complex Transatlantic Web of Women Writers." *Gaskell Society Journal* 19 (2005): 52-68.

Spivak, Gayatri Chakravorty. "Three Women's Texts and a Critique of Imperialism." *Critical Inquiry* 12.1 (1985): 243-61.

Stoneman, Patsy. "Inside Out: *Jane Eyre* on the Victorian Stage." *Brontë Studies: The Journal of the Brontë Society* 34.2 (2009): 147-154.

Thormählen, Marianne, ed. *The Brontës in Context.* Cambridge: Cambridge UP, 2012.

Tunc, Tanfer Emin. "Disease and Desire: Disciplining Encoded Homoeroticism in *Jane Eyre* and 'The Yellow Wallpaper'" *Foreign Literature Studies/Wai Guo Wen Xue Yan Jiu,* 31.1 (2009): 40-49.

Vanden Bossche, Chris R. "What Did Jane Eyre Do? Ideology, Agency, Class and the Novel." *Narrative* 13.1 (2005): 46-66.

Warhol, Robyn R. "Double Gender, Double Genre in *Jane Eyre* and *Villette*." *SEL: Studies in English Literature, 1500-1900.* 36.4 (1996): 857-75.

Wilson, Cheryl A. "Female Reading Communities in *Jane Eyre*." *Brontë Studies: The Journal of the Brontë Society* 30.2 (2005): 131-39.

Zonana, Joyce. "The Sultan and the Slave: Feminist Orientalism and the Structures of *Jane Eyre*." *Signs* 18.3 (1993): 592-617.

About the Editor

Katie R. Peel is an assistant professor of English at the University of North Carolina at Wilmington. Her teaching and research areas include women's studies and Victorian, young adult, children's, queer, and Holocaust literatures. Her essay "The Inadequacy of Closure in Charlotte Brontë's *Jane Eyre*, or, Why 'Reader, I Married Him,' is One of the Most Disappointing Sentences in Victorian Literature" appeared in Salem Press' *Critical Insights*: *Good and Evil*. In addition to writing about *Jane Eyre*, she has also published on her first love, *Villette*. She is currently working on an essay about the adaptation of George Eliot's *Daniel Deronda* for young readers.

Contributors _____

Joanne Cordón is an adjunct professor at the University of Connecticut. Her research interests include the novel, the eighteenth-century theatre, and women's studies. She has published in *Frontiers: A Journal of Women's Studies*.

Jennie-Rebecca Falcetta is assistant professor of Liberal Arts at Massachusetts College of Art and Design in Boston. While her scholarship generally falls within the bounds of modernist studies, Falcetta's interests lie as far afield as the Brontës and Medieval literature. Her publications include articles on Marianne Moore, Virginia Woolf, and Thomas Malory. Most recently, she contributed an article about teaching Millennial students to the collection *Generation X Professors Speak: Voices from Academia* (Scarecrow, 2013).

Mary Isbell is a lecturer in English and Theater Studies and a postdoctoral associate in Interdisciplinary Performance Studies at Yale University. Her book project explores the material conditions of nineteenth-century amateur theatricals, in order to recover the "theatrical" as a distinct type of period performance and to document the widespread popularity of the practice within diverse social groups, including aristocrats, middle-class families, university students, office clerks, and sailors aboard naval vessels. With Judith Hawley, she co-directs the international interdisciplinary network known as RAPPT (Research into Amateur Performance and Private Theatricals). Her work has been published in *Leviathan: A Journal of Melville Studies* and is forthcoming in *Victorian Literature and Culture*.

Jonathan Kotchian is a Marion L. Brittain postdoctoral fellow in the School of Literature, Media, and Communication at the Georgia Institute of Technology (Georgia Tech). He is revising his first book project, which shows how the figure of the superior author in early modern England co-evolved with satire. His second book project, which continues his investigation of "insider" literature, accessible only to certain readers or viewers, explores the relationship between concepts of intelligence and literary taste. His interests range from Shakespeare and Milton to using theatrical training techniques in his literature and composition classes.

Katherine Montwieler teaches eighteenth- and nineteenth-century British literature, women's studies, and contemporary fiction at the University of North

Carolina Wilmington. Her publications include articles on Mary Shelley, Claire de Duras, Charles Dickens, and Elizabeth Barrett Browning. She is currently working on a study of Fanny Imlay, sister of Mary Shelley and daughter of Mary Wollstonecraft.

John O'Hara received his MA from the University of North Carolina Wilmington and currently teaches English both there and at Cape Fear Community College. His research interests include science fiction, speculative realism, and British literature of the nineteenth century.

Thomas Recchio is professor of English at the University of Connecticut, where he teaches courses in: Victorian literature; the material forms of the novel, including serialization, illustrated editions, cheap editions, and so on; and contemporary adaptations and various re-writings of Victorian novels on film, on stage, and in current popular fiction. He is the author of *Elizabeth Gaskell's Cranford: A Publishing History* (Ashgate 2009) and the editor of the Norton Critical Edition of Gaskell's *Mary Barton* (2008). His articles have appeared in *Victorian Studies*, *Dickens Studies Annual*, *Studies in the Novel*, *Nineteenth-Century Theatre and Film*, and *The Gaskell Journal*, among others. Most recently, he has completed a book chapter, called "Adapting *Mary Barton*: History, Research, Possibilities", for a forthcoming volume called *Adapting Gaskell: Screen and Stage Versions of Elizabeth Gaskell's Fiction*.

Mara Reisman is an assistant professor of British literature and women's literature at Northern Arizona University. Her scholarly interests and teaching areas include twentieth- and twenty-first-century British and Irish literature and British, Irish, and American women's literature. She is also interested in film and television adaptations of contemporary British fiction. Reisman has published articles on Fay Weldon, Jeanette Winterson, Stella Gibbons, Jennifer Johnston, and Joan Schenkar, and she has guest edited a special issue of *LIT: Literature Interpretation Theory* on contemporary British women writers. She is currently working on a book-length project on Fay Weldon's fiction, titled *Waging War on Social Conventions: Fay Weldon, Feminism, and British Culture*.

Amanda T. Smith is an assistant professor in the Department of Language and Literature at Southwestern Oklahoma State University, where she teaches Composition and Editing and serves as the editor of *Westview*, a semiannual literary journal. She holds an MA in English from the University of Colorado and PhD in English from the University of Connecticut, where she served as the managing editor of *LIT: Literature Interpretation Theory*, a peer-reviewed academic journal published quarterly by Taylor & Francis. Her recent article, "'A Keen Sense of the Ridiculous': Comic Reframing and the Laughter of Sisters in Ella Hepworth Dixon's *My Flirtations*," appears in *Women's Writing* 19.1.

Meghan Sweeney is an associate professor of English at the University of North Carolina Wilmington. She teaches courses on children's and adolescent literature, critical theory, women in literature, and popular culture. Her recent publications include an article on Disney Princesses and web culture and an essay on pedagogy. She is working on a manuscript that addresses the ways that weddings are sold to American girls through books, costumes, toys, games, and websites and how these items help girls feel connected to an appealingly adult world but also establish constrictive notions about consumption and gender identity.

Barbara Frey Waxman is a professor of English at University of North Carolina Wilmington. Her scholarly interests include Victorian literature, nineteenth-century British novel, multicultural memoirs, American multicultural literature, and literature about aging. She has published essays on the work of George Eliot, Mary Shelley, William Wordsworth, Toni Morrison, and Eva Hoffman, among others, and she has written two books about the literature of aging, *From the Hearth to the Open Road: A Feminist Study of Aging in Contemporary Literature* (Greenwood Press, 1990) and *To Live in the Center of the Moment: Literary Autobiographies of Aging* (University of Virginia Press, 1997). She also edited a collection of essays, *Multicultural Literatures through Feminist/Poststructuralist Lenses* (University of Tennessee Press, 1993).

Cala Zubair received her PhD in Sociolinguistics from Georgetown University and is currently an assistant professor at SUNY Buffalo, where she teaches language- and culture-themed courses. Her research is directed towards various sociolinguistic and structural components of Sinhala language varieties. Her ethnographic studies among Sinhalese youth examine register formation, gendered slang constructions, and language ideology. She also focuses on Sinhala syntax and semantics via research on (in)volitive verbs, causative/inchoative alternations, and non-canonically case-marked subjects.

Index

Abbott, H. Porter 213
Abdiel xi, 161, 162, 163, 164, 165,
     166, 167, 168, 169, 170, 171,
     173, 174, 175
Abraham, Nicolas 113, 126
Abrupt, Absurd, Unconventional:
     Jane and Rochester Against
     the Victorian Conversational
     Landscape xi, 176
active virtue 163
Acton, Dr. William 202
adaptation xii, 159, 210, 211, 213,
     214, 217, 218, 223, 224, 225,
     269
admonishment 157
agency 6, 64, 65, 84, 93, 120, 123,
     197, 206, 244, 246, 247, 258
Agha, Asif 191
Agnes Grey 51, 52
Alfred, Lord Tennyson 238
Allegories of Empire 48, 98
Allegories of Empire: The Figure of
     Woman in the Colonial Text
     48, 98
Allegories of Reading: Figural
     Language in Rousseau,
     Nietzsche, Rilke, and Proust
     48
Allott, Miriam 12, 60, 61, 62, 63,
     143, 208, 266
ambition 152, 153, 162, 169, 170
American Christianity 146
American Economic Review 47
American Sociological Review 191
Anathematised Race: The Governess
     and Jane Eyre, The 197, 209,
     268
Angel in the House, The 207, 248,
     253, 258, 259
Angel of Lowood, The 195

Angels 169, 263
anger x, 64, 65, 70, 77, 78, 88, 92,
     93, 95, 96, 192, 194, 199, 200,
     201, 206, 208
Antoinette 96
Approaches to Teaching Brontë's Jane
     Eyre 159, 160
Apter, Emily 42, 48
Arabian Nights, The 15
Arac, Jonathan 45
Arawak Indians 32
Arcades Project, The 45
Areopagitica 167, 171, 175
Armstrong, Nancy 93, 96, 172, 174,
     193, 194, 208, 266
Around 1981: Academic Feminist
     Literary Theory 260
Association for the Aid of Milliners
     and Dressmakers 7
Athenaeum 18
Atlantic Islands: Madeira, the
     Azores, and the Cape Verdes
     in Seventeenth-Century
     Commerce and Navigation,
     The 46
Atlantic Islands, The 46, 48
Auerbach, Nina 249, 254, 260
Aurora Leigh 131, 143
Austen, Jane 53, 61, 62, 63, 65, 96,
     186, 191, 210
authority 37, 56, 95, 108, 109, 140,
     163, 164, 165, 167, 168, 169,
     170, 171, 172, 173, 174, 177,
     193, 194, 195, 198, 218, 248
autobiography 37, 51, 59, 240
Autobiography of Jane Eyre, The 51
autonomy 29, 95, 118, 123, 203, 207,
     243, 244, 245, 252
Aylott and Jones 18

Baird, Robert 44
Bakhtin, Mikhail 193, 208
Bank, Rosemary K. 225
Barreca, Regina 193, 194, 208, 209
Beaty, Jerome 171, 174
*Becoming a Heroine: Reading About
    Women in Novels* 7, 12, 208
Bell, Currer 3, 11, 18, 51, 245, 265
Bell, Rob 159, 160
*Beneficent Usurpers: A History of the
    British in Madeira, The* 46
Beneficent Usurpers, The 46, 47
Benjamin, Walter 45
Bennett, Ashly x, 58, 60, 64, 94
Bertha xi, xii, 4, 5, 9, 10, 24, 25, 31,
    34, 46, 47, 54, 57, 58, 62, 86,
    87, 88, 89, 90, 93, 96, 97, 101,
    114, 115, 118, 119, 120, 124,
    125, 128, 130, 133, 135, 136,
    137, 142, 143, 192, 200, 201,
    202, 203, 205, 206, 211, 225,
    234, 235, 236, 241, 243, 244,
    246, 250, 251, 252, 254, 255,
    256, 258
Bible, The 163, 216
Bicknell, Andrew 159, 160
Biddle, Anothony J. Drexel 46
bildungsroman 36, 57, 159
Bilger, Audrey 200, 205, 208
Bitternutt Lodge 255
Blackstone, William 232
Blackwood's Magazine 15, 62
Blessing, Carol 174, 175
Bloom, Harold 56
Bodenheimer, Rosemarie 58, 60
Bodichon, Barbara 7
Bolt, David 5, 12, 266
Book of Acts 154
Book of English Trades, A 26
Book of Genesis, The 216, 232
Book of Revelation, The 216, 232
Boone, Joseph 241
Boulger, G. S. 45

Bowery Theatre 220, 225
Branwell, Elizabeth 14
*Breath of Fresh Eyre: Intertextual
    and Intermedial Reworkings of
    Jane Eyre, A* 5, 13, 268
bride 61, 157, 208, 211, 215, 231
Bridewell Palace 235
Brocklehurst, Mr. 80, 129, 146, 147,
    149, 194, 214, 217, 248
Brontë's Jane Eyre xi, 3, 50, 61, 110,
    128, 133, 159, 160, 192, 213,
    226, 241, 243, 260, 266, 267,
    269
Brontës: The Critical Heritage, The
    12, 60, 61, 62, 63, 143, 208,
    266
Brooke, Dorothea 252
Brougham, John xii, 210, 226
Browning, Elizabeth Barrett 131,
    143, 271
Brown, Laura 95
Brownstein, Rachel 7, 12, 198, 207,
    208
Bubel, Katharine 59, 60
Bunyan, John 163
Burney, Fanny Anne 32, 46
Burns, Helen 37, 65, 74, 80, 117,
    123, 145, 147, 151, 167, 195,
    197, 249
Butler, Judith 47

Calvin, John 146
*Cambridge Introduction to Narrative,
    The* 213
Capital 23
Casey, Margaret 155
Cassandra 252
Cass, Jeffrey 174, 175
*Caught in the Act: Theatricality in the
    Nineteenth-Century English
    Novel* 211, 226

charade 211, 212, 215, 218, 223, 224, 225, 230, 231, 232, 233, 234, 235, 236
Charadized Relationships 231
Charadized' Relationships in Jane Eyre 242
Charlotte Brontë and Women's Culture 209
Charlotte Brontë: Feminine Heroine 209
Charlotte Brontë: The Imagination in History 208
Charlotte Brontë: The Self Conceived 62, 241
Chase, Karen 125, 126
Chase, Richard 54, 60
Chaucerian Polity: Absolutist Lineages and Associational Forms in England and Italy 46
Chichilnisky, Graciela 47
childhood 6, 59, 74, 105, 122, 125, 129, 193, 198, 213
Christian Remembrancer 3, 12, 51, 62
Chronicle of Higher Education, The 11, 13
Cinderella 206, 236, 241, 266
Clarissa 83
class xi, xii, 6, 7, 8, 10, 11, 24, 30, 34, 56, 78, 101, 102, 114, 116, 117, 126, 129, 137, 139, 142, 143, 146, 176, 177, 183, 186, 188, 197, 198, 199, 205, 210, 220, 223, 227, 229, 231, 235, 237, 239, 248, 270
Clergy Daughters School 15
Colls, Robert 47
Colonel Dent 215
Colonialism and the Figurative Strategy of Jane Eyre 45, 143
colonization 25, 28, 32, 33, 37, 140

Columbia History of the British Novel, The 209
Commoners: Common Right, Enclosure and Social Change in England, 1700–1820 45
communication 46, 67, 68, 71, 73, 108, 109, 190, 212
companionate marriage 230, 231, 238, 240
Comparative Perspectives on Slavery in New World Plantation Societies 46
compassion 119, 126, 151, 257
Comus 163, 174, 175
Consuming Anxieties: Consumer Protest, Gender and British Slavery, 1713–1833 45
conversation ix, xi, xii, 58, 75, 106, 108, 176, 177, 178, 181, 183, 189, 190, 213, 224, 239, 253, 259
Coontz, Stephanie 241
Cordón, Joanne ix, 14, 270
Cornhill Magazine 20
Corn Laws 34
Corpus of the Madwoman: Toward a Feminist Disability Studies Theory of Embodiment and Mental Illness, The 241
Critic 18, 205
Critical Inquiry 242, 268
Critical Insights: Good and Evil in Literature 260
Crosby, Alfred 32
Crosby, Alfred W. 46
Crystal Palace 19
Cultural Materialism: On Raymond Williams 47
curls 129, 130, 131, 147
curtains 100, 101, 210

Dalton, Timothy 159, 160
Daniel, Clay 163

Daniel Deronda 210, 269
Davis, Jim 225
death 14, 17, 19, 32, 57, 89, 99, 100,
    101, 103, 108, 137, 138, 142,
    147, 156, 169, 198, 200, 205,
    229, 235, 236, 240, 264
deforestation 25, 27, 28, 29, 31, 33,
    44, 46
dependence 85, 91, 104, 137, 239
Derrida, Jacques 59
Desire and Domestic Fiction: A
    Political History of the Novel
    208
Dialogic Imagination, The 208
Diederich, Nicole A. 57, 61
Diedrick, James 173, 175
discourse 11, 59, 65, 66, 67, 96, 133,
    148, 151, 176, 182, 183, 188,
    189, 213
Dodd, Philip 47
domesticity 43, 93, 139, 159
Donaldson, Elizabeth 235, 241
Dowager Lady Ingram 221
Downey, John 224
dramatic adaptation 217, 223, 225
Dr. Gibbons 26
Duke of Wellington 17
DuMaurier, Daphne 228
Duncan, T. Bentley 46
Durham, Charles W. 169, 175

Eagleton, Terry 55, 61, 266
Eberhart, Connie L. 163, 175
Ecological Imperialism 32, 46
Ecological Imperialism: The
    Biological Expansion of
    Europe, 900–1900 46
Ecological Monographs 46
Economic History Review 47
economics 101, 102, 276
education 7, 14, 15, 117, 129, 130,
    131, 139, 140, 141, 145, 196,
    249, 250, 253

Edward VI 235
egalitarian 124, 176, 177, 186, 258,
    259
egalitarian marriage 258
Eiland, Howard 45
Eliot, George 53, 95, 96, 97, 210,
    252, 260, 269, 272
Emeljanow, Victor 225
Emerson, Caryl 208
Emma 95, 96, 142, 144, 265
emotion 64, 67, 72, 76, 86, 93, 94,
    96, 153, 201, 230
English Furniture from Charles II to
    George II 26, 45
Englishness: Politics and Culture,
    1880–1920 47
equality xi, 39, 57, 102, 103, 104,
    107, 163, 164, 177, 186, 190,
    199, 259
Era 51, 52, 62
Eshton, Amy 215
Eshton, Louisa 215
Essays of Virginia Woolf: Volume I
    1904-1912, The 209
Evangelicalism 146, 149, 159
Evangelicalism at Lowood 159
Examiner's 51
Explicator 226
Eyre Affair, The 60, 61

Fairfax, Mrs. 117, 123, 130, 132,
    142, 143, 177, 178, 180, 184,
    212, 250, 251
fairy tale 229
faith 145, 149, 151, 157, 159, 199,
    252
Falcetta, Jennie-Rebecca xi, 145, 270
Family, Sex and Marriage in
    England, 1500-1800, The 242
Federico, Annette R. 4, 175
feeling 11, 14, 55, 56, 64, 70, 72, 74,
    78, 80, 82, 86, 93, 117, 151,
    166, 173, 207

female 3, 4, 5, 7, 11, 27, 36, 40, 51,
    56, 59, 64, 92, 93, 95, 100,
    102, 113, 115, 116, 117, 124,
    147, 182, 186, 193, 194, 198,
    202, 205, 206, 221, 232, 238,
    240, 245, 246, 247, 249, 257,
    259
femininity 60, 99, 100, 105, 249, 253
feminism 4, 35, 40, 51, 57, 58, 60,
    64, 66, 92, 95, 161, 174, 244
Feminisms: An Anthology of Literary
    Theory and Criticism 47
feminist consciousness 244, 245,
    246, 247, 252, 254, 255, 256,
    258, 260, 277
Feminizing the Fetish:
    Psychoanalysis and Narrative
    Obsession in Turn-of-the-
    Century France 48
Ferndean 7, 10, 12, 24, 25, 26, 27,
    43, 44, 101, 124, 205, 206,
    238, 239, 243, 259
Fetterley, Judith 246
Fforde, Jasper 60
Final Payments 155, 160
Flaubert, Gustave 54
Folklore: An Encyclopedia of Beliefs,
    Customs, Tales, Music, and
    Art, Volume 1 226
Fonblanque, A.W. 51
For Better, For Worse: British
    Marriages, 1600 to the Present
    241
Forcade, Eugene 52
Fordyce, James 198
foreignness 130, 136, 140, 142
Forests: The Shadow of Civilization
    45
Foucauldian 65
France 48, 131, 132, 133, 134, 135,
    138, 139
Franklin, J. Jeffrey 152, 159
Fraser's 52, 62

Freedgood, Elaine x, 23, 44
French Revolution 139
Freud, Sigmund 47, 194, 208
From Hellshire to Healthshire: The
    Genesis of the Tourist Industry
    in Jamaica 49
Fromkin, Victoria 191
Fruitless Trees: Portuguese
    Conservation and Brazil's
    Colonial Timber 23
Functions and Disorders of the
    Reproductive Organs, The 202
furniture 24, 25, 26, 27, 33, 34, 41,
    42, 44, 47, 234

Galasinski, Dariusz 191
Gallagher, Catherine 48
Gallagher, John 47
Gallagher, Susan VanZanten 159
Gallop, Jane 260
Garfinkel, Harold 191
Gaskell, Elizabeth x, 14, 19, 53, 99,
    104, 110, 264, 271
Gateshead 24, 25, 101, 113, 115, 116,
    125, 138, 193, 208, 217, 244,
    247, 248
gender xi, 6, 7, 8, 11, 28, 40, 51, 56,
    57, 58, 59, 60, 67, 94, 101,
    133, 146, 159, 172, 198, 205,
    230, 236, 240, 246, 248, 251,
    252, 259, 272
Gender and Literary Voice 209
gender roles 146, 172, 230, 236, 248,
    251, 259
Genette, Gérard 81
G. F. Asprey 46
Gilbert, Sandra 13, 61, 64, 97, 109,
    116, 118, 126, 175, 203, 208,
    228, 234, 241, 245, 260, 267
Gillis, John R. 241
Glen, Heather 208, 267

Goblin Ha-Ha: Hidden Smiles and Open Laughter in Jane Eyre, The 193, 209

God xi, 3, 53, 59, 102, 146, 149, 150, 151, 154, 155, 156, 157, 158, 161, 164, 165, 166, 167, 169, 170, 171, 172, 173, 174, 175, 203, 207, 256

Goffman, Erving 56, 204

Gordon, Mary 155

Gospel 149, 152, 155, 156, 157

governess 10, 16, 56, 58, 117, 128, 131, 137, 139, 140, 141, 182, 184, 186, 192, 197, 222, 244, 250, 251, 255, 263

Governesses' Benevolent Institution 7

Gray, Frances 195, 208

Great Exhibition 19

Greatheart 162, 170

Great-Niece's Journals, A 46

Greenfield, Sidney 46

Gregory, Desmond 46

Gregory, John 200

Greg, W. R. 7, 13

Grundrisse 35, 47

Gubar, Susan 4, 13, 56, 61, 64, 97, 101, 109, 126, 160, 161, 175, 193, 208, 211, 226, 245, 260, 267

Gulliver's Travels 29

Haden-Guest, Stephen 46

Hale, Margaret x, 100, 104

Hanson, Ellis 95

Harleth, Gwendolen 210

Harrison, Robert Pogue 28, 45

Hateley, Erica 60

Heidegger, Martin 23

Heilman, Robert B. 55

Herman, David 95

Herndl, Diane Price 47

hero 80, 81, 164, 198, 199, 228, 243

heroine 40, 55, 64, 83, 92, 95, 100, 104, 113, 119, 123, 125, 145, 155, 157, 158, 173, 176, 192, 194, 198, 199, 204, 205, 207, 208, 217, 228, 240

Hidden Story 142, 144

Higman, B. W. 48

History of British Birds 100

History of English Forestry, A 45

Hobbes, Thomas 194

Hodgson, James 35

Holdridge, Leslie R. 46

Holquist, Michael 208

Hope, Trevor 60

houses x, 29, 101, 113, 114, 115, 116, 124, 125, 251

How Novels Think 93, 96

Huang, Mei 241

Human Nature and De Corpore Politico 209

humor xi, xii, 192, 193, 194, 195, 196, 199, 200, 201, 202, 203, 204, 205, 206, 207, 208, 255

Hunt, Linda C. 209

Hypothetical Focalization 79, 80, 95

I Corinthians 150, 151

Ideas in Things: Fugitive Meaning in the Victorian Novel, The x, 44

Illustrated Junior Library 4

immorality 51, 52, 131, 134, 137, 139

imperialism 34, 35, 58, 59, 114, 115, 123, 124, 233

Imperialism at Home: Race and Victorian Women's Fiction 48, 143

Imperialism of Free Trade, The 47

Impressions and Experiences of the West Indies and North America in 1849 44

Industrial Reformation of English Fiction: Social Discourse and

Narrative Form, 1832–1867, The 48
industry x, 43, 109, 170
Ingram, Blanche 30, 88, 91, 118, 186, 199, 211, 252
inheritance 10, 104, 152, 157, 204, 244, 259
Interaction Order: American Sociological Association, 1982 Presidential Address, The 191
interrogation 177, 178, 179, 181, 217, 259
Isbell, Mary xii, 210, 270
isolation 100, 101, 104, 109, 121, 124, 238, 239

Jafari, Morteza 57, 61
James, Henry 53, 54
James, N. D. G. 45
Jane Eyre: an Autobiography 241
Jane Eyre and the Secrets of Furious Lovemaking 203, 208
Jane Eyre, from Governess to Girl Bride 61, 208
Jane Eyre: 'Hazarding Confidences 209
Jane Eyre on Stage 210, 213, 225, 226
Jane Eyre on Stage: 1848-1898 210
Jane Eyre on Stage, 1848-1898: An Illustrated Edition of Eight Plays with Contextual Notes 226
Jane Eyre: The Temptations of a Motherless Woman 56, 268
Jane Laughs Last: Developing Feminist Humor in Charlotte Brontë's Jane Eyre xi, 192
Jefferson, Gail 191
John the Apostle 149
John the Revelator 158
jokes 196

Jokes and Their Relation to the Unconscious 194, 208
Jones, Robin 193, 205
Joyce, James 54

Kaplan, Carla 58, 61, 95, 97
Kaplan, Cora 92, 97
Kapurch, Katie 60, 61, 267
Keynes, John Maynard 35
Kotchian, Jonathan xi, 161, 270

Laclos, Choderlos de 82
Lady Eastlake 3
Lady Ingram 214, 221, 222
LaMonaca, Maria 154, 159, 160
Landow, George 146, 160
Language 39, 40, 50, 80, 106, 130, 131, 136, 140, 143, 148, 153, 154, 176, 177, 182, 183, 188, 229, 233, 236, 239, 247, 248, 251, 253, 258, 259, 272
Language and Literature 60, 271
Language and Social Relations 191
Lanser, Susan 65, 95, 97
Lau, Beth 159, 160, 175
Laughing Feminism 200, 208
laughter 114, 192, 193, 195, 196, 200, 201, 202, 203, 205, 206, 208
Laughter of Maidens, the Cackle of Matriarchs: Notes on the Collision Between Comedy and Feminism, The 209
Law and Order 4, 13
Lean In: Women, Work, and the Will To Lead 11, 13
Leaves from a Madeira Garden 32, 46
Leavis, Q.D. 54, 61
Lefebvre, Henri 45
Lerner, Laurence 58, 62, 96, 97
Les Liaisons Dangereuses 82

Letters of Charlotte Brontë 16, 17, 19, 20
Levenson, Michael 125, 126
Lewes, George Henry 9, 19, 51, 62
Life of Charlotte Brontë, The 14, 20, 61, 264
linguistics 176
Literature of Their Own, A 56, 63, 95, 98, 245, 260
Literature of Their Own: British Women Novelists from Brontë to Lessing, A 63, 95, 98, 245, 260
Little Women 147
Litvak, Joseph 211, 226
Lolita 96
London, Bette 47, 59, 62
London Review of Books 47
London Times 35
Long Hoeveler, Diane 159, 160, 175
Lord Ingram 218, 222, 223
Lorimer, James 128
love 3, 6, 15, 16, 17, 57, 60, 91, 102, 107, 108, 122, 131, 133, 142, 145, 148, 149, 151, 153, 154, 155, 156, 157, 158, 165, 166, 168, 190, 200, 201, 219, 229, 230, 232, 237, 238, 240, 243, 254, 255, 256, 257, 258, 259, 269
Love Wins: A Book About Heaven, Hell, and the Fate of Every Person Who Ever Lived 159, 160
Lowood 24, 30, 65, 74, 77, 78, 101, 116, 117, 118, 123, 129, 130, 131, 139, 141, 146, 147, 152, 157, 159, 167, 177, 179, 180, 183, 184, 194, 195, 196, 200, 206, 208, 214, 217, 221, 244, 248, 249, 253
Lowood Institution 146

Lowood School 24, 30, 65, 74, 117, 177, 194, 248
Lynn, Sir George 215

Macropolitics of Nineteenth-Century Literature: Nationalism, Exoticism, Imperialism, The 45
Madeira 10, 25, 26, 27, 28, 31, 32, 33, 35, 40, 41, 43, 44, 45, 46, 47, 104
Madeira and the Beginnings of New World Sugar Cane Cultivation and Plantation Slavery: A Study in Institution Building 46
Madeira: Its Scenery, and How to See It 45
Madwoman and Blindman: Jane Eyre, Discourse, Disability, The 5, 12
Madwoman in the Attic, The 4, 5, 13, 56, 57, 58, 61, 92, 97, 109, 126, 158, 160, 175, 208, 211, 226, 245, 260, 266, 267
Magazine of Domestic Economy, The 238
mahogany 24, 25, 26, 27, 28, 31, 33, 35, 40, 41, 42, 44, 45, 47, 48
Man, Paul de 48
Mansfield Park 210
Manwood, John 29
March, Beth 147
marriage xii, 5, 6, 7, 10, 14, 17, 56, 57, 59, 61, 99, 101, 102, 103, 107, 109, 137, 138, 142, 152, 153, 154, 155, 157, 158, 171, 189, 190, 198, 199, 203, 205, 206, 207, 211, 214, 215, 219, 227, 229, 230, 231, 232, 234, 235, 238, 239, 240, 244, 245, 246, 247, 251, 252, 254, 255, 256, 257, 258, 259

Marriage, a History: From Obedience to Intimacy or How Love Conquered Marriage 241
Married Women's Property Act 232
Marshall, Woodville 38
Marshall, Woodville K. 48
Martineau, Harriet 19
Marx, Karl 23
Mason, Bertha 24, 25, 31, 46, 47, 57, 86, 89, 93, 96, 114, 118, 119, 125, 136, 225, 250
Mason, Richard 34, 211, 254
Matrimonial Causes Act 232
Maurier, Daphne du 50
Maynard, John 35, 174, 175
McLaughlin, Kevin 45
mentoring 113, 114
Merteuil, Mme. De 82
metalanguage 176
Metalanguage: Social and Ideological Perspectives 191
Mettinger-Schartmann, Elke 5, 13, 268
Meyer, Stephenie 50
Meyer, Susan 38, 45, 48, 133
Middlemarch 60, 146, 252, 260
Miller, Lucasta x, 99
Miller, Shawn William 23
Mill on the Floss, The 95, 96
Mills and Boon 228
Milton, John 161
Mines and Collieries Act 8, 50
Miss Gryce 214
mission xi, 139, 153, 157, 172, 233, 243, 258
Miss Scatcherd 77, 78, 168, 214, 217
Miss Temple 37, 117, 123, 139, 195, 196, 197, 207, 214, 249
Miss Wooler 16
mistress 7, 10, 12, 104, 120, 125, 128, 133, 135, 139, 154, 204, 243, 245, 257, 259
Moglen, Helen 241

Montwieler, Katherine vii, x, 4, 113, 270
Moore, Isabel 155, 156
Moroney, Maryclaire 241
Morton, Samantha 159
motherhood 157
Mr. Brocklehurst 80, 129, 146, 147, 149, 194, 214, 217, 248
Mr. Oliver 30
Mrs. Fairfax 117, 123, 130, 132, 142, 143, 177, 178, 180, 184, 212, 250, 251
M. Teclaff, Eileen 46
Myths of Power: A Marxist Study of the Brontës 55, 61, 266

Nabokov, Vladimir 96
Nandrea, Lorri 93, 95
Narrative Discourse 81, 97
narrative form 10, 75, 84
nationality 129, 133, 135, 138, 141
Neeson, J. M. 30, 45
neologism 131
New Brunswick 47, 241
New Casebooks: Jane Eyre 209
New Criticism 54
Newgate Prison 19
New Historical ix
New Historicist 56
Newman, Beth 63, 251, 260
New Perspectives on Women and Comedy 209
New Testament 148
New York xii, 11, 12, 13, 20, 45, 46, 61, 62, 63, 96, 97, 98, 109, 110, 126, 143, 144, 160, 174, 175, 191, 208, 209, 241, 242, 260, 266, 268
New York Times 11, 13
Nicholls, Arthur Bell 17, 264
Nicholson-Smith, Donald 45
Nicolaus, Martin 47
Nightingale, Florence 252

Nineteenth-Century Literature 45,
  62, 97, 209
*Non-Anomalous Nature of Anomalous
  Utterances, The* 191
North American 32, 63
North and South x, 99, 100, 103, 104,
  107, 109
Northanger Abbey 95, 96
North British Review 128
*North-South Trade and the Global
  Environment* 47
Note on Charlotte Brontë, A 53, 63
Noyes, Dorothy 212
Nussey, Ellen 16, 263
NWSA Journal 241

obedience xi, 108, 161, 162, 163,
  164, 165, 166, 167, 168, 169,
  170, 171, 172, 173, 174, 196,
  258, 283
objects x, 25, 28, 36, 42, 44, 105,
  129, 143, 152, 207, 250
Oedipal 56
O'Hara, John x, 50, 271
Ohio State University Press, The 94
Oliphant, Margaret 53, 62
Oliver, Rosamond 257
*On Longing: Narratives of the
  Miniature, the Gigantic, the
  Souvenir, and the Collection*
  48
orphan 10, 57, 100, 135, 138, 155,
  184, 201, 235, 243
Ottoman Empire 59

Pagan 257
Pamela 83
Paradise Lost xi, 15, 161, 164, 174,
  175
Parliamentary Blue Books 8, 9
passion x, 3, 99, 100, 101, 102, 104,
  105, 106, 107, 108, 109, 133,
  155, 173, 192, 201, 227, 228,
  245, 255, 256
*Passion and Economics in Jane Eyre
  and North and South* x
pastoral 43
paternity 135
Patmore, Coventry 113, 248
patriarchal values 246, 247, 259
Paul, T.H. 225
Peel, Katie R. 260
Pell, Nancy 56, 62
Penry-Jones, Rupert 159, 160
Pensionnat Heger 16, 263
performance xii, 68, 82, 131, 174,
  196, 211, 212, 216, 218, 219,
  224, 225, 231, 248, 252, 263,
  270
Peterson, M. Jeanne 117
Phelan, James 95, 96
physical touch 154, 155
Pilgrim's Progress, The 15
Plain Jane's Progress 126, 241
play 55, 159, 169, 181, 183, 186,
  204, 210, 211, 212, 214, 217,
  218, 219, 220, 221, 223, 224,
  225, 228, 230, 235
*Pleasures of Submission: Jane Eyre
  and the Production of the Text,
  The* 47, 62
*Politeness: Some Universals in
  Language Usage* 191
Politi, Jina 133
Poole, Grace 118, 224, 225
Poovey, Mary 47, 48, 56, 128, 197,
  199
power 3, 7, 25, 27, 39, 46, 51, 52, 58,
  66, 94, 95, 100, 103, 109, 113,
  115, 124, 125, 151, 156, 165,
  169, 170, 182, 183, 190, 191,
  193, 194, 196, 198, 199, 200,
  204, 206, 229, 230, 231, 232,
  234, 235, 236, 237, 240, 244,

246, 247, 249, 251, 252, 253, 254, 255, 256, 260

Premodern Places: Calais to Surinam, Chaucer to Aphra Behn 47

Prendergast, Christopher 47

Pride and Prejudice 95, 96, 146

Production of Space, The 45

Professor, The 18, 19, 20, 50, 264, 265

Project Muse 241

Proper Lady and the Woman Writer: Ideology as Style in the Works of Mary Wollstonecraft, Mary Shelley, and Jane Auste, The 191

Psychic Life of Power: Theories in Subjection, The 47

psychoanalysis 57, 58

Quarterly Review 12, 53, 63, 128, 192, 241

Queen Victoria 3, 9, 12

Radway, Janice 5, 13

Rai, Amit 93, 97

Rapunzel 229, 241

Rasselas 75, 76, 149

Raymond Williams and Colonialism 47

Reading the Romance: Women, Patriarchy, and Popular Literature 5, 13

Rea, Joanne E. 226

Rebecca xi, 50, 95, 145, 215, 216, 219, 228, 232, 270

Recchio, Thomas x, 99, 271

Reed, John 38, 100, 115, 126, 137, 162, 194, 247

Reflecting the Audience: London Theatregoing, 1840-1880 225

refuge 103, 114, 238

Reisman, Mara xi, 128, 271

religion 151, 158, 160, 174, 245

Renk, Kathleen Williams 58, 62

rereading xii, 145, 240

resistance xi, 58, 95, 125, 166, 167, 244, 245, 250, 255, 256, 259

Resisting Reader: A Feminist Approach to American Fiction, The 260

Resisting Reader, The 246, 260

Reverend Brocklehurst 117

Reverend Casaubon 145

revision xii, 59, 68, 90

revolt 77, 161, 163, 164, 165, 166, 236, 251

Rhys, Jean 59, 256

Rich, Adrienne 6, 13, 56, 62, 268

Richardson, Samuel 83

Richmond, George 15

Rigby, Elizabeth 3, 12, 53, 128, 140, 143, 192

right obedience 161, 162, 163, 164, 166, 168, 169, 170, 171, 172, 173, 174

Right Obedience and Milton's Abdiel in Jane Eyre xi, 161

Rise of Free Trade Imperialism: Classical Political Economy, the Empire of Free Trade and Imperialism, 1750–1850, The 47

Ritvo, Harriet 45

Rivers, Mary 150, 189

Rivers, St. John xi, 5, 52, 103, 123, 145, 147, 149, 159, 162, 203, 236, 243, 256

Robbins, R. G. 46

Robinson, Ronald 47

Rochester, Bertha 101, 192, 201

Rochester, Edward 114, 128, 228, 243, 246

Rodas, Julia Miele 5, 12, 58, 62, 266

Roe Head 16, 18, 263

Rolt, Margaret S. 46

romance 5, 50, 55, 56, 58, 60, 88, 95, 109, 197, 198, 199, 200, 208, 228, 240
Ross, Diana 48
Rowling, J. K. 11
Royal Navy 29
Rubik, Margarete 5, 13, 268
Rubin, Vera 46
Ruth x, 99, 266, 267

Sandberg, Sheryl 11, 13
Sand, George 53
Schegloff, Emanuel 191
scholarship ix, x, 4, 29, 54, 55, 270
Schwartz, Nina 59, 63
Secret Garden, The 227
Sedgwick, Eve Kosofsky 66, 67, 97
Sedley, Amelia 95
self-defense 193, 196
Self-Help 40
self-interruption 176, 182
self-preservation ix, 195, 203
self-repair 176, 183
Semiology and Rhetoric 48
Semmel, Bernard 47
servants 101, 113, 114, 116, 118, 124, 134, 197, 210, 212, 221, 222, 224, 250
Severn, Julia 129
sexual harassment 252, 253
sexual tension 105
shame x, 58, 64, 65, 66, 67, 68, 69, 70, 71, 72, 73, 74, 75, 76, 77, 78, 79, 80, 81, 82, 83, 84, 85, 86, 87, 88, 89, 90, 91, 94, 95, 96, 114, 121, 133, 134
Sharp, Becky 65, 95
Sharpe, Jenny 38, 48, 98
Shaw, Harry E. 95
Shell and the Kernel, The 113, 126
Shelley, Mary 186, 191, 271, 272
Shirley 19, 50, 264, 265

Showalter, Elaine 56, 95, 136, 195, 202, 245
Shuttleworth, Sally 101, 110
Signs 48, 63, 241, 242, 268
Signs: Journal of Women in Culture and Society 48
Simplest Systematics for the Organization of Turn-Taking for Conversation, A 191
Sins of the Mother: Adèle's Genetic and National Burden in Jane Eyre xi, 128
Slate 228, 242
slavery 25, 27, 28, 31, 32, 38, 39, 41, 126, 170
Smiles, Samuel 40
Smith, Adam 66, 67, 70, 97, 98
Smith, Amanda T. xi, 192, 271
Smith, Margaret 20, 55, 63, 175
Snowe, Lucy x, 6
social critique 193, 206
social relations x, 27, 35, 44, 64, 66, 84, 94
Spacks, Patricia Meyer 200, 209
Speak what we think': Women Writers 209
spectacle 220
spectator xii, 14, 67, 71, 72, 77, 211, 213
Spectator 52, 62, 223
speech 58, 69, 95, 103, 105, 140, 148, 165, 185, 186, 187, 190, 217, 218
Spivak, Gayatri Chakravorty 47, 242, 268
stage xii, 39, 50, 66, 83, 122, 135, 137, 193, 201, 212, 216, 217, 218, 220, 224, 225, 226, 231, 234, 271
Standard Edition of the Complete Psychological Works of Sigmund Freud, The 47
Sternlieb, Lisa 196, 209

Stewart, Susan 41, 45, 48
St. John xi, 5, 45, 52, 103, 123, 143,
    145, 147, 149, 150, 151, 152,
    153, 154, 155, 156, 157, 158,
    159, 162, 163, 164, 166, 168,
    169, 170, 171, 172, 173, 174,
    203, 204, 207, 227, 236, 243,
    244, 256, 257, 258, 259
St. John Rivers xi, 5, 52, 103, 123,
    145, 147, 149, 159, 162, 203,
    236, 243, 256
Stone, Lawrence 242
Stoneman, Patsy 210, 225, 226, 268
Story Logic 95, 97
Strachey, James 47
Studies in English Literature 61, 63,
    97, 208, 268
Studies in Ethnomethodology 191
sugar 27, 32, 33, 113, 118
*Sultan and the Slave: Feminist
    Orientalism and the Structure
    of Jane Eyre, The* 63, 242
Superwoman Myth, The 11, 13
survival xii, 6
Sussman, Charlotte 27, 45
Suzanne, Laura 159
Sweeney, Meghan xii, 227, 242, 272
Swinburne, Algernon Charles 53, 63
symbolic settings 244
Symonds, R. W. 26, 45
sympathy x, 64, 65, 66, 67, 70, 71,
    72, 73, 75, 76, 77, 85, 88, 92,
    93, 94, 95, 104, 152, 159, 256

*Tales of Glass Town, Angria, and
    Gondal* 18, 20
Tatar, Maria 119, 126
Taylor, Ellen 46
Taylor, Frank 43
Taylor, Mary 16, 263
Temple, Miss 37, 117, 123, 139, 195,
    196, 197, 207, 214, 249
Tennant, Emma 142, 144

Thackeray, William 19, 63, 98
*That Better Part Which Cannot Be
    Taken From You': Varieties of
    Christian Experience in Jane
    Eyre* xi
*Theatre Culture in America, 1825-
    1860* 225
Theory of Moral Sentiments 67, 70,
    98
Thickstun, Margaret Olofson 174,
    175
third story 245, 250, 251
Thomas-Stanford, Charles 32, 46
Thomas, Sue 47
Thornfield Hall 25, 86, 87, 113, 114,
    117, 118, 125, 210, 212, 214,
    215, 216, 218, 221, 225, 252
Thornton, John 105, 107, 108
Thorpe, Adam 35, 47
*Three Women's Texts and a Critique
    of Imperialism* 47, 233, 242,
    268
Tiedemann, Rolf 45
Todd, Janet 98, 209
Torah 250
Torok, Maria 113, 126
Trade, Government and Society 48,
    49
*Trade, Government and Society in
    Caribbean History* 48
*Tradition Counter Tradition: Love
    and the Form of Fiction* 241
Transforming the Cinderella Dream
    241
transgression 195
trauma x, 113, 114, 119, 120, 121,
    125
*Treatise of the Laws of the Forest,
    A* 29
*Tropical Extravagance of Bertha
    Mason, The* 47
tuberculosis 32, 147, 148, 159, 263,
    264

Tuden, Arthur 46
Tulliver, Maggie 65, 95
Twilight 50, 60, 61, 267

*Unabashed:Essays on Women and
    Humor in British Literature*
    208
Uncle Eyre 10
Uncle Tom's Cabin 147
undergraduate xii, 229, 230, 231,
    236, 237, 240
Uneven Developments 47, 48, 56, 62,
    144, 268
*Uneven Developments: The
    Ideological Work of Gender
    in Mid-Victorian England* 47,
    56, 62, 144, 268
Up in the Eyre 242

Value of Laughter, The 209
Vanity Fair 48, 51, 95, 98, 143
Varens, Adèle 118, 120, 128, 184
Varens, Céline 129, 134, 189
Vegetation of Jamaica, The 46
Victorian Conventions 182
Victorian England 47, 56, 62, 113,
    114, 144, 190, 268
Victorian era 53, 250
Victorian Literature and Culture 48,
    266, 270
Victorian Web 159, 160
Villette x, 6, 19, 50, 54, 63, 99, 142,
    208, 264, 265, 268, 269
Vindication of the Rights of Woman, A
    173, 175
Vinhatico 33, 45
violence 27, 28, 43, 44, 64, 90, 101,
    105, 109, 113, 114, 115, 116,
    118, 120, 165, 251
Virginia Quarterly Review 241
Viswanathan, Gauri 47
vocation 103, 104, 131, 151, 153
Volanges, Cécile 82

*Vox Populi': The St. Vincent Riots and
    Disturbances of 1862* 48
Vulcan 159

Wallace, David 46
walnut 24, 42, 45
Warhol, Robyn 57, 63, 268
Warner, Michael 87, 98
Wasikowska, Mia 3, 13
Watson, Melvin R. 54, 63
Waxman, Barbara xii, 243
wedding 17, 109, 118, 119, 206, 212,
    214, 215, 216, 219, 240, 255
Wesley, Charles 146
Westminster Review 8, 9, 52, 62
Whipple, Edwin Percy 53, 63
Whitcross 30
Why Are Women Redundant 7, 13
Wide Sargasso Sea 59, 61, 256, 267
Wilde, Oscar 66
Wilt, Judith 199, 209
Winter, Jessica 242
wit 192, 193, 198, 199, 200, 202,
    203, 205, 206, 207, 208, 243
Wollstonecraft, Mary 173, 175, 186,
    191, 271
*Woman and the Demon: The Life of a
    Victorian Myth* 260
*Woman's Portion: Ideology, Culture,
    and the British Female Novel
    Tradition, A* 209
Women and Laughter 208
Women and Work 7, 12
*Women's Place: Home, Sanctuary,
    and the Big House in Jane
    Eyre* x, 113
wood 23, 24, 25, 26, 31, 33, 34, 42,
    43, 48, 250
*Wood: A Manual of the Natural
    History and Industrial
    Applications of the Timbers of
    Commerce* 45

Woolf, Virginia 53, 63, 113, 192, 209, 270
working women 6, 7, 122
World Geography of Forest Resources, A 33, 46
Wright, John K. 46
Wright, Terrence 105

Wuthering Heights 3, 51, 52, 54, 55, 61
Wyatt, Jean 57, 63

Zlotnick, Sue 139
Zonana, Joyce 48, 59, 63, 242, 268
Zubair, Cala xi, 176, 272